Th

The modern state is hugely important in our everyday lives. It takes nearly half our income in taxes. It registers our births, marriages and deaths. It educates our children and pays our pensions. It has a unique power to compel, in some cases exercising the ultimate sanction of preserving life or ordering death. Yet most of us would struggle to say exactly what the state is.

The new edition of this well-established and highly regarded textbook continues to provide the clearest and most comprehensive introduction to the modern state. It examines the state from its historical origins at the birth of modernity to its current jeopardized position in the globalized politics of the twenty-first century. Subjects covered include:

- state and economy
- states and societies
- states and citizens
- states within the international system
- 'rogue' and failed states.

Thoroughly updated and revised with two new chapters, students will continue to find *The Modern State* a provocative introduction to one of the most important phenomena of contemporary life.

**Christopher Pierson** is Professor of Politics at the University of Nottingham.

# The Modern State

Second edition

**Christopher Pierson**

 Routledge
Taylor & Francis Group

LONDON AND NEW YORK

First published 1996
by Routledge
11 New Fetter Lane, London EC4P 4EE

Simultaneously published in the USA and Canada
by Routledge
29 West 35th Street, New York, NY 10001

Reprinted 2000, 2002

Second edition 2004

*Routledge is an imprint of the Taylor & Francis Group*

© 1996, 2004 Christopher Pierson

Typeset in Baskerville by
BOOK NOW Ltd
Printed and bound in Great Britain by
T.J. International Ltd, Padstow, Cornwall

*British Library Cataloguing in Publication Data*
A catalogue record for this book is available from the British Library

*Library of Congress Cataloging in Publication Data*
Pierson, Christopher.
  The modern state/Christopher Pierson.– 2nd ed.
    p. cm.
Includes bibliographical references and index.
1. State, The. I. Title.
  JC11.P54 2004
  320.1–dc22                     2003021058

ISBN 0–415–32932–9 (hbk)
ISBN 0–415–32933–7 (pbk)

**Still for Ailsa, Lewis and Meridee**

# Contents

# Acknowledgements

The author and publisher are happy to acknowledge permission to reproduce the following material in the book:

David Held and Polity Press for Figure 2.1, derived from 'The development of the modern state', in S. Hall and B. Gieben (eds) *The Formations of Modernity*; B. Turner and *Sociology* for Tables 5.1 and 5.2, derived from 'Outline of a theory of citizenship', *Sociology* 24, 2, 1990.

The first edition of this book was written with the support of the University of Stirling, the Public Policy Program/Research School of Social Sciences at the Australian National University in Canberra, the Carnegie Trust for the Universities of Scotland and the British Academy. This revised edition was written in the School of Politics at the University of Nottingham. I am happy to record my appreciation of the support I have received from all these quarters.

The book is still dedicated to Lewis, Ailsa and Meridee, who have had to weather a lot more than a Scottish winter.

Chris Pierson
*Nottingham, 2003*

# Introduction

That academic division of labour which once (and briefly) split the social sciences into the discrete study of the state (political science), economy (economics) and society (sociology) is breaking down. Of course, such a division was never watertight. It is absent from most classical political theory and from the founding texts of both classical political economy and the sociological tradition. At a more mundane level, students of social policy, for example, have long had to consider the ways in which state, economy and society interact. Increasingly, students of sociology are required to understand the basic laws of motion of the state, just as students of politics and economics are required to place political and economic institutions in their appropriate social context. With these old lines of intellectual demarcation breaking down, it is now widely recognized that, in most developed societies, the state has probably been the single most important social, economic *and* political force.

Ironically, this renewal of interest in the analysis of the state has coincided with a very widespread decline in popular and intellectual faith in its competence and, for some, the belief that we are witnessing the 'twilight of the state'. Critics from both right and left have increasingly condemned the state as inefficient, ineffective and despotic. Meanwhile, commentators from a very diverse range of political positions have encouraged us to believe that the state is an increasingly archaic form, yielding to markets or global networks or simply being swept up and away in a coming clash of civilizations. Yet, for all this critical interest, the very basic task of establishing what we mean by 'the state' remains unresolved. Debates about the 'proper' nature of the state have raised some of the most important and difficult problems in the whole of the social sciences: the relationship between value judgements (the normative) and matters of fact (the empirical), between internal (endogenous) and external (exogenous) explanations of societal development, between contingency and determination, between generalizing and individualizing methodologies. But in all these areas, too, it seems as if there are many more questions than answers. Indeed, at times our sense of the importance of the state and its contemporary problems appears to be matched only by a pervasive frustration at its sheer ungraspability.

Some of the questions that surround the state are certainly difficult. After all, the finest minds that have devoted themselves to these questions over two millennia have failed to generate any totally persuasive answers. Yet it is hardly to be doubted that an already difficult issue has sometimes been made much more impenetrable by accretions of wilful obscurantism. My ambition in this book is not so much to resolve as to try to make sense of these disputes and, without doing too much violence to their originators, to make them accessible and meaningful to the uninitiated reader. It's worth saying at the outset, too, that I think that states are still very important and very far from withering away.

In Chapter 1, I confront the question of defining the state. Here we are faced with a bewildering range of options, including the rather tempting (and sometimes well-argued) case for dropping the idea of the state altogether. We shall see that the simplest 'one-line' definitions of the state have not generally fared well. Most commentators are agreed that the state is multifaceted and many accept that it is a little fuzzy around the edges. Nor (fortunately) is a watertight definition of the state a precondition for discussing it. In his authoritative text *State Theory,* Jessop saves a definition of the state until page 341 and immediately follows this up with six substantial qualifications (Jessop 1990: 341–2)! While we shall not find any uniform agreement upon a precise definition of the state, I shall suggest that there is at least a 'cluster' of characteristic ideas, institutions and practices around which many commentators isolate their working definitions of the modern state. This should at least help us to focus upon a clear range of topics that are 'state related'.

In Chapter 2, I set out the case for insisting that the state must be understood historically and review some of the most important recent attempts to do so. In part, this judgement about the historical specificity of states is already contained in my decision to focus upon the *modern* state. With this qualification, the state is *already* placed in a particular historical *locale*. But even states more generically belong to a particular time and place. It is clear that, for most of its history, humankind functioned without even a very primitive form of state. In line with much recent historical sociology, I shall argue that modern states can only be properly understood in a historical context: clearly one way of getting a better grasp upon the nature of states is to trace the paths of their historical development. It underpins the judgement that the proper object of our study is not *the* state, but states placed in an international order of unequal and competing states. This helps us to avoid some of the problems that have arisen (e.g. in both structural-functionalism and functionalist forms of Marxism) from seeing the state in purely functional terms. This emphasis upon the historically unique does not, however, prevent us from identifying some common features and processes in the evolution of a range of modern states.

A further way to approach the problem of simultaneously delimiting and understanding the state is to consider it in terms of its relation to other forces and actors. This, very broadly, is the approach that I adopt in the central chapters of the book. In each of these chapters, I assess the state in terms of its relationship to a key term which it is frequently seen either to complement or to confront. In Chapter 3, I consider the relationship between states and societies. I seek to adjudicate between *state*-centred and *society*-centred accounts of states' development and try to identify the nature of the societies with which states are said to interact. In the end, states and societies prove to be tightly enmeshed in ways which make any straightforward account of one *determining* the other unsustainable. In Chapter 4, I turn to the relationship between states and economies and, more especially, the relationship between states and markets. Here we find that, for all the seismic changes of recent years, and even in the context of an increasingly global market economy, states remain decisive economic players. Again, it proves impossible convincingly to disentangle state and economy. In Chapter 5, I consider the relationship of the state to its members. Are they primarily 'citizens' or simply 'subjects'? Can the state be made democratic and can it be made to treat all its citizens equally? In Chapter 6, I make explicit my concern with the international order within which individual states are (sometimes quite perilously) located. In some approaches (above all, the 'realist' school of international relations), this is the context in which we can understand the 'real' nature and activity of states. Upon this account, making war, threatening war, forging alliances and entering into diplomacy are the central activities of states which are essentially turned outward in discharging their primary responsibility: that is, the defence of the territorial integrity and 'national interest' of a given state. But we shall see that the international arena is also subject to change and that new forms of state activity and even new forms of statehood are being increasingly brought into play.

In Chapter 7, I discuss some of the most important changes and challenges that states face in the early twenty-first century. These include the rise of new modes of governing (governance), the increase in multi-levelled governance, the development of policy networks and policy transfer. I also consider the ways in which government beyond and above the state is changing, assess the claims made about new dysfunctional state forms ('rogue states' and 'failed states') and discuss the nature of the non-state security challenge to the integrity of the modern states' system.

In the Conclusion, I return to the question of the future of the state. Some suggest that the classical state is in decline as its characteristic tasks are either devolved downwards on to a sub-national level, or reappropriated by market forms of exchange, overwhelmed by the power of external economic forces or replaced by the discharge of state functions by supra-national organizations. Are we in fact witnessing the twilight of the state or simply the metamorphosis of old powers into new forms? To anticipate just a little, I argue that we are still living in an era of big government and that states continue to be the most important purveyors of systematic violence.

# 1 Modern states

## A matter of definition

A US Supreme Court judge hearing an obscenity case had to decide what was meant by 'pornography'. Admitting that he could not define it, the judge insisted nonetheless that 'I know it when I see it' (cited in Hawkins and Zimring 1988: 20). We may feel the same way about the modern state. We might find it difficult to give a precise and comprehensive definition of the state, but we think we recognize it when it flags us down on the motorway, sends us a final tax demand or, of course, arranges for our old-age pension to be paid at the nearest post office. We may also think that we recognize the long arm of the state as CNN shows us a group of marines raising their national flag over some distant corner of windswept desert. Stateless persons, refugees and asylum-seekers have a very keen sense that it makes a real difference to live beyond the jurisdiction (and protection) of the state. From the mandatory certification of our birth (which should have taken place under medical circumstances prescribed by the state) to the compulsory registration of our death, we tend to feel that the state is (nearly) always with us. Even in Anglo-Saxon countries, everyday political discussion is replete with appeals to, condemnations of and murmurings about the state. Rather like the judge, we think that we know the state when we see it, yet it proves extremely difficult to bring it under some brief but generally acceptable definition. '*Everybody* agrees', so Berki argues, that 'the modern state . . . is a rather baffling phenomenon' (Berki 1989: 12). At times, it seems that collective bafflement is about as far as the agreement reaches.

A number of commentators, from quite differing political traditions, circumvent this problem by refusing any explanatory value to the category of 'the state'. More empirically minded political scientists ask us to focus upon 'governments' and the 'political system', abandoning the suspiciously metaphysical realm of 'the state' for institutions and practices which can be measured with due 'operational rigor' (Almond *et al.* 1988: 872; Easton 1981). Others, who are much more critical of the prevailing social order, insist that talk of the state actually serves to *conceal* or *obscure* the exercise of political power. According to Abrams, 'the state is not the reality which stands behind the mask of political practice. It is itself the mask which prevents our seeing political practice as it is' (Abrams 1988: 58). Some follow the brilliant and iconoclastic French thinker Michel Foucault (1926–84) in arguing that the state may be 'no more than a composite reality and a mythicized abstraction'. What matters for

Foucault is not so much the state as the much more generic practice of the 'art of governing' and the corresponding idea of *governmentality*. The state is just one site of the practice of governing (understood as the management of 'the conduct of conduct'). To focus attention exclusively upon the state is to fail to capture the full range and intensity of governing practices that permeate and mediate the entire body politic (Foucault 1994).

It is important that we do not lose sight of these rather unorthodox views (and we return to Foucault's argument in Chapter 3). Most political scientists, political sociologists and political economists, however, have felt that there are political structures, institutions and practices which it makes sense to try to explain under the rubric of the state. While their attempts to do so are very diverse, there has been a surprisingly broad area of agreement about what constitutes the essential elements of the modern state. In this chapter, I will try to establish the most important features of this shared understanding of the modern state.

## Approaches to the modern state

We can think of analysis of the state characteristically having asked two kinds of questions. The first and more normative or evaluative question is: What should the state be and what should it do? This invites us to consider the proper terms for establishing and maintaining any political authority, for defining the appropriate relationship between the state and its members and the acceptable limits of state action. This has been the major concern of political philosophers. The second and more 'fact-based' or empirical question asks: What are states actually like? This is the question that has most often been addressed by political scientists and political sociologists. In practice, the two approaches cannot be so neatly separated. For many commentators, description and evaluation overlap. For both advocates and opponents, what states are *really* like does imply something about what we can (reasonably) suppose that they *should* be like. Nonetheless, our primary focus here will be upon the second type of question, though with a recognition that more evaluative claims are never far away.

Initially, we may think about these explanations rather crudely in terms of those which focus primarily upon the organizational *means* adopted by the modern state and those which concentrate upon its *functions*. Still the most authoritative source for the first of these approaches is the work of the German political sociologist and economic historian Max Weber (1864–1920). Active in the early years of the twentieth century, Weber established many of the parameters of statehood which are still common to discussions a century later. A starting-point for Weber, which contrasted with much earlier thinking, was that the state could not be defined in terms of its goals or functions, but had rather to be understood in terms of its distinctive *means*. Thus, he argued:

> The state cannot be defined in terms of its ends. There is scarcely any task that some political association has not taken in hand, and there is no task that one could say has always been exclusive and peculiar to those associations which

are designated as political ones. . . . Ultimately, one can define the modern state only in terms of the specific *means* peculiar to it, as to every political association, namely, *the use of physical force.*

(1970a: 77–8; second emphasis added)

For Weber, *the modern state* was a particular form of *the state* which was, itself, a particular form of a more general category of *political associations.*

> A compulsory political organization with continuous operations will be called a 'state' insofar as its administrative staff successfully upholds the claims to the *monopoly* of the *legitimate* use of physical force in the enforcement of its order. . . . [The modern state] possesses an administrative and legal order subject to change by legislation, to which the organized activities of the administrative staff, which are also controlled by regulations, are oriented. This system of orders claims binding authority, not only over members of the state, the citizens, most of whom have obtained membership by birth, but also to a very large extent over all action taking place in the area of its jurisdiction. It is thus a compulsory organization with a territorial basis. Furthermore, today, the use of force is regarded as legitimate only so far as it is either permitted by the state or prescribed by it. . . . The claim of the modern state to monopolize the use of force is as essential to it as its character of compulsory jurisdiction and continuous operation.
>
> (1978a: 54–6)

These economical definitions help us to isolate several of the most important (if contested) features in all subsequent discussions of the mechanisms of the state:

1  (monopoly) control of the means of violence
2  territoriality
3  sovereignty
4  constitutionality
5  impersonal power
6  the public bureaucracy
7  authority/legitimacy
8  citizenship.

To these, I shall add a ninth category: taxation. I will discuss each of these in turn.

### (Monopoly) control of the means of violence

Weber gives great prominence to control over the means of violence as a defining characteristic of the state. Indeed, his very briefest definition sees the state as 'a human community that (successfully) claims the *monopoly of the legitimate use of physical force* within a given territory' (Weber 1970a: 78). In fact, control over the means of violence has long been a concern for those whose primary interest is in the 'reality' of states' practices. Thus, Thomas Hobbes (1588–1679), the Englishman who many see as the first theorist of the authentically *modern* state, was insistent that, to avoid collapse into civil war, individuals needed to establish over themselves 'a Common Power, to keep them in awe, and to direct their actions to the Common Benefit'. It seemed to Hobbes that 'the only way to erect such a Common Power . . . is to conferre all their power and strength upon one Man, or upon one Assembly of men' and to ensure that the wielder of this 'Common Power' – the 'great Leviathan' – 'hath the use of so much Power and Strength conferred on him, that by terror thereof, he is inabled to forme the wills of them all, to Peace at home, and mutuall ayd against their enemies abroad.' Once established, the authority of this 'Common Power' proceeds not from consent but from force: 'Covenants being but words, and breath, have no force to oblige, contain, constrain, or protect any man, but what it has from the publique Sword' (Hobbes 1968: 227–31).

Writers in the Marxist tradition have also stressed the importance of the state as organized violence, but for them this is primarily an expression of the intense antagonisms generated by a society divided into classes. Friedrich Engels (1820–89) articulates the classically Marxist view that the state is an expression of the contradictions of a society divided by irreconcilable class differences. The existence of the state is an admission that 'society has become entangled in an insoluble contradiction with itself, that it has split into irreconcilable antagonisms which it is powerless to dispel.'

> But in order that these antagonisms and classes with conflicting economic interests might not consume themselves and society in a fruitless struggle, it became necessary to have a power seemingly standing above society that would alleviate the conflict and keep it within the bounds of 'order'. This power, arisen out of society but placing itself above it, and alienating more and more from it, is the state.
>
> (Engels 1978: 752)

Of course, as Weber himself was well aware, 'the use of physical force is neither the sole, nor even the most usual, method of administration of political organizations' (Weber 1978a: 54). If we look around the contemporary world, we see great variation in the levels of direct physical intimidation that states offer to their citizen-subjects: compare, for example, the Netherlands with Indonesia or Sweden with China. Even the most violent states of modern times (e.g. Stalin's Soviet Union, Hitler's Germany) did not impose their rule by physical force alone. Nor did Weber argue that the state would necessarily reserve to itself all the lawful use of violence. In the USA, for example, citizens have a constitutional right to carry lethal weapons and many states sanction (limited) violence exercised by disciplining parents against their children. Feminist critics have long argued that states frequently fail to uphold their monopoly of violence in restraining the perpetrators of domestic assaults upon women (Dobash and Dobash 1992). What Weber does see as essential to the state is its status as 'the sole source of the "right" to use violence' (Weber 1970a: 78). Thus, those who exercise violence within the jurisdiction of a state may do so only under the express dispensation of that state. Normally, however, the state will seek to impose its will through the managed consent of its population – an aspect of legitimation to which we return below. Nonetheless, Weber insisted, 'the threat of force, and in the case of need its actual use . . ., is always the last resort when other [methods] have failed' (Weber 1978a: 54). As Hobbes had it, 'command of the Militia, without other Institution, maketh him that hath it Soveraign' (Hobbes 1968: 235). Under many constitutions, the harshest and most lethal remedies are reserved for those who challenge the integrity of the state itself (i.e. those who commit the crime of treason). Yet, even a quite minor breach of the authority of the state (e.g. failure to disclose certain driving documents to the police) may finally result in incarceration. In Berki's irreverent formulation: 'Tell the judge, a ridiculous old fogey dressed up in theatrical garb, to bugger off and leave you alone; you see where you will end up' (Berki 1989: 18). As we shall see, states' practice is usually a mixture of (managed) 'consent backed by coercion' (see below, pp. 60–3).

In fact, as a number of more recent commentators have suggested (see Mann 1993a: 55; Giddens 1985: 189), the state may never actually attain Weber's monopolization of violence within its jurisdiction, even if we include those forms of violence which are 'licensed' by the state. Organized crime and domestic battery are but two forms of chronic violence within contemporary societies which evade effective control by the state. The same commentators point out the extent to which the apparatus of the state's physical violence (above all, the armed forces) is institutionally isolated from many other areas of state activity. There may, nonetheless, be a relationship between the extent of monopolization of violence achieved by the state and actual levels of violence in society. Indeed, the more effectively is the use of force *monopolized* by the state, the less frequent may be the actual resort to violence. This was certainly the supposition of Hobbes and of many of those who have experienced the peculiar horrors of civil war. In Hobbes's view, the individual did a good deal when he [*sic*] surrendered almost all of his natural liberties to an authoritarian sovereign, since this was the only way of avoiding society descending into a war of all against all in which his life would famously be 'solitary, poor, nasty, brutish, and short' (Hobbes 1968: 186).

More important than the actual monopolization of violence may be the inauguration of a unitary order of violence. In Chapter 2, we shall see that many commentators trace the emergence of the modern state to the historical transition in Europe from forms of feudalism to absolutism. Crudely put, this is a transition from societies built upon multiple sites and sources of power to societies premised on a single legitimating structure. Feudalism is often represented as a pyramidical social formation built upon personal ties of fealty in which the wielders of power at any level depended upon their capacity to mobilize the resources (including armed force) controlled by many lesser power-holders. In such a model, power was not unified in the monarch but diversified among a hierarchy of lesser nobilities. It was also an order in which separate powers and jurisdiction applied to those in religious orders. An important part of the coming of the modern state was the move away from this multi-centred and pluralist structure of powers towards a single (absolutist) centre of power ruling over an undivided social order.

Fundamental to this process of the centralization of state power was the increasing *pacification* of society. To some extent the monopolization of violence within the state was matched by a pacification of relations in society. This was certainly a part of Hobbes's justification for the individual's subjecting himself to 'the great Leviathan'. Of course, in ways that I have already indicated, this pacification of society was always quite partial. Violence and the threat of violence continued to be a chronic feature of daily life. Yet, there is considerable evidence (in the face of the common-place claim that our societies are becoming increasingly violent) that the rise of the state coincided with a reduction in the levels of violence in day-to-day life. In part, this had to do with the new forms of surveillance and control that were becoming available to an increasingly powerful state. Premodern states could be extra-ordinarily arbitrary and despotic, but the range of their power was drastically limited. Genghis Khan was a fearful despot, but surely not the equal of Stalin, once famously described as 'Jenghiz [*sic*] Khan with a telephone' (Maclean 1978: 159). As Giddens points out, it was crucial too that the rising economic order (of capitalism) was one in which violence was extruded from the core economic relationship – the sale of labour power (Giddens 1985: 181–92). Of course, Marx insisted that the *establishment* of capitalism, the process of primitive accumulation, was 'written in the annals of mankind in letters of blood and fire' (Marx 1965: 715). Marxists saw the growth of imperialism as a very bloody business and expected that the revolution which would see capitalism replaced by socialism would be a violent one. Yet, the liberal capitalism described in Marx's *Capital* was one in which it was economic necessity, not the threat of violence, that drove workers into an exploitative contract with their capitalist employers.

## Territoriality

A second and seemingly straightforward feature of modern states is that they are geographic or geo-political entities. States occupy an increasingly clearly defined physical space over which they characteristically claim sole legitimate authority. Once again, this is a feature of statehood which is recognized by a wide range of writers (from Hobbes through Engels and Weber to contemporary theorists such as Mann and Giddens). Indeed, a clearly defined territoriality is one of the things that marks off the state from earlier political forms, such as premodern empires (i.e. those empires which were not the external domain of already established nation-states). These early empires were extensive and powerful political formations, but their territorial limits tended to be set by ill-defined frontiers rather than by the clearly demarcated borders with which we are familiar (Giddens 1985: 49–50). Rule was concentrated at the centre of the empire. The outlying areas tended to be a source of tribute rather than the objects of permanent and tightly managed administration. Considerable autonomy was allowed to local systems of governance, so long as the expectations of the imperial power could be satisfied.

Modern states defend their territorial integrity with a quite ferocious jealousy. At times, states have been willing to go to war over seemingly valueless tracts of land or uninhabitable islands, apparently unmindful of the considerable costs and the sometimes very limited benefits. The south-eastern corner of Europe has been repeatedly riven by civil war over the competing territorial claims of a number of aspirant states. Elsewhere in the world – in Kashmir, or the Indonesian provinces of Aceh or Irian Jaya, for example – claims to state authority continue to be fiercely contested. In addition, states lay claim not just to jurisdiction over a particular tract of land, but also to the minerals that lie beneath it, to the coastal waters that surround it (and to their economic product), to the airspace above it and, most importantly, to the people who inhabit it. States have not been an omnipresent form of human organization. Even upon the most expansive definition, the majority of people through most of human history have not lived in states. Nonetheless, we now live on a planet which is almost universally divided into (competing) state jurisdictions. There can hardly be a rocky outcrop anywhere which has not been claimed by at least one jurisdiction (and often by several).

This raises a number of further points. First, states do not exist in isolation. They are by their very nature part of *a system of competing states*. Frontiers might abut unclaimed territory, but borders are necessarily the dividing line between one state and another. The territoriality of states, their claim to monopolistic powers of adjudication within their boundaries and the existence of an international order premised upon competing nation-states, is definitive of one of the most important general approaches to the state – international relations. The sub-discipline of international relations invites us to focus our studies of the state, first and foremost, upon the *external* and *international* relationships of a series of competing sovereign states operating within an unruly international order. We shall return to this approach in Chapter 6.

Second, while the globe is finite and almost every inch of it is now under some state's jurisdiction, this does not mean that particular states are permanent features of the world's landscape. Those of us who live in one of the historically longer-standing states may think of states once having been founded as lasting in perpetuity. But this is not so. Tilly records that 'the Europe of 1500 included some five hundred more or less independent political units, the Europe of 1900 about twenty-five' (Tilly 1975: 15). Rather more remarkable is the redrawing of the map of European states between 1980 and 1995. Thirty-three nations competed in football's European Nations' Cup in 1992. Just four years later, there were forty-eight contestants, including separate teams from Slovakia and the Czech Republic and two national teams from within the borders of the former Yugoslavia! (*Sunday Times*, 23 January 1994). Or consider the statehood of one of Europe's central political actors: Germany. Founded little more than a hundred years ago, the country was split into two states for nearly half of that time and resumed its existing borders only in 1991. And in the twenty-first century, new states continue to appear, including, for example, East Timor, which reached full statehood on 20 May 2002.

Third, as the territory occupied by the state became ever clearer, so did the tendency to identify states with *nations*. The international order is increasingly recognized as one consisting of nation-states. This is, in both theory and practice, an extremely contentious and confused area. At this point, it may be useful to try to distinguish between conceptions of the *nation*, *nationalism* and *the nation-state*. *The nation* may be taken to describe 'a collectivity existing within a clearly demarcated territory, which is subject to a unitary administration' (Giddens 1985: 116). In Greenfeld's usage, the nation describes 'a *unique* sovereign people' (Greenfeld 1992: 8). *Nationalism*, by contrast, describes identification within an 'imagined community' (Anderson 1991). According to Giddens, it is 'primarily psychological, [expressing] the affiliation of individuals to a set of symbols and beliefs emphasising communality among the members of a political order' (or, we might add, of those *aspiring* to form a distinct political order) (Giddens 1985: 116). In Greenfeld's account:

> National identity in its distinctive modern sense is . . . an identity which derives from membership in a 'people', the fundamental characteristic of which is that it is defined as 'a nation'. Every member of the 'people' thus interpreted partakes in its superior, elite quality, and it is in consequence that a stratified national population is perceived as essentially homogeneous, and the lines of status and class as superficial. This principle lies at the basis of all nationalisms.
>
> (Greenfeld 1992: 7)

We return to the difficult question of the relationship between nations, nationalisms and the nation-state in Chapter 2.

## Sovereignty

Greenfeld's discussion of the nature of nationalism raises a third core component of the state – its supposed *sovereignty*. Hinsley (1986: 1, 26) defines sovereignty as 'the idea that there is a final and absolute authority in the political community', with the proviso that 'no final and absolute authority exists elsewhere.' The essence of sovereignty is not that the sovereign may do whatever it wishes. After all, even the most unbridled of states cannot make pigs fly. Rather, it is the idea that, within the limits of its jurisdiction (set by the division of the world into a series of similarly sovereign nation-states), no other actor may gainsay the will of the sovereign state. Modern usage is often seen to derive from the French philosopher Jean Bodin (1529–96), but still the most uncompromising statement of this position is that found in Hobbes's *Leviathan*. For Hobbes, once the members of the commonwealth have come together and agreed to constitute a sovereign power to rule over them, the powers of that sovereign are almost unlimited. The terms of the contract are irrevocable and, since members of the commonwealth have mutually willed the creation of the sovereign, they are deemed to have vicariously willed all of its actions. Since the initial agreement is between the members of the commonwealth (to create a sovereign power) and not between individual subjects and that sovereign power, 'there can happen no breach of Covenant on the part of the Soveraigne; and consequently none of his subjects, by any pretence of forfeiture, can be freed from his Subjection.' Since 'he that doth any thing by authority from another, doth therein no injury to him by whose authority he acteth . . . whatsoever [the sovereign] doth, it can be no injury to any of his Subjects.' It is true 'that they that have Soveraigne power, may commit Iniquity; but not Injustice, or Injury in the proper signification' (Hobbes 1968: 230–2).

Even for Hobbes, however, there are limitations upon the lawful authority of the sovereign. 'It is manifest', so he argues, 'that every Subject has Liberty in all those things, the right whereof cannot by Covenant be transferred.' So,

> if the Soveraigne command a man (though justly condemned) to kill, wound, or mayme himself; or not to resist those that assault him; or to abstain from the use of food, ayre, medicine, or any other thing without which he cannot live; yet hath that man the Liberty to disobey.

And there is one further substantial qualification of the powers of the sovereign: 'The Obligation of Subjects to the Soveraign, is understood to last *as long, and no longer*, that the power lasteth, by which he is able to protect them. (Hobbes 1968: 268–9, 272; emphasis added).

Subsequent discussion of sovereignty and the state may be seen to have moved in three directions. First, there has been an aspiration, consonant with the brief discussion of nationalism above, to relocate the site of sovereignty not in the state or the government, but rather in *the people*. Although the other great seventeenth-century English political theorist John Locke (1632–1704) was far from being an untrammelled democrat, he certainly held sovereign power to be much more subject to the will of its citizens. In contrast to Hobbes, he maintained that some form of continuing endorsement of government (however passively expressed) was needed for it to exercise proper and lawful authority. A much more radical position was adopted by Jean-Jacques Rousseau (1712–78), who argued that the principle of sovereignty should be retained, but that it should be relocated in the sovereign people. Certainly, advocates of democratization of the last two centuries have often made their case in terms of *legitimate* sovereignty residing in the people. Those states which are based upon some founding constitutional settlement often posit the sovereignty of the people as their first principle. Thus, the founding authority for the constitution of the USA rests famously with 'We, the people . . .' (McKay 1993: 305). The location of sovereignty in an unreconstructed constitution, such as we enjoy in Britain, is much more ambiguous.

A second development has been manifest in the attempts not so much to deny as to *apportion* sovereignty. This is, perhaps, clearest in the constitutional principle of the *separation of powers*, under which the functions of government (most usually divided between executive, legislative and judicial tasks) are allocated to differing institutions and persons. The principle is at its clearest in the US constitutional order, in which the powers of the president, the congress and the supreme court are clearly set out with the intention that no one branch of government should be able to dominate the others. Of course, this may be read as a simple refutation of the Hobbesian idea of sovereignty, i.e. that of all lawful authority residing in one institution or even one person. On the other hand, if the people are held to be sovereign, it may seem that this is but a convenient system for ensuring that the apparatus of government, to which the sovereign devolves its powers for a time, should perform its task effectively without that concentration of power which might pose a threat to the properly sovereign people. Alternatively, we may view such a constitutional order as one in which it is not the particular branches of government but the constitutional order itself which is sovereign.

The third development must be considered rather more unambiguously as a counter-movement against the idea of sovereignty. We have seen that democracy may be seen as a way of expressing the wishes of the sovereign people. In a more 'realist' tradition, democracy has sometimes been represented as a mechanism for exercising constraint over an apparatus of government in which *de facto* sovereignty is seen to reside. From the advocates of 'protective' democracy in the nineteenth century – such as Bentham (1748–1832) and J. S. Mill (1806–73) – to the 'democratic elite' theorists of the twentieth century – above all, Joseph Schumpeter (1883–1946) – the democratic process is one through which the people, who are not in fact sovereign, exercise some sort of constraint upon those state actors with whom real sovereignty rests. There is also a long-standing fear of the democratic sovereign retraceable all the way to Aristotle (384–322 BC). For some, the very real popular legitimacy of the democratic state makes it, if anything, more to be feared than an authoritarian but 'illegitimate' state. Liberals and conservatives, in particular, have seen, not very far behind the idea of popular sovereignty, the prospect of 'the tyranny of the majority'. For conservatives, the principal threat has been to the established order of property; for liberals, it is a challenge to property and individual liberty. For both, the legitimating force of a truly popular democracy is a threat to minorities. We have then, complementing the claims for popular sovereignty expressed through the extension of democratic institutions, a counter-movement stressing the inviolability of certain personal rights and an inviolable private space within which the state should not interfere. Paradoxically, we sometimes find argument and counter-argument voiced by the same individual (as famously in the case of J. S. Mill), as well as calls for a constitutionally self-limiting state, a state which should legislate to constrain its own powers of intervention.

Finally, it is worth stressing that the territoriality and, more especially, the effective sovereignty of modern states were transformed by a series of technical changes which profoundly altered the state's capacity for surveillance and control. New forms of administration, new techniques for record-keeping, new technologies for the transmission and processing of both people and information gave the modern state powers to govern which were simply unavailable to more traditional states. It was one thing for the pope to assert his authority as the head of all Christendom, but something else for officers of the state to have more or less instantaneous access to the personal details, criminal records and credit status of each of its citizens. According to Giddens, 'surveillance as the mobilizing of administrative power – through the storage and control of information – is the primary means of the concentration of authoritative resources involved in the formation of the nation-state' (Giddens 1985: 181). We need to be careful here. Giddens is not saying that changing technology *caused* the development of modern states. Rather, technological change made available to the modern state forms of surveillance and control which simply had not existed under more traditional state formations.

### Constitutionality

In much 'official' discourse about modern states, constitutions and the 'constitutionality' of the political order enjoy considerable prominence. In this context, constitutions are often taken to describe the basic 'rules of the game' of the political process. In many polities, there is a single document or set of documents that lays out and, often at the same time, justifies the state's basic political arrangements. The constitution establishes 'the laws about making laws' and may be presented as actually creating or, at least, securing the existence of the state itself. In some states, perhaps in the USA above all, the whole political process is sometimes presented in 'official' explanations as little more than the day-to-day operation of 'the constitution'. This narrowly constitutional account of the modern state is what one might expect to hear (in a truncated form) from a tour guide at the House of Commons or on Capitol Hill, or from a practising politician in a particularly pompous mood and with the tapes running.

Political commentators, be they academics, journalists or 'ordinary citizens', have been rather less persuaded that the constitutional model gives a very 'realistic' account of what states really do. The severest critics, such as Lenin (1870–1924), have seen claims about constitutional governance as an ideological gloss through which the minority who exercise *real* power through the state and its monopoly of violence seek to conceal this fact from the subject population (Lenin 1960). The 'realist' school of international relations, inasmuch as it has been at all concerned with constitutionality, has tended to see this as a rather decorous fiction drawing attention away from the 'real' business of politics, i.e. a largely non-constitutional clash of powers and interests. Some (perhaps most notoriously the inter-war German theorist Carl Schmitt) have stressed the importance of establishing who is sovereign in *exceptional* periods, i.e. when constitutional government is suspended. Certainly, there is a reasonable suspicion that the very best of constitutions are no match for the will of a usurping sovereign. The Soviet constitution of 1936 'guaranteed' extensive liberties to Soviet citizens. But this proved no great impediment to Stalin's reign of terror. Even those who have been willing to give rather greater weight to constitutional accounts (such as the US political scientists Robert Dahl and Charles Lindblom) have doubted that the actual working of constitutional arrangements looks very much like these idealized descriptions.

Nonetheless, 'constitutionality' rather more broadly conceived is an extremely important component of the idea of the modern state. We have seen that Weber writes of the modern state possessing 'an administrative and legal order subject to change by legislation'. The idea that the state constitutes a distinct and rule-governed domain with powers which are (at least formally) distanced from society and the economy is distinctively modern. Most modern states do indeed exercise a form of power which, at least formally, is public, rule-governed and subject to lawful reform. These characteristics may be as often honoured in the breach as in the observance, but they do nonetheless help to locate the state in modernity. In pre-modern states, social, economic, patriarchal and political powers were largely undifferentiated. Their activities could be justified as *explicitly* arbitrary, absolutist, theocratic and dynastic in ways which modern states generally cannot. The idea of constitutionality thus points us towards a number of further characteristic features of modern statehood (differentiation from society and economy, 'impersonal' power, bureaucratic organization and so on). But it is an idea that has also done an enormous amount of work in more *normative* accounts of the modern state. It has been an abiding concern of political philosophers to establish what (if anything) justifies the state's claim to the loyalty of its subjects. Is there anything more than 'might' that makes the state 'right'? This raises questions about the legitimacy of the state, the nature of its authority and the nature of its obligations to its citizens and of its citizens to it.

### *'The rule of law' and the exercise of impersonal power*

Of the essence, for those who stress constitutionality, is the idea that a constitutional political order would mean 'not the rule of men, but *the rule of law*'. There is a very ancient claim in political theory that a good polity is one which is ruled not by the subjective and arbitrary will of particular men [*sic*], but by the objective determination of general and public laws. According to Kant (1724–1804), 'the state is a union of an aggregate of men under rightful law' (cited in Dyson 1980: 107). Especially in the continental European tradition, we find that state activity is often characterized as a special form of (public or administrative) law, an arrangement under which 'public law regulates the interrelationships of public authorities with the "subjects"; private law regulates the relationships of the governed individuals among themselves' (see Dyson 1980; Weber 1970b: 239). Admittedly, some commentators have always been much more concerned with the state's actual capacity to uphold its own laws than with what would make them 'rightful' (e.g. see Kelsen 1961). But it is widely argued that, within a constitutional order, those who exercise state power must do so in ways which are themselves lawful, constitutional and constrained by publicly acknowledged procedures. They are generally seen to act not upon a personal basis, but rather because of their public position as the occupants of particular offices of state.

This aspiration to lawful government should not be conflated with the aspiration to extend democracy. Not only do the calls to make governance constitutional long *precede* any very widespread appeal to make it more democratic, but they have also often been advanced as a way of protecting certain individual or corporate interests *against* the encroachments of democratic governments. However, it is of the essence that, under a law-governed regime, politicians should themselves be subject to the constitutional order and the laws which they have themselves helped to make and enforce. Even under so centralized and sovereign a state as in the UK, government ministers may still be arraigned by the courts if they fail to abide by their own rules (however limited may be the effect of such judgments). From this, we may derive the central (if rather idealized) principles of legality and lawfulness as characteristic modes of state activity, of the state as an impersonal power, of politicians and civil servants as the (temporary) occupiers of particular public posts.

## *The public bureaucracy*

For Weber, it was of the essence that the administration of modern states would be *bureaucratic* (Weber 1978a: 217–26; 1978b: 956–1005). In fact, Weber saw bureaucracy as the generic form of administration in all large-scale organizations of modern society (including, for example, the modern capitalist corporation and the modern army) and this was, in its turn, a particular form of the more general process of rationalization which Weber identified with modernization itself. It established the administration of the modern state as quite distinct from those forms that had preceded it. The public bureaucracy, in Weber's celebrated description, can be isolated around the following features:

1   that bureaucratic administration is conducted according to fixed rules and procedures, within a clearly established hierarchy and in line with clearly demarcated official responsibilities;
2   that access to employment within the civil service is based upon special examinations and that its effective operation is dependent upon knowledge of its special administrative procedures – a good deal of the power of the civil service rests upon its specialized knowledge and 'expertise';
3   that bureaucratic management is based upon a knowledge of written documents ('the files') and depends upon the impartial application of general rules to particular cases;
4   that the civil servant acts not in a personal capacity, but as the occupier of a particular public office.

Office-holding in the civil service is seen as a 'vocation', subject to a special sense of public duty, and involves the individual civil servant in a clearly defined and hierarchical career path, usually with 'a job for life' (Weber 1978a: 220–1; 1978b: 956–63).

There were great bureaucracies in the premodern world (e.g. in ancient Egypt and China), but, for Weber, the modern predominance of bureaucratic organization is a product of the coming of a fully monetized market economy. The reason for its 'success' lies in 'its purely technical superiority over any other form of organization'. Bureaucracy is 'formally the most rational known means of exercising authority over human beings . . ., the needs of mass administration make it today completely indispensable.' According to Weber, 'bureaucracy inevitably accompanies modern *mass democracy*' and 'everywhere the modern state is undergoing bureaucratization.' He insists that 'it is obvious that technically the great modern state is absolutely dependent upon a bureaucratic basis. The larger the state, and the more it is or the more it becomes a great power state, the more unconditionally is this the case.' Furthermore, 'once fully established, bureaucracy is among those social structures which are the hardest to destroy' (Weber 1970b: 232; 1978a: 223; 1978b: 971, 983, 987).

Weber was quite ambivalent about the idea that bureaucracy (along with the more general process of rationalization characteristic of modernity) represented 'progress'.

He recognized that the treatment of individuals and their particular circumstances as just so many 'cases' to be processed according to 'the rules' has a cost in terms of the quality of our humanity. He was also fearful that the 'routinization' and rule-guidedness which was appropriate to large-scale administration might spill over into the more properly dynamic and value-laden sphere of 'politics proper'. He was certainly concerned about the consequences of a regime in which civil servants usurped the proper function of the politician (see Beetham 1985). The routinized terror of the bureaucratized authoritarian state was to become a prominent theme of twentieth-century fiction (from Kafka to Havel). The dullness and rule-boundedness of public officials has become one of the standing jokes of modernity. Much more at variance with Weber has been the widespread claim that, in practice, bureaucracy is a drastically *inefficient* means of administration. Rather than being grindingly efficient, bureaucracies (in the public sector above all) have been depicted as chronically inefficient. Above all, neo-liberal or 'New Right' critics have insisted that bureaucracies are almost universally *less* efficient as a means of administration than are markets. Bureaucrats are seen as rent-seekers who exploit the monopoly of provision by the state to extract greater material rewards for themselves from a system which tax-paying citizens cannot escape. This view has now spread well beyond the New Right to become a part of the new governing common sense of the twenty-first century, often classified under the label of the 'new public management'. Bureaucracy is very far from disappearing. Indeed, a whole new breed of bureaucracies has been established to manage the new surveillance practices that new public management creates. Nonetheless, there have been enormous changes in the ways in which public services are delivered (and we shall consider these further in Chapter 7).

### Authority and legitimacy

Issues of authority and legitimacy are quite central to the appraisal of the modern state. No state can survive for very long exclusively through its power to coerce. Even where power is most unequally distributed and the possibilities for coercion are at their greatest – for example, in a prisoner-of-war camp – the subordinated can always exercise *some* level of non-compliance, and, across time, the maintenance of social order is 'negotiated'. How much more is this the case for a state governing many millions of subjects in a comparatively open society? A stable state requires that, for whatever reason, most of the people most of the time will accept its rule.

At this point, it may be useful to turn again to Weber. In *Economy and Society*, he offers the following definitions:

> **Domination** (or **'authority'**) is the probability that a command with a given specific content will be obeyed by a group of persons.

> **Legitimacy** describes 'the prestige of being considered binding'.

> **Legitimate authority** describes an authority which is obeyed, at least in part,

'because it is in some appreciable way regarded by the [subordinate] actor as in some way obligatory or exemplary for him'.

(Weber 1978a: 53, 31)

Authority and legitimacy imply that, under normal circumstances and for most people, the actions of the state and its demands upon its population will be accepted or, at least, not actively resisted. Without *some* level of legitimacy, it is hard to see that any state could be sustained, and consequently a great deal of work goes into defending the state's claim to exercise not just effective power, but also legitimate authority.

Virtually all states have sought to make their rule appear legitimate. Sometimes the appeal has been to tradition (to a 'natural' order which is said to have governed since time immemorial and/or to have been ordained by God) or to the charismatic qualities of a particular leader (or indeed to both). But what is most characteristic of the modern state is not just the greater weight given to *legal* authority – to the state's embodiment of abstract legal principles enforced through an impartial bureaucratic and judicial apparatus – but, above all, to the idea that the state embodies and expresses the (sovereign) will of the people. In Weber's interpretation, legal authority rests 'on a belief in the legality of enacted rules and the right of those elevated to authority under such rules to issue commands' (Weber 1978a: 2, 15). Within such an account, citizens are seen to attribute legitimacy to the modern state on the grounds that it is the appropriate embodiment of 'a consistent system of abstract laws' impartially administered by a rule-governed and non-partisan civil service.

Roughly speaking, we can isolate two types of question about legitimate authority. First, there is the question that has dominated much of classical and contemporary political theory: i.e. under what circumstances can the state's actions be considered 'valid'?, and, consequently, under what circumstances should the citizenry obey or, indeed, be made to obey? A second set of questions is more empirical: Why has the state sought to present its actions as legitimate? How do states uphold their claim to legitimacy? Why do people obey?

Since the question of political obligation has been a major problem – in some accounts, *the* major problem for political theorists of the past four centuries (at least) – and since this is not a text in political philosophy, I can give only the briefest indication of where the difficulties lie. Although the problem is older than modernity, it is posed in a peculiarly acute way in the modern period. There was a time when legitimacy might derive from religious authority or simply the custom and practice of a long-established order. In the post-Enlightenment world, these forms of legitimacy are, at least in principle, very largely rejected (though the attempt to re-establish theocratic states in our own time perhaps challenges this assumption). It seems that the justification of the modern state has normally to be rational and perhaps legal-rational in character. It has also tended, in the West at least, to proceed from certain beliefs about the integrity and autonomy of the human individual. At its simplest, the issue is this: What are the grounds that would justify an agency (such as the state) forcing individuals to do things which they do not wish to do? Of course, one perfectly respectable response (that of most anarchists) is that there are *no* circumstances under which such an imposition could be justified and that, consequently, the state is *never* legitimate. Among those who reject anarchy, probably the most popular response has been to argue that the state is legitimate to the extent that it expresses the authentic will of its population. Thus, the state is not a usurpation of the freedom and autonomy of individuals where it is simply the (collective) representation of our individual wills. In obeying the state, we are simply obeying the dictates of our *own* wills vicariously expressed.

Of course, this rather vulgar formulation hardly does justice to four hundred years of accumulated political wisdom! It raises many more questions than it could possibly answer (not least about how our individual wills may be aggregated and how consent can be maintained across time) and it distracts from the fact that political thinkers have taken a radically different view of the sorts of political institutions to which such a supposition about the state might give rise. It does, however, help to point us towards a ubiquitous feature of arguments about the contemporary state: i.e. that the modern state is widely seen to be legitimate inasmuch as (but no more than) it represents 'the will of the people'. Of course, in *institutional* terms this carries us no further forward. Hobbes and Rousseau, for example, might be thought to justify the state on the basis of 'the will of the people', but to radically different effects. But we might wish to argue that there is here an underlying premise – that we should obey the state because it is an indirect or derived expression of our own wills – that straddles many disparate traditions in modern Western political thought.

We should be clear about what this means. It certainly does *not* mean that all modern states are 'truly' popular or democratic. Indeed, there is again a perfectly respectable view (held by many Marxists and anarchists among others) that *no* modern state is democratic. If democracy is defined as a political order in which all the people themselves rule and rule themselves directly, no contemporary state can qualify as democratic. We know, too, that many of the most authoritarian regimes of the twentieth century have claimed that their right to rule derived from their being an expression of the 'real' will of the people, without or even in defiance of the 'empirical' will of the population expressed through duly constituted electoral procedures. Military regimes across the globe, even those that have held power for many years, characteristically describe themselves as 'preparing the way for a restoration of democratic government'. The argument is not that states in modernity are genuinely an expression of the will of their peoples, but rather that it is perceived to be important that they should present themselves as such. Just as the thief, to take Weber's example, acknowledges the legitimacy of laws of property when he seeks to conceal his breach of them, so does the state acknowledge the validity of 'popular legitimacy' when, however disingenuously, it commends its own actions as an expression of the popular will.

As we turn to the question of the capacity of states to uphold their claim to exercise legitimate authority, we need further to distinguish two senses of legitimacy. For the most part, political theorists and philosophers have been concerned with establishing the conditions that would make the state's rule justified in terms of some more or less externally validated rational criteria. For actual states, it is much more important that they should be able to maintain the general population's belief in the legitimacy of their claim to rule. Indeed, even this is to claim too much for the state's interest in legitimacy. For states, it will usually be enough that the great majority of the population do not actively regard the existing form of governance as illegitimate – and that they do not act collectively upon this premise. Consider the classification developed by Held:

> We may obey or comply [with the instructions of the state] because:
> 1    There is no choice in the matter (*following orders*, or *coercion*).
> 2    No thought has ever been given to it and we do it as it has always been done (*tradition*).
> 3    We cannot be bothered one way or another (*apathy*).
> 4    Although we do not like the situation . . . we cannot imagine things being really different and so we 'shrug our shoulders' and accept what seems like fate (*pragmatic acquiescence*).
> 5    We are dissatisfied with things as they are but nevertheless go along with them in order to secure an end; we acquiesce because it is in the long run to our advantage (*instrumental acceptance* or *conditional agreement/consent*).
> 6    In the circumstances before us . . . we conclude that it is 'right', correct', 'proper' for us as individuals or members of a collectivity: it is what we genuinely *should* or *ought to* do (*normative agreement*).
> 7    It is what in ideal circumstances . . . we would have agreed to do (*ideal normative agreement*).
>
> (Held 1989a: 101)

All of these constitute reasons for which subjects may obey the state. Only one is unambiguously related to the threat of force, but only a further two rely in any strong sense upon the view that the state's authority is legitimate. Citizens are busy people. They want to hold on to their jobs, to make love, to play football and to walk the dog (though not necessarily in that order and certainly not all at the same time). It is enough for the state that they should not spend their time thinking critically about the legitimacy of the state and making this the basis of coordinated political action (see Mann 1970). It may, of course, be in the state's interests to *encourage* this political indifference, as it always has, by supporting whatever is the contemporary equivalent of the Romans' 'bread and circuses' (perhaps sponsoring a National Lottery and a broadcasting regime dominated by 'reality TV').

This said, there is still a residuum of legitimacy which the state must seek to deliver, and, given the general scepticism that is expressed above, it is worth pointing out that many modern states do have some plausible claim to legitimacy. I have already indicated that there are perfectly respectable grounds for arguing that existing Western 'democracies' are not really democratic at all. Much more common, though, is the view that, while very imperfect, the sorts of institutions which we associate with Western liberal democracy – fixed-term elections, 'free' competition between parties, lawful opposition, constitutional arrangements for the scrutiny of government activity and so on – represent real, if rather limited, popular achievements. Democratic elite theorists, for example, argue that, while this is still 'government by elite', we the people do get to choose by which elite we should be governed and are, from time to time, constitutionally empowered to change our collective mind. They insist that, limited as it is, this is about the most democratic order we can hope to achieve in large-scale modern societies. Even those who believe that much more democracy is possible would probably concede that what we have so far is valuable, hard won and better than the absence of any constitutional constraint upon the activity of the state.

Democracy is a very powerful ideology in contemporary societies. Indeed, some might suppose that in a 'post-ideological' world it is the one ideology that remains. Certainly, in many contexts other than the state, we are as individuals willing to accept decisions that go against our own personal will and judgement, if we feel that such decisions have been made by an appropriate community to which we belong with due freedom of discussion and information and through properly constituted democratic procedures. Acquiescence with the state is an amalgam of indifference, deference, fear, instrumentality and active consent. For all the inadequacies of liberal democracy, we should not underestimate the extent to which citizens, when they *do* think about the legitimacy of the state's actions (usually in a rather piecemeal way), accept that democratic procedures do give the state some authority to act as it wishes and do place us under some (albeit limited) obligation to obey. But we should remember that states are typically very jealous of their monopoly over the means of violence and no state relies exclusively upon its power to persuade. The character-istic form of state action, as the Italian Marxist Antonio Gramsci (1891–1937) observed, is 'consent backed by coercion' (see below, pp. 60–3).

### Citizenship

Citizenship is one of the oldest terms of political discourse, probably as old as the idea of the political community itself. In essence, the citizen is one who is entitled to participate in the life of the political community. Citizen status in the modern world typically denotes a mixture of entitlements or rights of participation and a series of attendant obligations or duties. In Held's helpful summary: 'Citizenship is a status which, in principle, bestows upon individuals equal rights and duties, liberties and constraints, powers and responsibilities [within] the political com-munity' (Held 1995: 66). Although the claims of citizenship first articulated in the city-states of the ancient world never quite went away, they burst onto centre stage in the modern world with the events surrounding the French Revolution of 1789. Revolutionary discourse was replete with appeals to citizenship and to the rights of the citizen. This republican approach to state and citizenship is neatly caught by Rousseau:

> The public person . . . formed by the union of all other persons was once called the city, and is now known as the *republic* or the *body politic*. In its passive role it is called the *state*, when it plays an active role it is the *sovereign*, and when it is compared to others of its own kind, it is a *power*. Those who are associated in it take collectively the name of a *people*, and call themselves individually *citizens*, in

so far as they share in sovereign power, and *subjects*, in so far as they put themselves under the laws of the state.

(Rousseau 1968: 61–2)

This captures the important sense in which modern claims of citizenship concern the transference of sovereignty. According to Turner (1990: 211), 'the transfer of sovereignty from the body of the king to the body politic of citizens is . . . a major turning point in the history of western democracies.' It suggests that, even, perhaps above all, in the revolutionary tradition, the entitlements of citizenship are complemented by the duty of the subject to obey the sovereign will. It also points to the association between an expanded citizenship and the shared identity of 'a people'. In Turner's usage, there are 'two parallel movements' in which 'a *state* is transformed into a *nation* at the same time that *subjects* are transformed into *citizens*' (Turner 1990: 208). Finally, the French revolutionary tradition makes clear that citizenship is a status which is (at least implicitly) *universal*. Thus we have an image of citizenship as empowering, universalistic, rights-based and tied to both democratization and an increasingly active role for the *nation-state*.

Citizenship has certainly been a key term in constituting the relationship of the state to its subject-members, but not always in just the ways that its more uncritical admirers have supposed. Thus, for example, the 'universalism' and 'participation' identified with citizenship have been extremely ambivalent. First, citizenship rights are not universal in the sense of 'natural rights' or 'human rights', which are often described as holding good at all times and in all circumstances, placing a general obligation upon those who are capable of satisfying them. Citizenship is normally acquired by the accident of one's place of birth and/or one's parents' citizenship. Not everyone residing within a given state's territory or under its jurisdiction will enjoy the status of a full citizen. Citizenship rights apply only to those who are fortunate enough to enjoy the status of citizen and can generally be redeemed only by the particular state to which such citizenship applies. In the mundane political world, disputes about citizenship have often been about the means of acquiring or the procedures for exclusion from this full citizen status and its attendant rights. At the same time, while citizens' rights imply an entitlement to some form of provision or restraint by the state, they are generally subject to interpretation or even revocation by state authorities. It is often an agency of the state which must decide to whom citizenship is to be attached and what substantively citizenship rights require. Citizenship is also seen to be 'exclusive' in at least two further senses. First, various categories of persons may be *formally* excluded from the status of citizen. This was for centuries the experience of women, to whom rights of citizenship (the right to enter into various forms of contract, to vote, to receive welfare benefits) were almost always granted some considerable time after men. Such formal exclusion remains important (especially for immigrant populations, émigré workers, political refugees and so on). But as formal equality has advanced, so have *substantive* differences of citizenship become more important. This, for example, is at the heart of feminist critiques of existing forms of citizenship (e.g. see Pateman 1988a; Phillips 1993; Lister 1993). Men and women may enjoy the same *formal* rights of access to the political process, but *actual* patterns of social organization – different working lives, provision of child care, the division of domestic labour – mean that men have *systematically* privileged access to the exercise of their citizenship rights. Existing evocations of citizenship are inadequate because of the particular way in which they conceive of the relationship between public life (the domain of citizenship) and the private sphere (which is conceived as politically 'off limits'). Citizenship helps to generate a distinctively modern conception of 'the public', but it is a public from which certain voices – defined by gender, ethnicity, sexual orientation or whatever – tend to be excluded.

Finally, since our concern is principally with the relationship of citizenship to the state, it is imperative to record that the strengthening of principles of citizenship may actually furnish *greater* powers to the state. This is not just because an extension of welfare citizenship, for example, puts enormous resources into the hands of the state, enabling it to control the basic life chances of many millions of its subjects. It is also that the rights of citizenship have been powerfully complemented by the *obligations* of citizenship. This was clear in the revolutionary tradition, where the invocation of the state's will as an expression of the collective will of all the citizens was seen to place a mighty obligation upon individual citizens to carry through the will of the state. Therborn (1977) has traced the association between the extension of political citizenship and conscription into the armed forces. Some strands of citizenship thinking – e.g. French republicanism or Soviet constitutional theory – show a strong sense that citizenship entails sometimes onerous duties (including compulsory military service) as well as rights. Citizenship is a double-sided process. In principle, its extension may empower individuals over and against the state. But, at the same time, it implies a strengthening of the authority and the obligation of the state's rule (now presented as the expression of the collective will of all the citizens). Many of these issues are developed in rather more detail in Chapter 5.

### Taxation

Taxation is mentioned but little discussed in Weber's account of the modern state. Yet the modern state as Weber describes it could not have existed without substantial and regular tax revenues. Indeed, the apparatus it requires, the relationship between tax-state and tax-subject it defines, and the sheer resources it generates make the consideration of taxation essential to any explanation of the modern state. We can begin from Braun's definition: 'taxes are regularly paid compulsory levies on private units to produce revenues to be spent for public purposes' (Braun 1975: 244). Of course, the extraction of resources from 'private units' is very ancient. The church tithe, for example, under which parishioners would pay a tenth of their 'income' to the clergy, long pre-dates the modern state, and, of course, the ancient and medieval world is full of stories of pillage, piracy and extortion. What distinguished these early forms of extraction was that they were occasional, sometimes quite random and often justified by little more than brute force or 'the right of conquest'. Before the eighteenth century, so Mann avers, tax collection was an 'expedient in times of emergency and even an abuse which as soon as possible should be replaced by income from public property, particularly domains, and by voluntary contribution' (Mann 1943: 225). Yet, the regime of the 'modern tax state', as Schumpeter (1954) calls it, carries all the hallmarks of Weber's modern state. It is systematic, continuous, legal–rational, extensive, regularized and bureaucratized.

For some commentators, such distinctively modern forms of well-regulated resource extraction become possible only with the emergence of a commercial market- or exchange-based economy. In earlier times, 'tax-farming', under which a ruler would sell off or award to a subaltern the right to make an income by extracting what resources he could from the local populace, had been common. Concealment or hoarding were equally common forms of resistance to this exaction. In the modern period, however, we move towards taxation uniformly applied by the state through officials who are responsible for collection, but whose income is not dependent upon these revenues. Modern accounting and banking procedures expose economic activity to state surveillance and expropriation (creating, in turn, the market for offshore tax havens and clever accountants). Indeed, as Giddens argues, the assessment and collection of taxation liabilities is one of the ways in which the state extends its penetrative surveillance of society (Giddens 1985: 157–9).

In some accounts, taxation (and the apparatus required to collect it) is one of the most basic constituents of the modern state, helping to mark if off from its 'feudal' predecessor. According to Schumpeter, 'without financial need the immediate case for the creation of the modern state would have been absent' (Schumpeter 1954: 24–5). This imperative is especially clear in the work of Tilly. In essence, Tilly's view of the development of the modern European state was this: 'War made the state, and the state made war.' Making war meant raising taxes.

> The building of an effective military machine imposed a heavy burden on the population involved: taxes, conscription, requisitions and more. The very act of building it – when it worked – produced arrangements which could deliver resources to the government for other purposes. . . . Thus almost all the major European taxes began as 'extraordinary levies' earmarked for particular wars, and became routine sources of governmental revenue.
>
> (Tilly 1975: 42)

None of the ambitions of state-makers could be realized without *extraction*, that is 'drawing from its subject population the means of statemaking, warmaking and protection' (Tilly 1990: 96). To simplify a complex historical story, we have a pattern something like the following. Proto-states make war. War is costly and requires a systematic and continuous process of extraction of resources. For the successful states, the process of extraction requires a larger state apparatus. The larger state apparatus requires more resources and thus a higher tax revenue and so on. Of course, royal courts could be very extravagant. Mann records that James I spent £15,593 on a bed for the infant Queen Anne! (Mann 1986: 458). But however profligate was the personal expenditure of kings and queens, these costs were generally dwarfed by the expenses of military activity. According to Tilly, 'the formation of standing armies provided the largest single incentive to extraction and the largest single means of state coercion over the long run of European statemaking' (Tilly 1975: 73).

As important as the sheer rise in revenue demands was the transformation of public indebtedness. Wars meant not just increased costs to be met in the present but also an increase in the public debt, and this had to be serviced by taxation payments outside times of active war-making. Mann observes that it was 'under Henry VIII that one important and permanent development occurred: Peacetime taxation' (Mann 1986: 57).

Upon Tilly and Mann's accounts, the development of the modern tax-state is full of unintended consequences. It was not that anyone wished to create a large fiscal state and extractive apparatus. It was rather a necessary by-product of the state's warlike ambitions. Once established, 'emergency' taxes proved increasingly difficult to remove. (In Britain, income tax started life as a temporary wartime expedient.) Once established, the public debt changed its character (so that by the mid-twentieth century it was seen as an instrument of governments' macroeconomic strategy). The state used taxation not just to raise revenue but also to encourage/discourage various forms of behaviour (imposing duties on alcohol and tobacco, offering tax relief for preferred family forms and so on).

Again, while the origins of modern taxation regimes may lie in the changing requirements of military activity, there is also some agreement that the pattern of public expenditure shifted in the later nineteenth and twentieth centuries. Despite the colossal costs of warfare in the twentieth century, and the extraordinary impact that the sheer costs of war have had in shaping the world since 1945, we can observe an underlying process of 'civilianization' in the changing balance of public expenditures over the last hundred years (Tilly 1990: 122–3). For most of the eighteenth century, military expenditure accounted for much more than half of all state expenditure in Britain. By 2000, this figure has fallen below 3 per cent (SIPRI 2002). At the same time, however impressive was the growth of state funding in earlier centuries (starting from an extremely low base), in volume terms this has been dwarfed by developments of the last hundred years. The tax take rose dramatically in the twentieth century from less than 10 per cent in 1890 to something more than 40 per cent by the 1980s (Peacock and Wiseman 1961: 42–3; *The Economist* 337 (1995), 7943) and there has been a transformation in the disbursement of these public funds. Of these changes, as we shall see in Chapter 2, the most remarkable has been the extraordinary growth of social expenditure – one of the most profound, if under-reported, developments of the twentieth century.

Of course, this wholesale transformation in the public finances has had a profound political impact not only upon the state, but also upon its subjects (as well as upon other potential political actors). Few people enjoy paying taxes – 'to tax and to please', so Edmund Burke (1729–97) argued, 'is not given to men' – and resistance against extraction is very ancient (Burke 1909). History before the rise of the modern state is littered with 'tax revolts' and 'peasants' rebellions' against unreasonable forms and levels of taxation. With the rise of the modern state, both the imposition of and the resentment against taxation became more systematic. While both Tilly and Mann, for example, argue that the militarization of the state was essentially turned *outwards* towards other states, the requirement to raise revenue certainly encouraged a more active policing of the *internal* order of nascent states. Control – military, judicial, civil and fiscal – was a commonplace of the modern tax-state. But, as in other areas of its activity, the modern state could not normally hope to extract resources by force alone, not least because the costs of compliance might make such a regime counter-productive. There was thus an increasing incentive to make the state's taxation regime appear *legitimate*. At the same time, we find a long-standing movement among those who bore the burden of taxation to gain some control over those who extracted their resources. To a certain extent at least, the story of the (partial) democratization of the modern state between the eighteenth and twentieth centuries can be understood in terms of the American rebels' famous insistence upon 'no taxation without representation'. For both rulers and ruled, it seemed that taxation might be more bearable if, at least formally, it could be construed as 'chosen by the people'.

Taxation is still a touchstone of the politics of the modern state. In Britain, the longest-serving prime minister of the twentieth century was brought down, at least in part, by her insistence upon reviving a premodern form of taxation – the poll tax (Butler *et al.* 1994). Modern British general elections are sometimes supposed to be won and lost on the basis of the projected headline rate of income tax. It is also widely argued that recent years have seen the growth of an increasing 'tax resistance' among democratic publics who feel themselves overburdened by a massive state apparatus. Certainly, the transformation of taxation (who pays and who benefits) helped to shape the grand contours of the politics of the second half of the twentieth century. Just as important, though a little less remarked upon, are the political constraints imposed by public indebtedness. Those who service the government's debt – and who may, unlike the general citizenry, decline to continue to do so – are in an extremely powerful position to establish the acceptable limits of the state's activity. It is the power that the servicing of the public debt places in the hands of fund-holders, banks and 'the markets' (rather than some 'bankers' ramp') which gives internationally mobile investors such a powerful lever upon the conduct of the state.

## Further reading

Anderson, B. (1991) *Imagined Communities*. London: Verso.

Gerth, H. H. and Mills, C. W. (eds) (1970) *From Max Weber*. London: Routledge & Kegan Paul.

Giddens, A. (1985) *The Nation-State and Violence*. Cambridge: Polity.

Hall, J. A. (ed.) (1986) *States in History*. Oxford: Blackwell.

Hobbes, T. (1968) *Leviathan*. Harmondsworth: Penguin.

Skinner, Q. (1989) 'The state', in T. Ball, J. Farr and R. L. Hanson (eds) *Political Innovation and Conceptual Change*. Cambridge: Cambridge University Press.

# 2    Placing the state in modernity

In the opening pages of this book, I made it clear that I should be concerned, above all, with the state in modern times. In Chapter 1, I dealt with some of the most important organizational and institutional features of this modern state. What I offered was less an *explanation* of the state's conduct than an attempt to establish the parameters of what have been seen characteristically as *states'* activities. In this chapter, I want to try to refine this understanding by investigating the *historicity* of the state. The state is not an eternal and unchanging element in human affairs. For most of its history, humanity got by (whether more happily or not) without a state. For all its universality in our own times, the state is a *contingent* (and comparatively recent) historical development. Its predominance may also prove to be quite *transitory*. Once we have recognized that there were societies *before* the state, we may also want to consider the possibility that there could be societies *after* the state. It may be that, under new circumstances, the state would simply give way to an alternative form of social organization. This has always been the aspiration of philosophical anarchists and various schools of supra-nationalism. More recently, it has re-emerged in the literature of globalization (discussed in Chapter 6).

I also made it clear at the opening of this book that the proper object of our study is not so much *the* modern state, but rather a number of states located in an international system of unequal and competing states operating within a distinctive, if rather fuzzy, 'modern period'. It is imperative then that we understand these states, their relations with each other and with other social forces, *historically*. Of course, such a history of modern states is bound to proceed at an extremely abstract and general level. It will obviously do very limited justice to the particularity of individual states. It should, however, allow us to establish clearly the conditionality, contingency and temporality of states. It may also enable us to confront the puzzle of how what was a contingent historical development should have given way to the present seeming universality of the state. If states are not an eternal and inevitable aspect of the human condition, how and why have they become so ubiquitous in the modern world?

## States and modernity

Treating the modern state historically requires that we establish a little more clearly what we mean by 'the modern' and 'modernity'. In making fuller sense of these terms, we face something of a divide between popular and academic discussion. In comparatively unreflective popular usage, 'modern' is still widely held to mean 'contemporary' and 'up to date'. A 'modernizer' is regarded as a reformer who wants to bring older ideas or practices into line with changing circumstances. On balance, when used in these senses, the 'modern' is still broadly positive in tone. In the academic world, the use of 'modern' and 'modernity' – and judgements about their consequences – is much more ambiguous. In academic discussion, modernity has come to have a much stronger identity with a discrete historical change and, correspondingly, a much weakened sense of being the 'permanent present'. A prominent trend for more than a century (and an abiding concern for many schools of sociology) has been the emergence of the modern world as an (admittedly extremely drawn-out) *event*. With varying levels of sophistication, the modern world, emerging somewhere between the fifteenth and eighteenth centuries, is contrasted with a traditional order that preceded it. In many accounts, this extended event, perhaps spreading across several hundred years, expresses an extraordinarily profound and rapid transformation in the human condition. Indeed, in many spheres of social life – not least in the ways in which actors perceive their own place within the social world – these were changes which could properly be called revolutionary.

Any number of features have been identified with the transition to modernity. The following list (which is very far from exhaustive) simply identifies some of the most commonly cited elements of this modernization:

- *industrialization*: the transition from an agrarian to an industrial society;
- *demographic transition*: transformation in the size and distribution of population;
- the *commercialization* and subsequent *commodification* of economic relationships that become more clearly differentiated from other aspects of social life;
- the *rise of capitalism*: the transition from a feudal to a capitalist economy or, more broadly, mode of production;
- the *growing social division of labour*, growing social and economic specialization (including the differentiation of economic and political functions);
- the *rise of scientific modes of thought* and their application to industrialized production and thence to social life more generally;
- *transformation in conceptions of rationality* (including *secularization*) and in beliefs about the plasticity of the physical and social world;
- the *transformation of modes of communication* for persons, goods and information;
- *urbanization*: the growth of characteristically industrial cities and a changed relationship between city and countryside;
- *democratization*: the expansion of political participation, with new political institutions and new forms of political legitimation (including appeals to socialism and nationalism).

Not everyone would agree that these are the most important features of the transition to modernity, and clearly not all of these changes carry the same explanatory weight. Nonetheless, even this rather crude and incomplete list should give an indication of the breadth and profundity of changes that have been identified with the emergence of the modern social order. Indeed, upon one respectable definition, sociology has been recast not as 'the study of society' but rather as the study of the processes of modernity (Giddens 1982). Of course, we are concerned above all with the emergence of *states* in modernity. To this extent, it might be thought that we should be concerned principally with those processes comprehended, perhaps rather generously, under the label 'democratization'. But, in fact, a whole range of changes much more broadly associated with modernity – transformation of the mode of production, changing relations between the city and countryside, the differentiation of the economic and the political, new technologies of communication and surveillance, etc. – had an impact upon the generation of distinctively modern state forms.

In placing the state in modernity, one further comment is in order. Modernity emerged not just at a particular time but also in a distinctive place – i.e. Europe – and it was essentially through the complex diffusion of this European development that modernity became a truly global phenomenon. Of course, it is important to guard against a crudely Eurocentric account of modernization. Clearly, the rapacious history of modernity is anything but the story of how the blessings of modern civilization were brought by beneficent Europeans to a grateful world. Nonetheless, it was in the most westerly reaches of the Eurasian land mass that those contingent developments which triggered the journey into modernity (for good and evil) took place. It is then justifiable (as well as convenient) that our investigation of the historical emergence of modern states should centre upon Europe.

## Modernity and postmodernity

For many of those who have discussed modernity – notably the founding figures of late nineteenth-century sociology and US political scientists in the post-war period – the coming of the modern world expressed not just a profound but also a *once-and-for-all* transformation in the human condition. But if, as I have suggested, modernity proves to be not the 'permanent present' but rather the contingent product of a particular time and place, there is the possibility that it too might be replaced by a new social order that is, in some sense, 'beyond modernity', or post-modern. In recent years, there has been a fierce debate in and around the academy about whether we still inhabit a social world that is defined by the processes of modernity. The battle has been joined between those who argue that we still occupy that social and philosophical space defined by the project of modernity and those who insist that the 'old' formations of modernity are now giving way to a new and distinctively postmodern epoch.

This feverish debate has often generated more heat than light. We can confine our consideration of it here to a few points that are relevant to making sense of the modern state. In essence, the politics of modernity is identified by its critics with totalizing political ideologies and accompanying 'projects' for wholesale social and political change. Modernity is seen as a creature of Enlightenment thinking, and to this extent it is driven by a belief in progress and the wholesale reformability of the social order in line with the dictates of reason (revealed according to the canons of scientific thought). The characteristic political project of modernity involves the attempt to transform social and political life so as to bring human practice in line with the forms of social organization that this reason dictates. In brief, the argument of postmodernists is that this (misconceived) aspiration to transform society in line with the dictates of reason has meant not 'utopia and progress' but 'dystopia and barbarism'. There is no revealed reason. There is no universal political project that reason dictates. The social world is not amenable to reconstruction in line with a willed human project. In practice, the attempt to carry through such transformations has issued in the most dreadful crimes against humanity, from genocide and mass starvation to the most intimate abuses of the human mind and body. For post-modernist critics, it is the modern state, perhaps above all the state as it developed in the socialist societies of the former Soviet Empire, that is the definitive expression of this misbegotten modernist political dystopia.

The claim that modernity's promise of progress and reason turn into their opposites is very vigorously contested. I shall not attempt to adjudicate this dispute here. The postmodernists' expectation that the modern state is (or, at the very least, should be) in decline is an issue to which we shall return in the closing chapter. For now, two points seem to be in order. First, the postmodernist challenge does raise the spectre of state forms *beyond* modernity with which defenders of the established order have had to engage. Second, postmodernist criticisms have chimed with, and perhaps contributed to, the acute disenchantment with states' performance that has been a general feature of political debate over the past twenty-five years. To this extent, it is part of a much more general 'retreat from the state' to which we shall return in later chapters. For now, I wish to return to the historical account of the emergence of the modern state.

## 'Traditional' states

Two points need to be made at the outset of this discussion. The first is to reinforce the claim that the state is a comparatively novel social development. Indeed, Mann (1986) argues that something less than 1 per cent of humanity's history has been lived out under even the most primitive of state forms. Second, the *modern* state is, even within this foreshortened history, a comparative newcomer. Tilly (1990: 2) dates the earliest 'traditional' states at around 6000–8000 BC. The earliest fully modern states emerged not much more than 300 years ago. Mann (1993b: 117–18) argues that developed nation-states are largely a product of the twentieth century, with many of them emerging only after 1945.

Traditional (i.e. premodern) states took a variety of forms. Eisenstadt lists the following: city-states, feudal systems, patrimonial empires, nomad or conquest empires, and 'centralised historical bureaucratic empires' (Eisenstadt 1963: 10). Of these, the most important in the European context in the period before the emergence of feudalism are probably city-states and the varying forms of traditional empire. The criteria according to which states in this earlier period are defined are generally less exacting than those applied to the state of modernity (and discussed in Chapter 1). Tilly, for example, defines states as 'coercion-wielding organizations that are distinct from households and kinship groups and exercise clear priority in some respects over all other organizations within substantial territories' (Tilly 1990: 1). In many ways, these traditional states were qualitatively different from their modern equivalents. They involved the capacity to exercise force and some element of territoriality. But, as Giddens notes, traditional states (especially the expansive traditional empires) were delimited not by clear borders but by much more indeterminate frontiers. They might exercise a sort of *rule* over a particular territory, but generally they lacked the administrative or military capacity to *govern* (i.e. to exercise day-to-day control and surveillance over their subject populations). The extraction of resources was important and might indeed be merciless, but it was based upon a system of tribute-taking or simple extortion rather than upon a regularized regime of systematic taxation. These traditional state forms generally lacked conceptions of sovereignty, monopolistic authority, nationality, constitutionality and so on. They also lacked the self-consciousness of themselves as states among other states which is characteristic of the state in modernity.

The lengthy historical transition from these traditional to modern state forms is neatly and summarily captured in Held's typification (Held 1992). Held identifies 'five main clusters of state systems':

- traditional tribute-taking empires
- feudalism: systems of divided authority
- the polity of estates
- absolutist states
- modern nation-states.

The broad historical parameters of these state systems are captured in Figure 2.1.

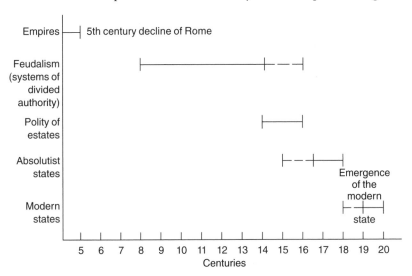

*Figure 2.1* Held's five main clusters of state systems.

Source: derived from Held (1992: 78).

## Before the modern state: feudalism

Since our account of the origins of the modern state can hardly begin at the beginning (given that the first 99 per cent of humanity's worldly sojourn has gone largely unrecorded), it may make sense to start in the epoch of feudalism. In fact, there is probably no more a consensus among scholars about the nature of feudalism than there is about its more extensively discussed successors – capitalism and socialism. In terms of its time and place, the agreement may actually be rather less. Our discussion, in focusing upon the grosser features of feudalism and its transformation, will do scant justice to these concerns. My intention in this and subsequent sections is simply to sketch in the very broadest terms the sorts of processes that may be seen to have precipitated the emergence of the early modern state.

At its simplest, we may think of feudalism as a social world of 'overlapping and divided authority', as a loosely structured system of personal and clientelistic relationships (of lord and vassal) which, taken together, form a famously pyramidical if rather fissiparous social hierarchy. Anderson offers this rather tighter definition:

> Feudalism typically involves the juridical serfdom and military protection of the peasantry by a social class of nobles, enjoying individual authority and property, and exercising an exclusive monopoly of law and private rights of justice within a political framework of fragmented sovereignty and subordinate fiscality, and an aristocratic ideology exalting rural life.
>
> (Anderson 1974: 407)

Using this rather precise definition, Anderson identifies feudalism as a *uniquely* European development, with Japan offering the nearest extra-European equivalent (Anderson 1974: 4, 12–13). While this geographical exclusivity is not universally accepted, there is some agreement that the distinctive features of European feudalism and its historical trajectory may help to explain the distinctive path to modernity in post-feudal Europe.

Feudalism is conventionally seen to have emerged out of the comparative murkiness of the 'Dark Ages' that followed the collapse of the Roman Empire somewhere around the eighth century AD. By the fourteenth century at the latest, it is seen to have been yielding to distinctively new forms of social organization, with 1,477 witnessing 'the collapse of the last great alternative "feudal" state, the duchy of Burgundy' (Mann 1986: 416). In Poggi's influential account (Poggi 1978, 1990), the roots of early feudalism lay in the admixture of the political institutions of Germanic tribal populations with half-remembered residues of the Roman Empire. It arose initially from the structures of military command: from the relationship between a tribal chief and his leading warriors (or *vassi*). Poggi identifies its expansion into a more general system of rule with the emergence of a new dynasty of Frankish rulers at the end of the seventh century (Poggi 1990: 36). The core constituent relationship of feudalism was the personal bond between lord and vassal, with land (and its people and product) – the *fief* – being gifted by the king or lord in exchange for the military support of the vassal and his retinue. This core relationship between lord and vassal might then be re-created by a number of 'sub-contracts' between nobles and lesser dignitaries. At the bottom of the pile, however, the vast majority of the population, by whom any economic surplus was generated, were seen as 'the objects of rule . . . never the subjects of a political relationship' (Poggi 1978: 23).

Although a prevalent academic interest in the transition from feudalism to capitalism has seen attention focused upon the feudal *economy*, in an important sense, the characteristic relationships of 'classical' feudalism were militaristic. At the same time they were unstable. The feudal king was *primus inter pares* (the 'first among equals'). Relationships of loyalty between lord and vassal could easily break down, and nobles might always be tempted to use their independent military resources *against* the prevailing feudal authority. The feudal regime was then characteristically fragile and acutely vulnerable to dissent and even open warfare. The distance this left between Europe at the millennium and the modern state form is graphically expressed by Tilly:

> The emperors, kings, princes, dukes, caliphs, sultans, and other potentates of AD 990 prevailed as conquerors, tribute-takers, and rentiers, not as heads of state that durably and densely regulated life within their realms. Inside their jurisdictions, furthermore, rivals and ostensible subordinates commonly used force on behalf of their own interests while paying little attention to the interests of their nominal sovereigns. Private armies proliferated through much of the continent. Nothing like a centralized national state existed anywhere in Europe.
>
> (Tilly 1990: 39–40)

The fragmentation of the feudal political order was exacerbated by two further features. The first was the 'universal' authority claimed and, to some degree, sustained by the Catholic Church. The Holy Roman Empire, inaugurated with the crowning of Charlemagne as emperor by the pope on Christmas Day AD 800, was to last (albeit rather vestigially) for the best part of a thousand years. It expressed a largely unrealized aspiration to conjoin secular and sacred political authority. The continuation throughout this period of a separate system of ecclesiastical courts was testimony to the divided authority of the feudal order. A second element undermining the capacity for the exercise of unified political power under feudalism was the centuries-long rise of towns and cities. Of course, city-states (especially those of northern Italy) were to become an important state form in their own right. What we have in mind here, however, is the much more general process of the growth of towns and cities, of the trade and commercial activities associated with them and the different class structures to which these gave rise. Increasingly, an essentially rural and aristocratic order – and the forms of extraction characteristic of it – was challenged by new and physically more concentrated social and material resources.

## The polity of estates

This changing role of towns and cities becomes more clear if we shift our attention forward to the phase Poggi describes as the *Ständestaat*, or 'polity of estates'. Not everyone follows Poggi in identifying this as a political form distinct from feudalism, but it does appear to describe a series of changes in 'late' feudal times (concentrated in the twelfth and thirteenth centuries) which foreshadowed the emergence of absolutism.

Poggi explains this development above all in terms of the new relationships and new needs that emerged in late medieval towns. The core lord–vassal relationship of feudalism was inappropriate in expressing the new collective or *corporate* needs of commercially influential town-dwellers. Their interest in trade led them to favour territorially more extensive forms of political organization (over traditional feudal arrangements). They sought representation of their collective or corporate interests (as *Stände*, or 'estates') rather than the purely personal ties of traditional feudalism. The polity of estates

> differed from the feudal system essentially in being more *institutionalized* in its operations, in having an explicit *territorial* reference, and in being *dualistic*, since it confronted the ruler with the *Stände* and associated the two elements in rule as distinct power centres.
>
> (Poggi 1990: 40–1)

Poggi describes the *Ständestaat* as an '*early-modern* system of rule'. But it is important not to get carried away with the modern-sounding elements in the polity of estates. It would be inappropriate, for example, to project back upon these late medieval institutions distinctively modern conceptions of legitimacy, sovereignty, territoriality and representation. It is appropriate, however, to see this as a prelude to the period of absolutism which we can legitimately describe as the proximate source of the modern state.

## Absolutism

There is considerable disagreement about whether the absolutist state belongs more properly to the 'traditional' or the 'modern' period. Indeed, Henshall (1992: 143–5) enters very serious reservations about the applicability of 'absolutism' to describe *any* historical state form. Poggi (1990: 42) describes the absolutist state unambiguously as 'the first major institutional embodiment of the modern state'. Giddens, by contrast, insists that, for all the changes that it wrought, 'the absolutist state is still . . . a traditional state' (Giddens 1985: 93). Given this disagreement, absolutism is perhaps best seen as a *transitional* form, albeit one that spanned several centuries. It began under what were clearly late feudal circumstances and was eventually overtaken by forms which are more or less universally regarded as 'modern'. Emergent in the sixteenth century, it was a dominating state form throughout the seventeenth century, generally yielding to more recognizably modern state forms only in the latter part of the eighteenth century or beyond. In England, where the absolutist phase was unusually short, it did not survive the seventeenth century. Indeed, it is not clear that 'constitutionalist' regimes, such as those that prevailed in England and Holland, were ever 'properly' absolutist. In many parts of Eastern Europe, by contrast, it was a powerful force well into the nineteenth century. Given its longevity and proximity to modernity, it is perhaps unsurprising that many of the most important characteristics of the modern state are recognizably products of absolutism and that, in some important respects, modern states are still recognizably 'absolutist'.

The sources of transition to the absolutist state are many and various. Held lists the following:

> Struggles between monarchs and barons over the domain of rightful authority; peasant rebellions against the weight of excess taxation and social obligation; the spread of trade, commerce and market relations; the flourishing of Renaissance culture with its renewed interest in classical political ideas (including Athenian democracy and Roman law); changes in technology, particularly military technology; the consolidation of national monarchies (notably in England, France and Spain); religious strife and the challenge to the universal claims of Catholicism; the struggle between Church and State.
>
> (Held 1992: 83)

Above all, absolutism was about the concentration and centralization of political power.

> Absolutism signalled the emergence of a form of state based upon: the absorption of smaller and weaker political units into larger and stronger political structures; a strengthened ability to rule over a unified territorial area; a tightened system of law and order enforced throughout a territory; the application of a 'more unitary, continuous, calculable and effective' rule by a single, sovereign head; and the development of a relatively small number of states engaged in an open-ended, competitive, and risk-laden power struggle.
>
> (Poggi 1978: 60–1)

The mixture of residual feudalism and emergent modernity that characterizes absolutism is most effectively captured in Anderson's magisterial *Lineages of the Absolutist State* (Anderson 1974). In its origins, so he argues, absolutism was 'essentially just this: *a redeployed and recharged apparatus of feudal domination*' (1974: 18). Absolutism is certainly related to the gradual transition from a feudal towards a capitalist political economy. It was not, however, a direct expression of the new powers of an ascendant urban merchant class (though it was, in part, a response to these new powers). Rather it constituted an attempt by the established landed nobility to protect their position in a period of increased commodification, more particularly in circumstances in which traditional labour-rents (and their attendant economy) were giving way to money-rents (and the consequent emergence of wage labour). The gradual disappearance of serfdom resulted in 'a *displacement* of politico-legal coercion upwards towards a centralized, militarized summit – the Absolutist State' (Anderson 1974: 19).

Anderson isolates five 'institutional innovations' that marked the arrival of absolutism. These were: a standing army (or, in the case of England, a navy); a centralized bureaucracy; a systematic and statewide taxation regime; a formal diplomatic service with permanent embassies abroad; and state policies to promote commerce and economic development. Of course, such developments were eventually to form important pillars of the definitively modern state. But in their origins, Anderson argues, they were a hybrid mixture of the modern and the archaic. Thus, for example, standing armies were established, but these were still based largely upon foreign mercenaries rather than upon conscription. Warfare and its economic role also disclosed a broadly mercantilist or even feudal expectation that economic aggrandizement was based upon the appropriation of land rather than the intensive development of trade and production. Similarly, the emergence of a permanent bureaucracy and taxation system sounds distinctly modern. But positions within the bureaucracy could still be purchased and even inherited. The 'taxation system' was still seen largely as a source of 'occasional' resourcing for wars, often 'subcontracted' to tax-farmers and resolutely concentrated upon the poor, in particular the long-suffering and, from time to time, rebellious peasantry.

Anderson calls diplomacy 'one of the great institutional inventions of the epoch' (1974: 37). Giddens describes it as 'the best single expression of the fact that a new type of state system had come into being' (1985: 85). For both, it marks out absolutism as 'the first international state *system* in the modern world' (Anderson 1974: 11). Such membership of a multi-state system is a quite essential point about states through modernity. For, as states became more centralized, their territorial claims more clearly defined and their jurisdictional competence more vigorously upheld, it was ever more apparent that individual states existed only as part of an international system of states with similar sorts of claims. This did not, of course, preclude vicious and extended warfare between states, but it did imply a recognition that this took place within an international order of several competing states. Giddens gives especial weight to this emergence of an international state system, coincident in his view with the development of 'what subsequently came to be called "international relations"' (1985: 86). With it came the idea of 'the balance of power' within the state system, the panoply of congresses and diplomatic missions and, above all, the recognition of 'the legitimacy of other states, none of which has the right to universalize its own elements of administration or law at the expense of others' (1985: 87).

## The 'outward face' of sovereignty

In some ways, this is but an expression of the 'outward face' of one of the most consequential of all developments under absolutism – the hugely strengthened claims of state *sovereignty*. We saw in Chapter 1 that the claim to sovereignty – defined by Hinsley as 'the idea that there is a final and absolute authority in the political community' – is one of the most significant determinants of the modern state. It is instructively in the political writing of the early absolutist period that we find the first systematic usage of sovereignty and, indeed, of the term 'the state' itself. The idea of sovereignty is often retraced to the publication in 1576 of the *Six Books* of Jean Bodin (1529–96), with anticipations being found in Machiavelli and even earlier writers in the republican tradition (see Skinner 1989; Bodin 1967). But, as we saw in Chapter 1, it is to Hobbes, writing in the mid-seventeenth century, that we look for the first unambiguous statement of the necessity of the absolute power of the sovereign.

In fact, the absence of external constraint is inscribed in the very term 'absolutism', and the claim to a more-or-less unlimited jurisdiction over a given territory has become one of the defining claims not just of the state under absolutism, but also of the modern state. In the absolutist period, this was expressed in the emergence of a new international order premised upon a number of sovereign states which recognize the legitimate existence of other sovereign states with their own jurisdictions, but accept no other and higher binding authority upon their bilateral relations. Held gives a summary account of the elements of this international order, often discussed under the rubric of the *Westphalian model* (named after the Peace of Westphalia of 1648, which brought to a close the Eighty Years' War between Spain and the Dutch, and the German phase of the Thirty Years' War):

1   The world consists of, and is divided by, sovereign states which recognize no superior authority.
2   The processes of law-making, the settlement of disputes and law enforcement are largely in the hands of individual states subject to the logic of 'the competitive struggle for power'.
3   Differences among states are often settled by force: the principle of effective power holds sway. Virtually no legal fetters exist to curb the resort to force; international legal standards afford minimal protection.
4   Responsibility for cross-border wrongful acts are a private matter concerning only those affected; no collective interest in compliance with international law is recognized.
5   All states are regarded as equal before the law; legal rules do not take account of asymmetries of power.
6   International law is oriented to the establishment of minimal rules of co-existence; the creation of enduring relationships among states and peoples is an aim only to the extent that it allows military objectives to be met.
7   The minimization of impediments on state freedom is the 'collective' priority.

(Held 1995: 78)

This Westphalian model has been enormously influential in treatments of the modern states' system, especially within the dominant realist paradigm in international relations. But it is important to report that not everyone is signed up to this account of the importance and integrity of state sovereignty. Foucault (1994), as we have observed, insists that sovereignty is the wrong place to search for the effective exercise of political power. Stephen Krasner (1999, 2001) has insisted that the Westphalian model has very little to do with either the Peace of Westphalia or, more importantly, the lived experiences of states in the subsequent 350 years. We shall return to these reservations in later chapters.

Of course, the rise of diplomacy did not mean the end of inter-state warfare. The networks of alliances, the desire to maintain the 'balance of power' and the feverish dynastic manoeuvring of the new diplomatic order could actually encourage armed conflict. Indeed, Anderson insists that 'the virtual permanence of international armed conflict was one of the hallmarks of the whole climate of Absolutism' (1974: 33). This warfare was fought increasingly between larger standing armies, under new organizational disciplines and with an enhanced military technology. The numbers of troops under arms in the emergent nation-states of Europe rose steeply between 1500 and 1700 (Tilly 1990: 79). According to Tilly, as 'armies expanded . . ., they became big business.' At the same time, and as a consequence, 'the ability to borrow became more and more crucial to military success' (Tilly 1990: 79, 86). He argues that it was largely through this process of war-making and its attendant peace-brokering that the essentials of the European states' system we still recognize today were forged. As Tilly observes, 'most of the European efforts to build states failed' (Tilly 1975: 38). What we see in the states' system of modernity, in Western Europe at least, is the residue of 'winners' in the state-making contest. The losers, from Burgundy to Sedan, are largely forgotten (see Spruyt 1994).

## The 'inward face' of sovereignty

Even more consequential (and terrifying) for its ordinary subjects was the trans-formed *inward-turned* face of state sovereignty under absolutism. An enduring feature of the Westphalian model was a recognition that the claim of states to jurisdiction within their own territories was absolute and that no external force had the right to intervene in the internal affairs of any state. Of course, this principle was repeatedly breached in practice as the more powerful states engaged in whatever was the historically appropriate form of 'gunboat diplomacy' in defence of the interests of their citizens (and corporations) abroad. In general, the peoples who inhabited that greater part of the world which lies *beyond* Europe were simply disallowed the integrity of statehood as European powers sought increasingly to colonize the globe. But for the subjects of increasingly sovereign European states, Leviathan loomed ever larger.

In this context, it is important to have in mind two differing aspects of state sovereignty. One is the nature of the state's *claims*; the other is the extent and nature of its *capacities*. In practice, the two tend to come rolled together, but it is helpful to make an analytic distinction between them. One thing that is new about the state's sovereign claim under absolutism is that all authority within a given jurisdiction is concentrated in a single place, classically in the divine person of the king. This aspiration is given its clearest expression in what is often seen as the definitively centralized state of the absolutist age – France. Maybe Louis XIV never did say 'L'état, c'est moi', but we can see what it was he had in mind. His successor, Louis XV, certainly said much the same thing, though rather less economically (see Louis XV, cited in Held 1992: 83). Perhaps even more important than this *claim* to a newly concentrated authority, however, was the *capacity* to sustain it. A despot might rule by decree – and to this extent his rule might be unqualified – but, without the means to carry out his will or indeed to *know* that his will was or was not being carried out, his actual exercise of power might be quite feeble.

In some ways, what was most important about absolutism was the extent to which the *capacities* for the exercise of sovereign will were increased. New forms of bureaucratic organization, new forms of communication, new apparatuses of surveillance, new methods of accountancy, new technologies of social control all increased the *infrastructural* power of the state. The individual subject might have had much to fear from the random violence of a despotic state or, without some means of maintaining the public peace, of anyone else. But in a premodern context, he or she might not expect to be routinely the object of the state's attention (and extraction). Of course, the infrastructural powers of the absolutist state were but a fraction of the huge intrusive capacity for surveillance of the modern state, but they do betoken the beginnings of this hugely consequential development.

## Paying for it

Questions of capacities bring us to the issue of resources. Waging war (successfully) was essential to state-making – and waging war is expensive. For states to flourish, they needed both resources of men and money within their jurisdiction *and* the capacity to extract them. They thus relied upon a wealth-generating economy and a sustainable system of taxation. In so far as these were interests of the absolutist state, they foreshadowed, albeit in miniature, what were to be overwhelming concerns of states in fully fledged modernity. As we saw in Chapter 1, Tilly argues that state-making was frequently a consequence not so much directly of warfare, as of the struggle over the extraction of resources through which the war-making ambitions of the state could be realized.

So the growth of the state was not just a product of its war-making activity. It was also (upon Tilly's account, perhaps even more so) a by-product of these aspirations: i.e. the apparatus required to extract the resources to fuel these ambitions. Of course, extraction could be in money or in kind (or some combination of the two). Tilly (1990: 30) charts three models of state-building: a *coercion-intensive* mode based on the direct extraction of resources (often from a largely peasant population); a *capital-intensive* mode, which relied upon compacts with capitalists to rent or purchase military force without a large extractive apparatus; and an intermediate *capitalized coercion* model where rulers did some of each. The *coercion-intensive* mode was most frequently found in Eastern Europe, while the *capital-intensive* was most often found in the affluent city-states of Western Europe. The *capitalized coercion mode*, which proved historically to be the most successful, was found in the large and powerful states of Western Europe, notably England and France.

As the resources required to fund successful state-making and state-maintaining grew, so did 'success' tend to fall to the most resourceful states. Increasingly, these tended to be the states in which capitalism was most fully developed. The relationship between capitalism and the coming of the modern state is a tricky one.

Arguments about who *really* rules in the modern liberal-democratic state (capitalists or governments) have raged for at least a hundred years. I return to these difficult questions in Chapter 3. For now, we may simply observe:

1   that the more successful states of the absolutist period tended to be found in the more affluent societies, and these generally had a well-developed capitalist sector;
2   that the coercive extraction of resources by the state in these economies was made more difficult by the increasingly less-qualified status of private property. At the same time we should note, however, that:
3   their extraction through the selling of public debt became easier;
4   the generation of this public indebtedness greatly strengthened the position of those who underwrote those debts, and these were generally the holders of (frequently international) capital.

Finally, we should record just how much the growth of taxation transforms the relationship between state and subject/citizen. State-making required increasing resources, and populations, whether of merchants or peasants, resented and resisted these impositions. But these exactions were, down to the earliest years of the modern state, comparatively modest. In recent years the Adam Smith Institute has taken to celebrating 'Tax Freedom Day', marking the end of that portion of a year's employment which the average employee has to complete in order to be able to meet his or her tax liability. In the UK in 2003, 'Tax Freedom Day' fell on 12 June, 170 days into the year and reflecting a composite tax rate of about 46.5 per cent (Adam Smith Institute 2003). As late as 1789, 'Freedom Day' for the average labourer in the UK would have fallen on 14 January! Even at the height of the (hugely expensive) Napoleonic Wars, the labourer's responsibility would have been discharged by the beginning of February (Tilly 1994: 288). Three points seem in order here. First, the modern state is a 'tax state' in a way that previous state forms, even absolutism, were not. Second, there is a downside to the historical process of democratization and enhanced citizenship to which we shall shortly turn. Historically, many people did not very much bother with the state because the state did not very much bother with them. In part, the aspiration to participate is a response to an increasingly interventionist state. Given this, it is worth observing that 'tax resistance', which is often described as a characteristic of the disenchanted citizens of overgrown welfare states, is as old as the state itself.

## From absolutism to the modern state

Under the mature absolutist state (and its constitutionalist contemporaries) we can see many of the features that were identified in Chapter 1 as characteristic of the modern state. This is true in at least the following five areas:

1   (monopoly) control of the means of violence
2   territoriality
3   sovereignty

4    bureaucracy
5    taxation.

These elements have been among the most essential underpinnings of the modern state. Yet even in a fully developed absolutism there was still an element of the 'archaic' in these features. Bureaucracy was still significantly unreformed (corrupt and pre-professional). Taxation was still comparatively episodic and unsystematic, in some countries still reflecting the immunity of traditionally privileged estates. Territoriality was increasingly well defined – e.g. with Spain, France and England established within recognizably modern borders. But the national unification of Germany and Italy was still a very long way off.

Other characteristic elements of the modern state were still more partially developed under absolutism. For example, it is a key idea of modern statehood that the state is something other (and more) than the persons in whom it is embodied. After all, governments and presidents may come and go, while the state persists. In some ways, kingship seems the very epitome of personalized rule. However, it is appropriate to think of royal rule in this period increasingly as personal but not patrimonial. There was a decreasing sense that the nation was simply the king's household writ large, a change which Skinner sees coming as early as the thirteenth century (Skinner 1989). With the establishment of a constitutional monarchy, in which divine right is explicitly rejected and the king is in some sense 'chosen' (as happened in the wake of England's 'Glorious Revolution' of 1688), we are moving to quite a different sort of regime. Yet under 'properly' absolutist circumstances, the division between state and office-bearers characteristic of modernity was quite partially developed. Similarly, we find under absolutism an increasing concern with issues of the authority and legitimacy of the state. But for much of the period – as with the claimed 'divine right of kings' – we find justifications which are archaic, often religious and insistently traditional (though even the perceived need to establish legitimacy will seem for some to be a distinctly modern concern). Weber insisted that the most characteristic form of legitimation under the modern state was the claim to be legal-rational. We can find anticipations of such a justification in the absolutist period – notably but not originally in Hobbes – but its full flowering really belongs to the defenders of the modern state.

A third aspect of the modern state, partially anticipated in the absolutist period, is the commitment to constitutionalism: i.e. the insistence that government should be conducted according to clearly established laws and that all participants should respect certain 'rules of the game'. There is clearly a tension between the idea of absolutism, defined in part as the absence of external authority, and the constitutionalist principle of 'limited government'. In part, this simply highlights the fact that our historical generalizations are too broad to do justice to the historical record. Some states, notably Holland and the UK, were constitutionalist at the time that continental absolutism was at its height. Absolutism persisted in the east of Europe after it had ceded to much more constitutionalist regimes throughout most of Western Europe. But, in fact, even 'high' absolutism contained presentiments of 'modern' constitutionalism. The much-vaunted rediscovery or reconstitution of the

Roman law, while it justified a sometimes untrammelled public power, also invoked the powerful rhetoric of the 'rule of law'. The exercise of public power might be unlimited, but it should not be arbitrary. A growing function of the state was to uphold lawful relationships within the society it governed, more especially maintaining the sanctity of contract and the claims of private property. It is hard to overestimate, especially, for example, in the German context, the impact of law as a mechanism for the evolution of the modern state. And, of course, as I have already stressed, in so far as sovereignty does imply a state that is, in the last instance, *above* the constitution, this continues to be an absolutely fundamental aspect of the *modern* state.

Finally, there is one element in the modern state configuration that is radically underdeveloped under absolutism – and that is the idea of citizenship. Of course, citizenship is not an invention of the modern period, but its distinctively modern invocation under the rubric of rights, universality and democracy is something new.

## The growth of the modern state

Investigating these and other areas as they manifest themselves in the modern state is the major purpose of this study. The sorts of breathtaking generalizations I have so far made in this chapter (covering more centuries than pages) will look even more illegitimate as we move into a modern period about which we think we know much more. What generalizations could possibly be applied to the UK, France and Germany over the last two centuries – not to mention Russia, Brazil and Lesotho? This is perhaps an appropriate point at which to repeat that I am concerned largely with European developments and that I am simply seeking to identify some broad and significant trends which help us to make sense of 'the modern state' – not to make generalizations which can be applied across a very disparate range of times and places. It is also worth stressing again that there is no single logic under which we can bring every state's experience, still less a single historical pattern of 'progress' towards modernity along which all the world's states can sensibly be placed.

Having sounded this caveat, I want in the closing pages of this chapter to identify some of the changes that we can find broadly represented across a whole range of states in modernity down to the most recent period. These issues will be treated in rather more detail in the central chapters of the book. Prospects for the future of the modern state are discussed in the closing chapter.

In looking at these very broad changes, perhaps the first thing to record is the sheer growth in the size of the modern state. In one sense, the story is very simple. States used to be tiny and now they are enormous. One of the earliest records of state income that we have shows annual revenue under Henry II of England in 1171–2 of £21,205 (Mann 1986: 418). In 2003/4, UK public expenditure stood at approximately £420 billion (HM Treasury 2003). Of course, both figures are fairly meaningless, but they certainly indicate growth! In fact, as late as 1890 in the UK, government expenditure (local and central) amounted to less than 10 per cent of GDP. It now takes up about 38 per cent of a hugely increased domestic product.

There is, however, some reason to doubt that the growth of the state is a simple story of 'onwards and upwards' – of expanding functions, increasing personnel and rising expenditure. In opposing such a story, Mann's revisionist account insists that, while states' budgets around 1700 were still relatively small (perhaps 5 per cent of GDP in peacetime, 10 per cent of GDP in wartime), they grew rapidly, if inter-mittently, throughout the eighteenth century, so that by 1810 the state was consuming somewhere between one-quarter and one-third of all national income (Mann 1993b: 116–17). He reports that 'these 1810 extraction rates are *identical* to those of the two world wars of the twentieth century and to the highest rates in the world today, those of Israel and Iraq' (Mann 1993b: 117). Thus, war-making in the late eighteenth century (above all during the Napoleonic Wars) saw levels of state activity of almost twentieth-century dimensions.

Mann's further argument is that the 'long nineteenth century' saw a *decrease* in state activities as a proportion of national economic activity: 'although the absolute financial size of states was growing at current prices and most were also growing modestly in per capita real terms, state fiscal size relative to civil society was . . . either static or declining' (Mann 1986: 370). In part, this was an artefact of rapid economic growth through the nineteenth century. But, for Mann, the principal explanation is in terms of the costs and patterns of war-making. The eighteenth century had been a war-torn century, culminating in the pan-European struggles with Napoleonic France. By contrast, the nineteenth century was to be, for Europe, and by contrast with both the eighteenth and twentieth century, a peculiarly pacific period. Thus, it was declining military costs that explain the fall in overall levels of state activity and extraction. Indeed, they conceal a secular growth in the *civilian* activities of the state, and the fall in states' size might have been more dramatic but for this growth in its non-military functions. Thus, the civilian element in state expenditure rose from about one-quarter in the 1760s to about three-quarters in the 1900s (Mann 1993a: 375).

The twentieth century saw a continuing rapid increase in the size and scope of the state. Mobilization for 'total war' had a dramatic and lasting impact on the size of states and their capacity for extraction. Peacock and Wiseman (1961) observe a 'ratchet effect' in which the 'exceptional' levels of extraction required by mass war-fare are never quite abandoned once the immediate military necessity has passed. The twentieth century also saw a transformation in the disposition of these public expenditures, with growing spending on those areas of social provision that have come to be identified with the 'welfare state'. In 1900, no more than one or two European states devoted as much as 3 per cent of GNP to social expenditure. By 1940, nearly all had reached social expenditure levels in excess of 5 per cent. In the early 1950s, this figure ranged between 10 and 20 per cent. By the mid-1970s, among the European welfare states, between one-quarter and something more than one-third of GNP was devoted to social expenditure. Even the most 'reluctant' welfare states saw a wholesale transformation of their public budgets. In the USA, total social expenditure rose from 2.4 per cent of GNP in 1890 to 20.2 per cent in 1981. Even in Japan, where an exceptional proportion of welfare is organized and delivered through private corporations, the social budget expanded from 1.4 per cent of GDP in 1890 to 16.2 per cent in 1985 (see Pierson 1998: 108–9). Thus, much of the remarkable overall growth in public expenditure of the twentieth century has to be attributed to the growth of the social budget, and this rapidly growing proportion of national wealth devoted to social welfare must itself be set against the background of a sevenfold increase in average per capita output in the cited countries over the past 100 years. The growth in this 'social' function of the state is one of the more remarkable and significant developments in the twentieth-century trajectory of the modern state.

## States and societies: infrastructural power and surveillance

These few bald statistics already attest to the scale of changes which the coming of the modern state has wrought. Whatever the 'prehistory' of states' expenditure, it is clear that, as little as 100 years ago, states consumed little more than 10 per cent of GNP. Today in some states, more than half of national economic product is consumed by the government. Almost nowhere in the developed world does this figure fall below 25 per cent. This period is also one in which the European state has been 'civilianized'. Armed forces, though still vital to the integrity of the state, now consume a much smaller part of their state's resources. Patterns of employment have also been transformed. In the twentieth century, public servants came to be numbered in their millions and the government became a major civilian employer. In most countries, the state took an increasingly active part in the management and sometimes the ownership of the national economy. Even where such intervention was limited, the role of the state as a large employer, big spender, and guarantor of the national currency gave it a preponderant economic role.

All of this increased activity had to be funded, and this has transformed levels and patterns of taxation. To take one example, income tax in the UK, which at the start of the twentieth century might have been described as a sort of 'wealth tax', now embraces millions and reaches down to include employees on quite modest incomes. These long-term changes in employment patterns, taxation regimes, patterns of public expenditure and so on have had, in their turn, a profound impact upon party political programmes and patterns of electoral support across all modern states.

A further, very general feature of the state's development in modernity has been its increasing penetration of the society over which it presides. A number of commentators have drawn attention to the way in which the French Revolution of 1789 embodies a more general transition from indirect towards a much more direct governance of the state over society and the individual. Giddens draws attention to the hugely enhanced powers of surveillance which the modern state has at its command. Mann comments upon the extended *infrastructural powers* of the modern state. The modern state is widely seen as an active and as a proactive state, increasingly managing, shaping, even creating its constituent population. Attention is drawn to the coincidence of the coming of the modern state with the rise of statistics (in origin, 'state-istics') and with a growing desire to measure, describe and variously investigate its population (Foucault 1994). For some, this development reached its definitive form in the totalitarian states of the old Soviet Union. Others saw much the same process taking place, albeit in a rather more benign form, in Western European states (Hayek 1976). Writing in the mid-nineteenth century, the

French anarchist Joseph Proudhon (1809–64) railed against these impositions of the modern state:

> TO BE GOVERNED is to be at every operation, at every transaction, noted, registered, enrolled, taxed, stamped, measured, numbered, assessed, licensed, authorized, admonished, forbidden, reformed, corrected, punished. It is, under pretext of public utility and in the name of the general interest, to be placed under contribution, trained, ransomed, exploited, monopolized, extorted, squeezed, mystified, robbed; then, at the slightest resistance, the first word of complaint, to be repressed, fined, despised, harassed, tracked, abused, clubbed, disarmed, choked, imprisoned, judged, condemned, shot, deported, sacrificed, sold, betrayed; and, to crown all, mocked, ridiculed, outraged, dishonoured. This is government; that is its justice; that is its morality.
>
> (Proudhon, cited in Miller 1989: 6)

Proudhon does not understate his case! But every citizen of a modern state knows what he means and most will have at least a sneaking sympathy for his outrage. Certainly, the modern state involves itself chronically in the most intimate details of its citizens' day-to-day lives in a way which would be unrecognizable to the subjects of even the most despotic of premodern states.

## Societies and states: citizenship and democracy

Yet the growing intimacy of state and society has not all been one-way traffic. Indeed, in the conflict between state and society not every resource has been in the hands of the state. Think, for example, of resistance to the UK poll tax introduced by Margaret Thatcher towards the end of the 1980s. Citizens took a number of steps to avoid payment: concealment, non-registration, lying, moving address, mass non-payment and direct resistance. In the end, the state was forced to back down, although, of course, the poll tax gave way to a new, less objectionable and less resistible form of extraction. In the end, the state got its money (see Butler *et al.* 1994). The more general point is that citizens and their organizations do have resources (information, money, loyalty, votes, the power to inconvenience) which enable them to negotiate, albeit on very (and varyingly) unequal terms, with the state.

The most benign account of this relationship stresses the increasing account-ability of the modern state to its empowered citizenry. Thus, in some accounts, the growth of the modern state is at the same time a story of enhanced citizenship and increasing democratization. These claims about citizenship are developed further in Chapter 5. But, most notably in the French tradition, citizenship is still more explicitly attached to a second generalization about the modern epoch – i.e. its characterization as an 'Age of Democracy'. In its most positive version, the argument is that what is distinctive about the modern state is that it is democratic. What justifies, indeed mandates, its greater social intervention is the fact that it is the representative expression of the will of its people. Upon such an account, it is, in fact, the state that is subject to the collectively expressed will of society. We shall see in subsequent chapters that it is hard to accept this judgement as it stands. Nonetheless, however inadequate we may wish to argue is the democratization of the modern state, the fact that modern states have taken a broadly representative democratic form is of the first importance. The claim of modern European states to be 'democratic' is clearly not wholly ungrounded.

Typically, modern European states (though it should be stressed *not* most modern states elsewhere) have developed as *liberal democracies*. That is, they mix representative democratic institutions (parliaments, presidencies and their local equivalents) with certain civil liberties arranged within broadly privately owned market economies. Norberto Bobbio defines the *political* element of liberal democracy around the following 'cluster of rules':

1   All citizens who have reached legal age, without regard to race, religion, economic status, sex, etc. must enjoy political rights, i.e. the right to express their own opinion through their vote and/or to elect those who express it for them.
2   The vote of all citizens must have equal weight.
3   All citizens enjoying political rights must be free to vote according to their own opinion, formed as freely as possible, i.e. in a free contest between organized political groups competing among themselves so as to aggregate demands and transform them into collective deliberations.
4   They must also be free in the sense that they must be in a position of having real alternatives, i.e. of choosing between different solutions.
5   Whether for collective deliberations or for the election of representatives, the principle of numerical majority holds – even though different forms of majority rule can be established (relative, absolute, qualified), under certain circumstances established in advance.
6   No decision taken by a majority must limit minority rights, especially the right to become eventually, under normal conditions, a majority.

(Bobbio 1986: 66)

Less widely articulated, but certainly equally important to the characteristic structure of liberal democracies, is the context of an economy based upon private ownership and 'free' markets – i.e. capitalism. Clearly, not all states in modernity have been liberal democratic. (The states of the former Soviet Empire were certainly not for the most part *liberal* democratic.) However, those modern nation-states of Western Europe which have been liberal democratic have been based upon broadly capitalist forms of economic organization.

The relationship between state and society is among the most difficult to adjudicate. Is the modern state really Proudhon's embodiment of almost every imaginable evil, with its hands at the throats of its citizens ready to throttle the very life out of them at the least sign of resistance, or is it, by contrast, the highest expression of the common good, the embodiment of the democratically expressed will of its empowered citizenry? In Chapter 3, I try to furnish some answers. At this point, though, it is worth reporting that what we have described are not the only ways in which relations of state and society may be mediated. In practice, state and society are not two sharply differentiated spheres. They are entwined, and establishing the flow of forces and resources between them will not always be straightforward.

## State and nation

One final element seems worth identifying at this (high) level of generality. It is that the states of modernity are typically nation-states (or, in some accounts, *national states* or even *state-nations*). The ubiquity of this nation-state form is nicely captured by Smith:

> In the modern world only one form of political community is recognized and permitted. This is the form we call the 'nation-state'. It is easy enough to discover. Nation-states have frontiers, capitals, flags, anthems, passports, currencies, military parades, national museums, embassies and usually a seat at the United Nations. They also have one government for the territory of the nation-state, a single education system, a single economy and occupational system, and usually one set of legal rights for all citizens.
>
> (Smith 1986: 228)

I confine myself here to four supplementary points. First, in Europe at least, states predate nations. Mann reports that the first European state-building can be found in the twelfth century (Mann 1986: 416–49). Greenfeld (1992: 3–9) attributes the first use of a recognizably 'modern' sense of nation to early sixteenth-century England. Nation-building has been extremely important for state-building, but it has not been identical with it. Conversely, prior state-building has helped to shape the differentiation of nations. As Tilly has it, 'the European state-making process *minimised* the cultural variation within states and *maximised* the variation among states' (Tilly 1975: 19; emphasis added). Second, it is important to remember the distinction between the *nation* and *nationalism*. Here, Giddens's classification is helpful. A nation describes:

> a collectivity existing within a clearly demarcated territory, which is subject to a unitary administration, reflexively monitored both by the internal state apparatus and those of other states.

Nationalism describes:

> a phenomenon that is primarily psychological – the affiliation of individuals to a set of symbols and beliefs emphasising communality among the members of a political order.
>
> (Giddens 1985: 116)

He concludes that, 'although sentiments of nationalism often coincide with the actual distribution of populations within states, and while those who govern modern states usually seek to promote such sentiment wherever possible, there is by no means always a clear correspondence between them.' In fact and in practice, state, nation, nationalism and ethnic identity often become co-mingled in what is a heady and sometimes explosive mixture. Although in reality ethnic identity is *socially* acquired, the idea that nationhood describes a community of *biologically* shared descent is an extremely powerful (and politically consequential) one. Smith suggests that, 'in an era of nationalism, states which have a divided ethnic core and rival ethnic pasts are generally weaker and less well-developed than their ethnically secure counterparts' (1986: 263). In almost every quarter of the globe, we can find political and military confrontations that arise from the contested claims of state and nationhood.

Third, nations are associated with characteristics that are more or less unique to the state in modernity. Thus, nations reflect claims of sovereignty at a particular level (not local, not cosmopolitan). They reflect the formalization of borders and the importance of a shared legal apparatus. They also evoke elements of the 'citizenship' side of the modern state: rights shared within a particular community, authority deriving from the will of the sovereign people, the state as an expression of this collective will and so on. Held (1995), for example, sees the discourse of 'the nation' as an important element in enhancing the legitimacy of the modern state. According to Anderson, 'far from the essence of metaphysical nations finding expression in nationalism, nations were created, and created comparatively recently, by nationalism and nationalists' (1986: 115).

Finally, and in the light of these considerations, it is worth reporting that there are few nation-states for whom the claimed identity between state and nation is very convincing. Smith concludes,

> If we mean by the term 'nation-state' that the boundaries of the state's territories and those of a homogeneous ethnic community are coextensive, and that all the inhabitants of a state possess an identical culture, then we will not be able to muster more than 10 per cent of existing states as candidates for the title of 'nation-state'. A few moments' reflection on the United Kingdom of Great Britain and Northern Ireland should convince us of the gulf that lies between the nation state and the state as nation.
>
> (Smith 1986: 228–9)

## Conclusion

The purpose of this chapter has been to illustrate the *historicity* of the (modern) state. Not all societies have been governed through states, not all states have been like modern states and not all forms of the modern state are the same. We have been able to identify some fairly common features in this historical story. I have repeatedly stressed the impact of the international order, of the military and of the apparatus of resource extraction. I have given rather less weight to the economic sources of states' growth, and these will be more fully developed in the coming chapters. I have also tried to show how purely contingent events may, through time, have a determining effect upon patterns of later development and the ways in which developments within one jurisdiction may have decisive consequences for developments elsewhere. In the course of time, the modern nation-state form became established almost throughout the globe – and I have tried to suggest some of the reasons for this. But it is important that this should not be collapsed into an 'onward-and-upward' evolutionary story starting in the impenetrable mists of time and culminating in Western Europe somewhere around 1989. The processes that led to the modern state were much more haphazard and accidental than such an account would suggest. At the same time, we do not need to abandon all attempts to explain what has taken place by insisting that everything is just as it happens to be and that no one thing is quite like any other. The mixture of contingency and causation which lies behind the modern state is neatly captured by Mann's idea of 'caging'. At various historical points, the future was 'open'. The actual direction of development was contingent. But once a choice had been made, certain previously available options were foreclosed and certain other paths became 'privileged'. The large-scale history of states is chiefly the story of this recurrent process of choices made and options delimited – a process of caging which finds us bound by the parameters of the modern state. It is to a more detailed investigation of these parameters and of the processes that operate within and between modern states that we must now turn.

## Further reading

Anderson, P. (1974) *Lineages of the Absolutist State*. London: New Left Books.

Held, D. (1992) 'The development of the modern state', in S. Hall and B. Gieben (eds) *Formations of Modernity*. Cambridge: Polity.

Mann, M. (1986) *The Sources of Social Power*, Volume I: *A History of Power From the Beginning to AD 1760*. Cambridge: Cambridge University Press.

Mann, M. (1993) *The Sources of Social Power*, Volume II: *The Rise of Classes and Nation States, 1760–1914*. Cambridge: Cambridge University Press.

Poggi, G. (1990) *The State: Its Nature, Development and Prospects*. Cambridge: Polity.

Tilly, C. (1990) *Coercion, Capital, and European States, AD 990–1990*. Oxford: Blackwell.

# 3   States and societies

In 1897, Otto Hintze, the distinguished German contemporary of Weber, insisted that 'the relationship between the state and society is one of the most obscure and controversial topics of science' (Hintze 1973: 154). A hundred years on, the relationship between state and society remains just as controversial and, despite or perhaps because of everything that has been written and said in between, not much less obscure. We have seen (in Chapter 2) that, for much of human history, drawing a distinction between state and society would not have made much sense. Indeed, for most of human history, conceptions of state and society in anything like their modern senses simply did not exist. We also saw that for many commentators the very origins of the state lie in its emergence as a particular institutional ensemble *differentiated from* society. It is perhaps natural, then, that we should so frequently find the pairing 'state and society' or, rather more pointedly, 'state versus society'. But, at the same time, the uncertainty we have already identified in attempts to define the essence of 'the state' is more than matched by the ambiguity that surrounds contemporary understandings of what constitutes 'society'. This, in its turn, helps to explain why their interrelationship should have remained so unclear.

## Identifying 'society'

*Society* is a core conception for all the social sciences (perhaps above all for sociology). Like many ideas in the social sciences, we tend to use it unreflectively and fairly indiscriminately, but may be hard pressed to give it a definition which is both watertight and corresponds to the full range of ideas and institutions that we wish it to convey. Some older textbooks have tended to identify society with a more or less bounded and unitary social *system*. Such a view has probably been easier to sustain where society is identified, as frequently it is, with the boundaries of the modern nation-state. Thus, to speak of 'French society' or 'Spanish society' may seem relatively unproblematic. But even on this most favourable analytical terrain, there may be problems. We speak in similar terms of 'British society', even though this does not correspond to the borders of any single nation-state. We speak as convincingly of 'Welsh society', even though Wales is still (and despite its assembly) essentially a 'stateless nation'.

The broader problem of isolating societies may be illustrated by repeating a thought-experiment invoked by Mann. Suppose we were to ask an individual: To what society do you belong? The answers we might receive would undoubtedly differ according to the context within which the question was asked. But it would certainly make perfectly good sense for the respondent to claim to belong to a large number of quite differing types of society. Thus, for example, the respondent might reply that he or she was a member of British society or Scottish society; she might insist that she 'belonged to Glasgow' or the Royal Society for the Protection of Birds or a local amateur dramatic society or the Society of Christ. In some contexts your respondent might describe herself as a member of (a) European society. Of course, both questioner and questioned would normally (though not always) be able to judge from a particular context what sort of response was appropriate. The real point is that society cannot be coterminous with the nation-state; that the boundaries of most societies are not as clearly demarcated as those that surround these states; that we are all members of multiple societies, some of which are much smaller and others larger than nation-states; and that all societies exist not as free-standing social systems, but within the context of a range of other overlapping and abutting societies. One of the most salient features of the present period – as we have already seen – is the extent to which we are increasingly members of societies which are larger than the nation-state, including, in some circumstances, a 'global society'.

This rather more flexible sense of society is captured by Mann, who renders it as 'a network of social interaction at the boundaries of which is a certain level of inter-action cleavage between it and its environment'. A society is 'a unit with boundaries, and it contains interaction that is relatively dense and stable; that is, it is internally patterned when compared to interaction that crosses its boundaries' (Mann 1986: 13). Giddens writes of societies as special types of 'social systems which "stand out" in *bas-relief* from a background of a range of other systemic relationships in which they are embedded.' He identifies society with:

- a specifiable *clustering of institutions* across time and space;
- an association between the social system and a specific locale or 'territory of occupation';
- the existence of normative elements that involve laying claim to the legitimate occupation of the locale;
- the prevalence, among the members of the society, of feelings that they have some sort of common identity.

Having established these parameters, Giddens repeatedly insists that the boundaries of societies are permeable and that, in the modern world, all societies exist 'within the context of *intersocietal systems*' (Giddens 1981: 44–6; 1984: 164–5).

This blurring of the limits of society is carried still further (in fact, almost to the point of elimination) in Jessop's treatment of society in its relationship to the state (Jessop 1990). In effect, Jessop wishes to deny the utility of operating with any conception of 'society in general'; 'society', as a generic expression, serves at best as an 'indeterminate horizon' within which various 'societalization projects' may be considered. He argues that 'the existence of a society cannot be taken for granted: it must be constituted and reproduced through more or less precarious social processes and practices which articulate diverse social relations to produce a "society effect".' Jessop refers to the political projects that are directed towards the generation of 'society effects' as 'societalization'. Our analytical attention should more properly be directed towards this process of 'societalization' – the endeavour to produce 'society effects' – than upon the 'indeterminate horizon' of society itself. This corresponds to Jessop's belief that the proper object of our study of states is not 'the state' itself (if such a unitary phenomenon can be said to exist), but 'state projects', those political undertakings which have as their intended outcome 'state effects'. In Jessop's account, then, the institutional integrity of both state and society are put in question and, if it were not too cumbersome, might suggest that we should recast the object of our study in this chapter as the relationship between 'statization' and 'societalization'!

This brief review of recent thinking on the nature of society has a number of interesting consequences. First, we see that the reservations that have been entered against a unitary conception of the state have been reproduced in questioning the unitary conception of society. At its limits, such a position suggests that we focus upon *processes* of the generation of state effects and society effects, rather than directly upon conceptions of state and society themselves. We find, too, that just as states have to be located in a multi-state and inter-state system, so too must societies be placed within an inter-societal context. We see also (most explicitly in Giddens's treatment) an overlap among the sort of criteria – territoriality, boundedness, legitimacy, collective identity – with which both state and society are identified. Since neither state nor society are straightforward conceptions, and since they seem to share some defining criteria in common, we cannot expect to find that the relationship between them is itself simple or clear-cut. We shall soon see that few contemporary commentators argue that it is.

## State and *civil* society

Before we move to a direct consideration of relationships between state and society, we have first, however, to deal with one rather special version of this relationship – that is, in terms of the contrast between the state and *civil* society. *Civil* society involves a quite distinctive characterization of the non-state sphere. It is an expression that belongs, above all, to modern normative political theory, though it seeks also to invoke an actual or, at the very least, an imaginable sociological reality. In modern times, we nearly always find it used in the couplet 'state and civil society', though sometimes accompanied by a third or further complementary term(s). As we shall see, its meaning, and its supposed relationship to the state, has been subject to enormous variation over the past three or four hundred years. At one time, perhaps as late as the middle of the eighteenth century, it was just another term among many for what we would now call the state. In more recent usage, i.e. through most of the last two hundred years, it has been used to define a realm outside of, often contrasting with or indeed counterbalancing, the jurisdiction of the state (though variously interconnected with it).

Simplifying what is a complex debate, we can isolate two distinctive positions that have dominated modern discussions of the state–civil society relationship. On the one hand there are those who see civil society as the benign sphere of (individual) freedom whose integrity needs to be jealously guarded against the incursions of a domineering state. This has often been tied to an argument for the sanctity of private property and some sort of restraint upon the authority of democratic decision-making. The second position has tended to see civil society as an anti-social 'war of all against all', economically necessary, but needing to be controlled and patrolled by a powerful state embodying a wider social and public interest. Rather too crudely, the first position is often associated with classical liberalism, the second with varying socialist traditions, especially a Hegel-indebted Marxism.

A significant difficulty in adjudicating this dispute arises from a lack of consistency about what counts as civil society. It has often been argued that for Marx, and to some extent for socialists more generally, *civil* society has been too closely identified with a *capitalist* or *bourgeois* society. (In German, the same words – *bürgerliche Gesellschaft* – cover both *civil* society and *bourgeois* society.) Certainly, for Marx, civil society's sphere of formal equality and freedom simply defined a social order in which the controllers of private capital were free to exploit the labour power of those who lacked these resources. *Real* freedom could not mean extending autonomy within civil society, but rather the abolition or *overcoming* of civil society itself. But this was certainly *not* because Marx was an admirer of the modern state. Rather, it was Marx's view that the division into state and civil society was itself an expression of the deep underlying contradictions which a capitalist society could not overcome. Certainly, for Marx (in contradistinction to Hegel), it was civil society rather than the state that was the dominant and determining element in the relationship. But this problem could not be overcome by strengthening the powers of the state. Rather, it could only be addressed through the transition to socialism in which process the division between civil society and the state – indeed, the existence of both as separate domains – would be overcome in forging the first society that could be described as a 'true democracy' (Marx 1975). Whatever have been the practical outcomes of those who have made their politics under the label of Marxism, and whatever the relationship between these practices and Marx's own work, it is not appropriate to see Marx as an advocate of the socialist super-state. In fact, it was other, more gradualist and reformist variants of socialism that have tended to have a more positive view of the role of the state as an expression of the general or public interest.

We shall return to a fuller treatment of the Marxist account of the state–society relationship later in this chapter. For now, we can concentrate upon the ambiguity that Marx's position illustrates in the meaning of civil society. Is civil society anything more than the (broadly conceived) economy? For Marx, it seems the answer is 'not much'. But the same might be said of some *(neo-)liberal* commentators on civil society. For them, the key freedoms exercised in civil society are the rights of private property. It is private property that forms a bulwark for the individual citizen against the claims of an over-mighty state. Thus, we can find on both right and left the view that the essence of civil society is its guarantee of the integrity of a market capitalist economy premised upon private property. The difference is that the right like it and the left do not.

If we move on to consider the contemporary advocacy of civil society, we tend to find civil society more broadly conceived. There is still plenty of variation in what is defined into civil society. But for most commentators it is something *more* than the economy. For some, it is actually something *other* than the economy. Among these contemporary advocates, a strong civil society tends to be invoked as a means of empowering citizens over and against a domineering state. But while we find characteristically a commendation of civil society as something that ought to be empowered over and against the state, we do not for the most part find the judgement that it ought to be expanded, so far as is possible, to exclude the state. Keane, for example, defines civil society in the following terms. It is

> an aggregate of institutions whose members are engaged primarily in a complex of non-state activities – economic and cultural production, household life and voluntary association – and who in this way preserve and transform their identity by exercising all sorts of pressure or controls upon state institutions.
>
> (Keane 1988: 14)

But 'actually existing civil societies' – dominated by white heterosexual males and private corporations – are seen to be inadequate to the task of reform without themselves undergoing substantial change. Indeed, the state may be required to intervene in civil society precisely to guarantee that citizens have the rights and opportunities that allow them to operate on a basis of reasonable equality within this non-state sphere. Keane summarizes this new relationship between state and civil society in the following way:

> Without a secure and independent civil society of autonomous public spheres, goals such as freedom and equality, participatory planning and community decision-making will be nothing but empty slogans. But without the protective, redistributive and conflict-mediating functions of the state, struggles to transform civil society will become ghettoised, divided and stagnant, or will spawn their own, new forms of inequality and unfreedom.
>
> (Keane 1988: 15)

A similar aspiration informs Cohen and Arato's advocacy of civil societies. They define civil society as 'a sphere of social interaction between economy and state, composed above all of the intimate sphere (especially the family), the sphere of associations (especially voluntary associations), social movements, and forms of public communication' (Cohen and Arato 1992: 440–2). Again, their principal ambition is to check a domineering state, though, in fact, they operate with a *threefold* account of the social order (state, economy and civil society) and are almost as concerned with the threat that existing forms of corporate capitalist economy pose to the integrity of civil society. Their aspiration is not to endorse a political strategy of 'society versus the state', but to guarantee the space in which a civil society, partially sheltered from the logics of both state and economy, may flourish. This agenda is nicely captured by Held, who insists that, for any politics with a transformative intent, the reform process must be one of *double democratization* in which 'state and civil society . . . become the condition for each other's democratic development' (Held 1987: 286).

More recently, we find a parallel attempt to invoke a *global* form of civil society (see Keane 2003). Global civil society operates above and beyond the boundaries of nation-states and domestic societies. Its initial inspiration is seen to have come from the success of those movements grounded in a vigorous civil society which proved so important in overturning the former socialist regimes of Eastern and Central Europe. Beyond this, it has drawn strength from the following:

> a heightening appreciation of the revolutionary effects of the new galaxy of satellite/computer-mediated communications . . . the new awareness, stimulated by the peace and ecological movements, of ourselves as members of a fragile and potentially self-destructive world system; the widespread perception that the imploding Soviet-type communist systems implied a new global order; the world-wide growth spurt of neo-liberal economics and market capitalist economies; the disillusionment with the broken and unfulfilled promise of post-colonial states; and the rising concern about the dangerous and misery-producing vacuums opened up by the collapse of empires and states and the outbreak of uncivil wars.
>
> (Keane 2003: 1–2)

Global civil society embraces 'charities, think-tanks, prominent intellectuals . . . campaigning and lobby groups, citizens' protests . . . small and large corporate firms, independent media, Internet groups and websites, employers' federations, trades unions, international commissions, parallel summits and sporting organisations'. Taken together these form 'a dynamic non-governmental system of interconnected socio-economic institutions that straddle the whole earth, and that have complex effects that are felt in its four corners' (Keane 2003: 8–9). This is the non-governmental sphere that corresponds to (and is at least in part invoked by) the emergence of a globalized political and economic order (which we discuss further in Chapter 4).

Although, as I have suggested, the discussion of civil society has primarily been one in normative political theory, many of the same issues are raised in mainstream discussions of the state–society relationship. It is to these that we should now turn.

## Society-centred states or state-centred societies?

In the rest of this chapter I outline six of the most important positions that have been adopted on the state–society relationship. The several schools of *pluralism* and the seemingly numberless variants of *Marxism* have tended to argue (in their very different ways) that society is the dominant term in this relationship, shaping or even determining the nature of the state. The approaches which I summarize here as *neo-liberal*, *élitist* and *institutional statist* argue, by contrast, that the state acts in pursuit of its own interests and may well have an independent role in shaping the nature of society. *Feminist* approaches have represented an important challenge to *all* these ways of thinking about the state–society relation. They have treated of the state–society relationship in very different ways which have in some cases amounted to a wholesale rejection of the explanatory (rather than obfuscatory) role of the state. In a final section, I consider briefly the unique and increasingly influential account of the state–society relationship developed in the work of Michel Foucault. In the closing pages of the chapter, I draw upon these several sources to attempt some provisional judgement on the state–society relationship. I begin with a discussion of pluralism.

### Society-made states: pluralism

As its name suggests, the key idea behind pluralism is plurality – diversity, variety, many-sidedness. Its core proposition is that power and resources within society (and, by extension, within the sphere of the state itself) are dispersed. Pluralism achieved prominence, indeed precedence, as an explanatory model for political science in the thirty years following the Second World War, a period in which US experience came to dominate the discipline. Its primacy went largely unchallenged in the period down to the late 1960s and it continues to be a prominent (if sometimes unacknowledged) explanatory paradigm. Now, like most other such positions, it is to be found qualified in any number of ways, giving rise to 'reformed pluralism', 'critical pluralism', 'radical pluralism', 'neo-pluralism' and even 'Marxist pluralism' (e.g. Smith 1995; Dunleavy and O'Leary 1987). My concern here is not to explore this growing diversity, but rather to explore relatively briefly the most commonly shared elements in the pluralist position on state and society.

   As a point of departure, we may observe that pluralism classically gives very little space to the idea of *the state*. Pluralists have always been very suspicious of such abstractions. They have generally wished to concentrate upon observable *behaviour* – the actions of individual citizens, social groups or government officials – and have avoided terms which are not 'operationalizable' and which they have tended to identify as abstracted (and untestable) philosophizing. They have been suspicious in both normative and empirical terms of the idea of a unitary and sovereign state and have held up the dispersal of power especially in US institutions – the constitutional separation of powers, federalism, the lack of disciplined national parties, the entrenched rights of individual citizens – as examples for much wider admiration and emulation. Correspondingly, their attention has been focused not upon states but upon 'governments' or, better still, upon the activities of particular groups and individuals involved in the discharge of public functions. Indeed, many of them have identified a sort of pluralism within the institutions of the state itself, a process Wilson (1977: 45) christens 'Whitehall pluralism'. Thus, different ministries, different agencies, even different cabinet colleagues are seen to be pursuing differing ambitions, bringing diversity and multiplicity to the very heart of government and state.

   For pluralists, the real source of democratic decision-making lies not in this disaggregated state but in a diverse society. What makes countries such as the UK and the USA good liberal democracies, in the pluralist view, is not so much their constitutional arrangements (though these are important), but rather the nature of the wider society within which these are located. Such societies are 'open'. Power is to be found in many different places. Different groups are able to mobilize very differing sorts of resources, and power is generally non-cumulative. Citizens are free to express themselves and to seek to organize and mobilize to advance their several interests. They enjoy a 'civic culture' which is tolerant, stable, mature and capable of accepting and reconciling differences of interest without resort to violent social and political conflict (Almond and Verba 1965). They also enjoy a widespread consensus about the 'basic rules of the political game'. This consensus is not an expression of shared substantive beliefs about what public policy should be. Rather it expresses a willingness 'to agree to disagree', accepting that there should be a diversity of interests within society and that other citizens should have an equal right to organize themselves around their different (and potentially) competing interests.

Such a pluralist regime also requires that citizens be willing to accept what is always an *interim* compromise between their several interests brokered by the public authorities. Under these circumstances, the principal mechanism of policy-shaping is not the individual citizen casting a vote in more or less frequent elections. The discipline of electoral accountability is an important one, but parties, especially the 'catch-all' parties in a two-party system, seek the broadest possible voter appeal and are quite ineffective in articulating the wide range of very particular interests that individual citizens wish to see pursued. For pluralists, the privileged mechanism shaping policy outcomes is the activity of *interest groups*.

Upon such an account, the making of public policy by governments is the end-product of a process of negotiation and accommodation in which citizens organized in groups to represent their interests exert pressure to realize their ambitions. If such a process is to be broadly democratic, it is clear that all interests should potentially be able to mobilize, that no group should enjoy such a command of resources that they are able to 'squeeze out' competing interests, and that the agencies of the state should be open, neutral and fragmented. No particular interest in society should have privileged access to the state or any of its parts. Very broadly, mainstream pluralists insist that these criteria are more or less satisfied in societies like ours. Few of them deny that some interests, above all business interests, do command disproportionate resources and governmental attention. This privileged status of business interests has been enough to drive some of the most distinguished pluralists (most prominently Dahl and Lindblom) out of the pluralist camp. Yet those who remain have always insisted that differing groups are able to command differing kinds of resources (business is generally strong on money but not necessarily in numbers) and that the differential influence of interest groups may be a reflection of the differing number of supporters and intensity of interests which they represent (Dunleavy and O'Leary 1987).

Pluralism has been under sustained intellectual assault for more than thirty years. Every one of its presuppositions has come under attack. Thus, it is argued that pluralists focus too narrowly upon observable actions (behaviour) to the exclusion of underlying asymmetries of power; that they ignore problems of the differential capacity to form interest groups; that certain groups have systematically privileged (and others effectively excluded from) access to the policy-making process; that particular agencies of government, if not the whole arena of state activity itself, have been effectively 'captured' by sectional social interests. In responding to many of these (often well-founded) criticisms, the lines that divide pluralism from the other positions considered here have become rather blurred. There is an excellent and extensive secondary literature on these questions (including Dunleavy and O'Leary 1987; Held 1987; Dearlove and Saunders 1991; Smith 1995). Rather than rehearse these arguments here, I want to devote a little more attention to pluralist views of the state.

I have already indicated that pluralists give comparatively little space to discussions of the state, and almost all of those who have commented upon their analysis insist that, in the pluralist framework, the state is 'under-theorized'. Certainly in some variants of pluralism the state is quite perfunctory. Public policy outcomes simply reflect the balance of forces in society registered (but in no way mediated) by the governing authorities. But there are more active versions of the state's role which are still broadly consonant with pluralist premises. Thus, the state may be 'neutral' between competing societal interests, but at the same time 'active' in seeking to balance, referee and mediate competing forces so as to generate stable forms of compromise which are, among other things, consonant with some overall sense of 'the public interest'. In this view the state may have a role as a 'mediator, balancer and harmonizer of [differing societal] interests' (Dunleavy and O'Leary 1987: 46).

Dunleavy and O'Leary also isolate a third pluralist model of the state: the broker state, which 'does not mirror its society, nor neutrally follow the public interest . . . [but envisages] public policy as the aggregation of pressure group activities going on inside the state apparatus' (Dunleavy and O'Leary 1987: 47). Upon such an account, we have a still more active role for the state. The state now seeks not only to reconcile competing societal interests, but also to do so in a way which is consonant with its *own* policy concerns. In cases where the balance of societal forces is close to equilibrium, the state may actually exercise a decisive role in shifting policy in one or other direction. Thus, 'state officials [may be] capable of manipulating the cleavages and interest groups in civil society; sowing division, and exploiting for their own purposes the cross-cutting cleavages and overlapping group membership which stabilize liberal democracy' (Dunleavy and O'Leary 1987: 48).

We see then that pluralists have actually come to work with a number of conceptions of the state (and, correspondingly, of its relation to society). These range from the supposition that the state is almost powerless to an account in which its representatives act quite consciously to shape the policy process in line with their *own* policy ambitions. What unites these pluralist positions, however, is the supposition that the original driving force of the state's activity arises from societal sources. States may be more or less active, but they are in essence reactive, at their most interventionist seeking to turn the tide of diverse societal initiatives to their own ends. We can still think of pluralism as an account in which society strongly determines what happens at the level of the state.

### Society-made states: Marxism

It is perhaps commonplace to think of Marxism as defining a unified body of political thought from which we might expect to be able to derive a single (and perhaps rather dogmatic) account of the state–society relationship. But such a supposition is quite misplaced. There has been no shortage of pretenders to the title of the 'one, true and authentic' Marxism, but the practical and theoretical history of Marxism actually discloses a bewildering diversity of analyses and strategies. This is certainly as true of Marxist accounts of the state–society relationship as it is of any other. It is a product of both the astonishing fecundity and the troubling ambiguity of Marx's own thinking on this question. Rather than map out all the pathways (including not a few culs-de-sac) that bring us to the current state of Marxist and 'post-Marxist' thinking on the state, I want to concentrate here upon some key trends established in the work of a comparatively small number of influential Marxist theoreticians.

Naturally, such a journey must begin with Marx (1818–83). For all the complexities in his work, it seems reasonable to argue that the underlying premise of Marx's position was that society determined the form and nature of the state. Indeed, in his earliest critical writings on Hegel, Marx insisted that the very existence of the state was the consequence of a society which was divided by social class. In a future society that had ceased to be based upon class, the state as a separate social sphere could be expected to 'wither away'. Yet, while the state was, in some sense, but a displaced expression of society, at the same time it had to exercise power over it. In Engels's words, the state was a power, arisen out of society but placing itself above it (Engels 1978: 752). The state had to use its powers to prevent a bitterly divided society from descending into open civil warfare. However, it did so not as a neutral peace-maker, but acting in the long-term interests of society's dominant class.

Although Marx was, of course, a great advocate of socialism, he was above all else an analyst of capitalism (and, naturally enough, of the capitalism of his own time). In his mature writings, we find at least two accounts of the state–society relationship under capitalism. The first and predominant view saw the state as essentially the instrument of society's ruling class – the capitalists or bourgeoisie. In a famous phrase from the *Communist Manifesto*, he claimed that 'the executive of the modern state is but a committee for managing the common affairs of the bourgeoisie' (Marx 1973a: 69). For Marx, capitalism was a social and economic system in which the wealth of the capital-owning bourgeoisie was derived from the exploited labour power of a propertyless working class of proletarians. Class struggle was endemic to such a society, and the state with its means of violence was there to control the outbreak of hostilities and to ensure that the interests of the exploiting minority, the capitalist class, were upheld. Following Marx's more general materialist conception of history, it was the economic or productive basis of society that determined its political forms. There were circumstances in which the state might act against the representatives of particular *fractions* of capital, but always the better to protect the overall interest of the capitalist class in general. Indeed, Engels formalized the notion of the state as an 'ideal collective capitalist', the sole agency able to represent the general and collective class interest of individual capitalists whose day-to-day competition could make effective cooperation difficult. This view was especially influential upon the first generation of Marxists who shaped its development in the period down to the Russian Revolution of 1917. Lenin described the state as 'a special force for the suppression of a particular class' (Lenin 1960: 392). Karl Kautsky (1854–1938), leader of the German Social Democratic Party (and once described by Lenin as 'the Pope of Marxism'), could not have been much clearer: 'the modern state is pre-eminently an instrument intended to guard the interests of the ruling class' (Kautsky, cited in Salvadori 1979: 42).

It is also possible to discern a second, less influential and less systematic account of the state–society relationship in Marx's writings. This view can be seen intermittently throughout Marx's career, from the early critique of Hegel to the late commentary on the experience of the Paris Commune (in 1871). It is perhaps most sharply drawn in *The Eighteenth Brumaire of Louis Bonaparte*, Marx's commentary on the coming to power of Louis Bonaparte in France between 1848 and 1851. Here, Marx suggests that, particularly in periods of intensified class conflict and when the contending forces are fairly evenly matched, the state may find itself able to exercise power to some extent *independent* of the will of the ruling class. To some extent, Marx reverts to his earliest critique of the state as parasitic upon society, condemning the 'enormous bureaucratic and military organization . . . this appalling parasitic body [which] enmeshes the body of French society like a net and chokes all its pores' (Marx 1973b). At the same time, he evokes the idea (to be taken up in later Marxist accounts of the state in 'exceptional' periods) that there may be times of acute peril in which the bourgeoisie 'gives up' its political power, the better to be able to secure its still more fundamental economic interests. But Marx never argues that the state can free itself entirely of its basis in the class structure of the society over which it presides, giving rise to the widely used formula in which the state under capitalism is said to be '*relatively autonomous*' of its class base. This formulation, with its suggestion that, within certain parameters, the state may act independently of those societal forces out of which it emerges, was particularly influential in the remarkable renewal of interest in the state among Marxist thinkers that began towards the end of the 1960s. It certainly opened up the way for those who wanted to argue that the state under capitalism might mean not so much the state of the capitalist class (the instrumental approach), but the state within a capitalist society (a structural approach) in which the requirement to maintain the long-term viability of the capitalist order might not tie the state and its agents to a particular class.

Peculiarly influential in the transition from the claims of a classical Marxism dominated by the instrumental approach to the much greater diversity of Marxist work on state and society of the last twenty-five years was the analysis of the inter-war leader of the Italian Communist Party, Antonio Gramsci. Writing from the prison to which he had been confined by the Italian fascists, Gramsci set out a quite distinctive Marxist view of the state–civil society relationship. Reflecting upon the defeat of the workers' movement in Western Europe that had followed upon the period of radical mobilization at the end of the First World War, Gramsci insisted that the mode of capitalist rule could not be reduced simply to the actions of a repressive state apparatus acting directly under the control of the capitalist class.

Gramsci argued that, under the 'advanced' form of capitalism that had developed in the West (and in contrast with the circumstances that had faced Lenin and the Bolsheviks in Russia), the normal form of rule was mediated through both state and civil society. The mundane rule of capitalism was not secured principally through repression and armed control of the population (though these options always remained available for 'emergency use'). Rather, the rule of capital was more normally (and securely) managed through the ideological and cultural domination of the subordinate classes within the institutions of civil society. Churches, newspapers, schooling, the structure of the family, cultural values, even reformist trades unions: these were the media through which both an ideological and a practical domination was maintained. Rule was a mixture of 'manufactured consent backed by coercion'. The elements of cultural and ideological control, the mobilization of consent, Gramsci called *hegemony*. Under normal circumstances, the bourgeoisie would seek to secure its rule not simply by imposing its will upon society, but rather by pursuing hegemonic *strategies* in which it would seek to win the support of secondary classes, even of elements within the working class itself, so as the better to secure its long-term domination.

Given the difficult circumstances under which Gramsci wrote – in prison and under the watchful eye of the censor – his usage of state and civil society is not entirely clear and consistent. At times, he distinguishes modes of rule through the state (associated with coercion, dictatorship, direct force) and civil society (associated with consent, hegemony and the institutions of managed consent). But he also wrote of 'the integral state' (*lo stato integrale*) or 'the state in its inclusive sense', which embraced rule mobilized through 'political society plus civil society'. This broader conception of the state is neatly caught by Gramsci when he identifies it with the 'entire complex of political and theoretical activities with which the ruling class not only justifies and maintains its dominance, but manages to win the active consent of those over whom it rules' (Gramsci 1971: 244).

The breach which Gramsci's thought represents with the rather mechanistic economism of an earlier generation of Marxist thought was a major influence in the revival of Marxist writing on state and society that blossomed from the late 1960s onwards. Some influential work of this later period (perhaps, above all, the work of Ralph Miliband) continued to draw upon an (albeit more subtle) version of the instrumentalist approach. But more characteristically it has taken up a number of Gramscian themes: the interweaving of state and society, the uniqueness of given nation-state formations, the mediation of rule through societal institutions, the importance of non-economic modes of rule, the struggle for hegemony, the pursuit of political strategies and so on. Among the most influential sources in this development has been the work of the Graeco-Parisian theorist Nicos Poulantzas (1936–78), whose celebrated debate with Miliband helped to launch the revival of Marxist interest in the state. Poulantzas was influenced not only by Gramsci, but also (among others) by the French structuralism of Louis Althusser. Much of his writing is rather inaccessible, but his last and most readable text, *State, Power, Socialism*, makes absolutely clear his breach with the presumption that the state is the instrument of the ruling class.

Indeed, much of Poulantzas's work is concerned with the elaboration of the idea of the *relative autonomy* of the state from the ruling class. His aspiration seems to have been to reconcile the central Marxist presumption that the state is, in some final instance, a *capitalist* state (in some way destined to reproduce the existing social and economic order), while insisting that it is not the state of the capitalist class. In so far as the state does act to reproduce capitalism, it does so not by being the embodiment of the will of the dominant capitalist class, but rather through its being 'the factor of cohesion' that holds together the capitalist social formation. At its simplest, the state realizes this mission through its capacity to 'organise and unify the dominant power bloc by permanently disorganising-dividing the dominated classes' (Poulantzas 1978: 140). In so doing, it may sometimes act against the immediate and/or economic interests of the capitalist class, when the needs of long-term capital accumulation require an *economic* price to be paid to secure the *political* compliance of non-ruling class interests. The state is constantly involved in the negotiation of compromise with secondary class elements and in the forging of hegemonic strategies through which the rule of capital may be retained. In contrast to the classical Leninist position (that 'the state is always the instrument of a single class'), Poulantzas is insistent that the state itself is 'constituted-divided' by the same divisions that characterize capitalist society more generally. Thus, state struggles may be played out in society, while societal struggles penetrate the very apparatus of the state itself.

Overall, we might characterize Poulantzas's work as an attempt to deploy greater analytic flexibility and historical sensitivity, a sense of strategic choices and an element of indeterminacy, within a framework that remains resolutely Marxist. In the end, it is not clear that Poulantzas was able to reconcile these several ambitions. In the period since his untimely death in 1978, this aspiration has been most systematically carried forward by the British social theorist Bob Jessop. His ambition has been to generate a synthesis which is ever more sensitive to the complexity of real-world social forces and ever more rigorous in its excision of the methodologically unsustainable elements in traditional Marxist thinking, while retaining a coherent theoretical basis premised in Marxian political economy. Bob Jessop abandons the perspective of a 'relative autonomy' of the state (related to some finally determinant force located elsewhere) and rejects the necessary primacy of class and the economy in favour of what he calls a 'strategic-relational' approach to the state. *Strategy* refers to the element of intentional action through which (structure-bounded) actors pursuing particular 'state projects' make and remake the state. This process is *relational* because the capacity to pursue particular state projects 'is not inscribed in the state system as such. Instead it depends upon the relation between state structures and the strategies which various forces adopt towards it' (Jessop 1990: 10). Thus, 'the State is not simply something towards which one must adopt a political strategy but is something (or better, a social relation) which can be fruitfully analysed as the site, the generator, and the product of strategies' (Jessop 1989: 3).

In Jessop's mature view, the field of contestation over state and society is extraordinarily complex. There is no single logic from which we may derive state activity. The reality of determinate outcomes (necessity) is tempered by a recognition of contingency (in terms of our incapacity to predict the complex paths through which these determinate outcomes will develop). The terrain of the state is contested by a diversity of social forces pursuing a diversity of social projects. It is not a unitary force but rather 'a specific institutional ensemble with multiple boundaries, no institutional fixity and no pre-given formal or substantive unity. . . . Any *substantive* unity which a state system might possess derives from specific political projects and struggles to impose unity or coherence on that system' (Jessop 1990: 267–8). The actual outcomes of struggles on the terrain of the state reflect the existing balance of social forces structured, in part, by the sedimentation of the outcomes of earlier struggles.

In the end (and as we saw earlier in this chapter), even the fuzzy lines defining state and society tend to disappear, as Jessop speaks of 'society effects' and 'state effects' and processes of 'statization' and societalization', rather than of state and society.

### State-made societies: neo-liberalism

So far, we have seen that both pluralists and the more orthodox of the Marxists argue, in their rather different ways, that it is the nature of society which 'in the final instance' determines the form of the state. For pluralists, this is generally a benign process (giving us a decent working model of democratic decision-making for large-scale and complex societies). The Marxists' judgement is much more negative: the state is a displaced expression of a society divided by class and exploitation. By contrast with both these positions, neo-liberal thinkers see the modern state as an increasingly domineering and malign influence, imposing itself upon society. They echo the fear that has been voiced at least since the time of Hobbes, that the modern state would come to be so powerful and so authoritative that it would crush all freedom and autonomy in civil society. They argue that the modern state has truly become 'a New Leviathan' (Radosh and Rothbard 1972).

The neo-liberal position on state and society is often expounded in the context of the historical evolution of state and society in Western Europe and North America in the half-century following the Second World War. For neo-liberals, the origins of the expanded state lie in the nineteenth century, but it is really in the twentieth century, and more particularly in this period since 1945, that states in Western Europe and North America have became too large and too powerful. The rise of this 'New Leviathan' was largely the consequence of the pursuit by parties of *all* persuasions of a broadly social democratic agenda, in which the state intervened ever more extensively in society to seek to increase levels of economic activity, to redistribute the fruits of economic growth and to underwrite the welfare status of its citizens. States extended their policies into more and more areas of social life, including the 'intimate' sphere of the family, promising to protect its subject-citizens from the exigencies of everyday life. The more the state intervened, the greater were the resources it had to extract from society. But the greater the scope of these interventions, so the neo-liberals have argued, the more frequently did they fail or have unintended and undesirable consequences. Eventually (some thirty years into the post-war world), the accumulation of failed government interventions and the raising of the resources to fund them triggered a process of government *overload*.

States were extracting more and more resources from society, so as to impose their unsuccessful agenda of reforms upon it. This was undermining the health of the economy, with the sustained growth of the twenty-five years following the Second World War yielding to problems of rising inflation and unemployment, lower growth and increasing public indebtedness.

Probably the most sophisticated and thoughtful exponent of the more general neo-liberal position on state and society was the Austrian political economist Friedrich Hayek (1899–1992). For Hayek, the key human values are freedom and justice. Democracy was important and Hayek undoubtedly considered himself a democrat (of a very particular kind), but he was still more an advocate of individual freedom, and certainly an opponent of the ideas of sovereign and unlimited government. A free and just society, he insisted, can be secured only on the basis of *catallaxy*, the term Hayek coined to describe 'the special kind of spontaneous order produced by the market through people acting within the rules of the laws of property, tort and contract' (Hayek 1982: II, 109). Freedom and justice could only be secured in a society of freely contracting individuals coordinating their actions through market-like transactions. This demanded a correspondingly very limited role for the state. 'Only limited government can be decent government', Hayek insisted, 'because there do not exist (and cannot exist) general moral rules for the assignment of particular benefits' (Hayek 1982: II, 102). The duty of the state is not to pursue its own ends but rather to provide the framework (of 'the Rule of Law') within which catallaxy or the market-ordered society may develop. Thus, the state ought properly to be limited to the maintenance of collective security against external threats, the preservation of the Rule of Law, provision of that very small number of public goods which cannot be efficiently delivered by the market and the relief of destitution. Its tax-raising powers ought to be limited to the funding of these few legitimate activities.

Yet, in practice, the state as it has developed over the past hundred years has systematically broken all these constitutional limits. Most damaging has been the working through of 'the pernicious principle of parliamentary sovereignty' (Hayek 1982: III, 3). Where parliament is sovereign, Hayek argues, governments become the plaything of organized sectional interests. Rejecting the claims of the pluralists, Hayek insists that, under these circumstances, principles and 'the national interest' will be abandoned in the attempt to mobilize a majority-creating coalition of particular interests against the *genuinely* common or public interest. Interest-group pressure on the state is not the means of reconciling and compromising a diversity of interests in society. Rather, it is the way in which organized interests are able to promote their well-being at the expense of the general (and disaggregated) citizenry.

These vices of unlimited government have been peculiarly damaging when the state has been captured by socialists and social democrats. First, socialists try to adjust the spontaneous order generated by market transactions, a project which Hayek depicted as hopeless, given the impossibility of adequate centrally organized knowledge of the infinity of market-like decisions. Interventions of the state in the market will *always* have sub-optimal outcomes and *always* lessen general social welfare. Second, social democrats' sponsorship of the welfare state and of particularistic legislation, most notably to confer privileges upon its allies in the organized labour movement, represents a break with Hayek's insistence that the law must be confined to rules of 'just conduct of universal application'. Third, socialists and social democrats intervene in the market and its outcomes to promote 'social justice' (Hayek 1982: II, 1). This is a mistake. Justice, Hayek insisted, is strictly *procedural* and can only refer to the proper enforcement of general rules of universal application without regard to its particular results. 'The mirage of social justice' which the socialists pursue is, at best, a nonsense and, at worst, pernicious and itself unjust. It means undermining the justice of the market, confiscating the wealth of the more successful, prolonging the dependency of the needy, entrenching the special powers of organized interests and over-riding individual freedom. Indeed, it is 'irreconcilable with the rule of law' and, in seeking to press state intervention beyond its legitimate minimum, socialists have been the worst offenders in 'giving democracy a bad name' (Hayek 1982: II, 86).

In recent years, the broad philosophical case that Hayek made out against the extended state and its interference in society has been supplemented by a more specific attack upon the characteristic structures of the state apparatus itself. Particularly influential have been the arguments of a number of critics (working within the general framework of public choice theory) who have contended that states are almost always a worse option than markets. They insist that there is an inherent tendency for states to grow beyond their desirable limits, that states will always tend to oversupply public goods and that those who staff the state apparatus will manage the public policy process so as to advance their own sectional interests at the expense of the wider society.

*Public choice theory*, located on the boundaries between economics and political science, has traditionally been concerned with collective or non-market forms of decision-making. When deployed by neo-liberals, it is taken to show that, under liberal-democratic procedures, collective choice through state actions, beyond that necessary minimum advocated by Hayek, will always tend to yield outcomes that are less efficient or desirable than outcomes determined by private choice in civil society through the medium of markets. The great weakness of decision-making procedures in the liberal-democratic state is that it encourages both governments and voters to be fiscally irresponsible. The individual making a private economic choice within the market has always to weigh costs against benefits. Public choice theorists argue that, in the political 'market', both voters and governments are able to avoid or at least to deflect the consequences of spending decisions and thus to seek benefits without taking due account of costs. Within the rules of the liberal-democratic game, it is then possible for both governments and voters to act rationally, but through their collective action to produce sub-optimal or even positively harmful consequences. This, it is suggested, may be shown in a number of ways.

First, it may not be rational for individual voters carefully to consider the full range of a prospective government's public policy, still less to consider the overall consequences of such policies for the national interest. The marginal impact of a single voter's decision is so limited that the opportunity costs of a well-considered decision would be unreasonable (Downs 1957; Olson 1982). Under these circumstances, no rational actor will normally press his or her consideration beyond a crude calculation of how the incumbent government has benefited the voter. Given this, it is in the interests of a government seeking re-election to ensure that the pre-election period is one in which as many voters as possible 'feel good'. Governments will then seek to manage the economy in the run-up to an election so as to lower inflation and unemployment and to maximize incomes (perhaps through lowering personal rates of taxation). In this way, a *political business cycle* may be established, with governments manipulating economic variables in the prelude to an election. Not only will this give misleading signs to the electors, but it will also undermine the long-term stability of the economy and will tend to increase the state's indebtedness (through an imbalance of spending and taxation). Under circumstances of two-party adversarial politics, such fiscal irresponsibility is unlikely to be challenged by the opposition, who are more likely to 'bid up' the electorate's expectations, promising 'more for less' in the attempt to unseat the existing government (Downs 1957; Alt and Chrystal 1983).

Clearly in a private economic market such overbidding would be constrained by the threat of bankruptcy. A corporation that sold goods and services at less than their cost of production would soon be forced out of business. But governments do not face this same constraint (at least in the short and medium term). By increasing the public debt, governments may defer the costs of their present spending upon future governments (and/or generations). This may have a damaging effect on the medium-term prospects for the economy – by encouraging inflation, squeezing out private-sector investment or whatever – but, while this runs against the overall public interest, it is not rational for either particular governments or particular voters to seek to stop it. Indeed, Olson argues that economic growth becomes a 'public good' for most interest groups. It is more rational to seek to extract a greater proportion of the national budget (through political pressure) than to seek to enhance the overall growth of the economy (Olson 1965, 1982; Rose and Peters 1978). In a number of other ways, this logic of collective action can be seen to furnish sub-optimal outcomes. Governments that are seeking to maximize their electoral appeal are driven to support the particularistic claims of well-organized interest groups and to satisfy the claims of special interests. The costs of meeting the claims of the well-organized are discharged upon a wider and unorganized society. The politics of voter-trading and political activism tend to lead to an expansion of government beyond that which is either necessary or desirable (Tullock 1976).

This oversupply of public services is further exacerbated by the nature of the public bureaucracy. First, the public bureaucracy is itself a powerful interest group, and public bureaucrats have a rational interest in maximizing their own budgets and departments. Second, the public bureaucracy does not normally face competition, or indeed any of the economic constraints of acting within a marketplace. Where costs are not weighed against benefits and where the utility maximization of bureaucrats is dependent upon the maximization of their budgets, the public choice theorists insist that there will be a chronic tendency for the public bureaucracy to oversupply goods and services (Niskanen 1971, 1973; Tullock 1976). This problem becomes still more acute when the monopolistic powers of the public bureaucracy are strengthened by an expansion of white-collar trades unionism, as happened, for example, in the much expanded British civil service in the period after the Second World War (Bacon and Eltis 1978).

Neo-liberals do not argue that the state–society relationship is all 'one-way traffic'. For example, they make much of the pressure that organized interests in society are able to bring to bear upon the state and the almost irresistible demands (which may even come from a majority of the electorate) to which governments find themselves obliged to defer. Rather, their argument is that a good society – one which can secure freedom and justice – must be founded upon the unforced interchange of uncoerced individuals in market-like transactions in a liberal civil society. The only legitimate function of the state, even the democratic state, is to secure the general conditions under which contractual relations between individuals will be upheld. Yet what we saw in the twentieth century were states consistently over-reaching themselves, seeking much more actively and expensively to govern the societies over which they preside. The consequences are a loss of freedom, a lack of justice and economic under-performance.

### State-made societies: élitism

Élitism – as the belief that society is and/or ought to be governed by a minority comprising the most able – is a very ancient idea in the study of human societies (retraceable all the way to Plato). It was revived with particular vigour around the turn of the twentieth century by a number of (mainly continental European) critics who challenged the optimistic expectations about a participatory democracy that had been expressed in the nineteenth century by both socialist and liberal thinkers. Perhaps the most prominent critic of the idea that an extension of voting rights would mean a real expansion of popular democratic decision-taking was the German theorist Robert Michels (1876–1936). In essence, his argument was that the coming of mass voting would not lead to mass empowerment because the influence of the masses would be mediated by political parties in which organizational and informational resources would be concentrated in the hands of a small leadership group. Somewhat notoriously, Michels wrote (in the context of the German Social Democratic Party) of an 'iron law of oligarchy' under which effective decision-making power in any large-scale organization, however formally democratic, would always come to rest with a small élite group, at the expense of rank-and-file members (Michels 1962).

The more general élitist argument was carried forward by two Italian social theorists, Gaetano Mosca (1858–1941) and Vilfredo Pareto (1843–1923). Mosca gives clearest expression to the 'inevitability' of government by élites:

> In all societies – from societies that are very meagrely developed and have barely attained the dawnings of civilization, down to the most advanced and powerful societies – two classes of people appear – a class that rules and a class that is ruled. The first class, always the less numerous, performs all political functions, monopolises power and enjoys the advantages that power brings,

whereas the second, the more numerous class, is directed and controlled by the first.

(Mosca 1939: 50)

In Pareto, we find the same emphasis upon rule by a minority, but also attention directed towards the 'circulation of élites'. Borrowing from Machiavelli, Pareto stresses the different qualities of those rulers he characterizes as 'foxes' (cunning, intelligent and consent-mobilizing) and 'lions' (unimaginative but resolute in their use of force). Broadly conceived, history consists in the circulation of these two types of governing élite.

The idea of the circulation of élites is also quite central to the model of 'democratic élitism' or 'competitive élitism' most frequently associated with the work of Weber and Joseph Schumpeter. In essence, the position of the democratic élitists was this: the 'classical' model of democracy, in which all citizens are equally involved in the making and implementing of collective decisions, is utopian. In reality, real decision-making power will always be concentrated in the hands of a small number of political decision-takers (hopefully) directing the actions of a large-scale bureau-cracy. The normal pattern of governance is one in which decisions are passed down from the governors at the top to the governed beneath them. An element of democratic accountability is retained, however, if there is competition for these élite positions and if those who currently hold élite positions face the possibility of losing office in some future electoral confrontation with an alternative élite. Democracy is not, therefore, a mechanism for expressing (and mobilizing) the popular will. It is the name for that form of competition for the votes of the electorate through which alternative élites compete for the right to rule. According to Schumpeter,

> democracy does not mean and cannot mean that the people actually rule in any obvious sense of the terms 'people' and 'rule'. Democracy means only that the people have the opportunity of accepting or refusing the men who are to rule them.

(Schumpeter 1976: 284)

It is clear, I think, how the general position of the élitists might lead to a view in which the state (directed by a powerful élite) dominates over and controls society (composed of a disaggregated and largely ineffectual mass). The position adopted by the competitive élitists suggests only a marginal adjustment of this relationship, with a very modest form of control exercised by the electoral base in endorsing a presumed-to-be predominant governing élite. Yet élitism, in itself, does not neces-sarily yield such a conclusion. Certainly, élitists reject the claims made for a participatory democracy, but this does not require that the state should dominate over society. For it is possible that differing social spheres may generate their *own* élites and that, for example, government élites may be counterbalanced by élites in the world of finance or business. This is certainly one way in which an amended form of pluralism (based upon a plurality of élites) has been defended (Vogel 1987). Yet, the more radical and critical theorists of élitism (from C. Wright Mills in the

USA of the 1950s to John Scott writing about contemporary Britain) have seen the several élites (in government, business, the military and the academy) as mutually reinforcing (sometimes coming together to constitute 'National Elite Power Networks') (Mills 1956; Scott 1991, 2001; Evans 1995). Thus, Scott, for example, concludes that 'Britain is ruled by a capitalist class whose economic dominance is sustained by the operations of the state and whose members are disproportionately represented in the power élite which rules the state apparatus' (Scott 1991: 151).

There is also the possibility, raised by the analysts of varying forms of 'corporatism', that society comes to be governed by the concerted action of a series of élites who enter into arrangements on the basis of their capacity to deliver the support of their own particular social base. The best known definition of corporatism in this context is that given in the 1970s by Schmitter:

> Corporatism can be defined as a system of interest representation in which the constituent units are organized into a limited number of singular, compulsory, non-competitive, hierarchically ordered and functionally differentiated categories, recognized or licensed (if not created) by the state and granted a deliberate representational monopoly within their respective categories in exchange for observing certain controls on their selection of leaders and articulation of demands and supports.
>
> (Schmitter 1974: 93–4)

Plenty of reservations have been entered against the claim that corporatism described a new and distinctive form of governance, and it is certainly the case that not all variants of corporatism are appropriately labelled 'élitist'. Normally, those interests which were held to be involved were the state, organized business and organized labour. It has always been argued that corporatism applied to a limited range of societies (above all in continental Europe and Scandinavia) and that possibly its time has now passed (though this last claim is keenly contested). (Among recent discussions, see Garrett 1998; Kitschelt *et al.* 1999; Coates 2000.) But it does, in principle, represent a distinctive way in which societal and state élites might coordinate their actions so as to deliver effective control over a wider society.

### State-made societies: 'institutional statism'

Increasingly influential in recent years has been the approach of 'institutional statism' or the 'structured polity'. For advocates of this approach, the golden rule is to 'bring the state back in' to political analysis (definitively in Evans *et al.* 1985). This suggests that the statists' position is above all a reaction against those who have given too much weight to the political influence of societal forces and especially against those who have abandoned the analytic category of 'the state' in favour of the more general appraisal of 'political systems' (see Almond *et al.* 1988). Their ambition is not generally to deny that society may have effects at the level of the state but rather to insist that the state apparatus may pursue its own interests, sometimes in defiance of interests in the wider society, and that any proper explanation of the state–society relationship must recognize the autonomous powers which comparatively small numbers of state actors are able to exercise. This requires a shift in emphasis away from 'social forces' towards studying the behaviour of (state) institutions. At the same time, and under the rubric of the 'new institutionalism', attention has shifted from formal descriptions of the state (of the kinds of constitutional conventions discussed in Chapter 1) towards a more empirical and nuanced view of the ways in which institutions of government *actually* work. This means looking at both institutions and the rules that govern them in terms of regular and regulated processes rather than the textbook formalities about 'how government works'. For example, at the heart of government it means a shift in attention from the rubric of 'prime minister and cabinet' towards the more complex network of powers and resources that make up the 'core executive' (see Peters 1999; Chapter 7).

The claims of the institutional statists are summarized with particular clarity in Nordlinger's study *On the Autonomy of the Democratic State* (Nordlinger 1981: 7). Here, he outlines the following general propositions:

- When state and societal preferences do not diverge, public officials invariably translate their own preferences into authoritative actions, and their preferences have at least as much explanatory importance as societal preferences.
- When state and societal preferences do not diverge, public officials periodically capitalize upon their autonomy-enhancing capacities and opportunities to reinforce societal convergence, deference, and indifference so as to forestall the emergence of preferences that diverge from the state's.
- When state and societal preferences diverge, public officials periodically capitalize upon their autonomy-enhancing capacities and opportunities to bring about a shift in societal preferences and/or the alignment of societal resources in order to make for non-divergent preferences [or] to free themselves from societal constraints, and they then translate their own preferences into authoritative actions.
- When state and societal preferences diverge, public officials periodically rely upon the inherent powers of the state to translate their preferences into authoritative actions.

'Two far-reaching assertions' underpin Nordlinger's position:

- Look at least as much to the state as to civil society to understand what the democratic state does in the making of public policy and why it does so.
- The democratic state is frequently autonomous in translating its own preferences into authoritative actions, and markedly autonomous in doing so even when they diverge from those held by the politically weightiest groups in civil society.

(Nordlinger 1981: 203)

A similar position has been developed through the last twenty years by Theda Skocpol, a US political sociologist and perhaps the most influential advocate of 'bringing the state back in'. Skocpol insists that she is 'not trying to substitute "political determinism" for "social determinism"'. But she does argue that 'socially determinist theories overlook the ways in which the identities, goals, and capacities of all politically active groups are influenced by political structures and processes', above all by the character of the state (Skocpol 1992: 47). In her account, 'state formation, political institutions, and political processes (understood in non-economically determinist ways) must move from the penumbra or margins of analysis and towards the center' (Skocpol 1992: 40). This is best done by developing a 'structured polity perspective'.

> A structured polity perspective holds that politicians and administrators must be taken seriously. Not merely agents of other social interests, they are actors in their own right, enabled and constrained by the political organizations within which they operate. . . . Both appointed and elected officials have ideas and organizational and career interests of their own, and they devise and work for policies that will further those ideas and interests, or at least not harm them.

State officials will not only seek to defend their existing interests in reacting to social initiatives. They may also be proactive.

> If a given state possesses no existing (or readily adaptable) capacities for implementing given lines of policies, political leaders are not likely to pursue them. But such leaders are quite likely to take new policy initiatives – conceivably well ahead of social demands – if the capacities of state organizations can be readily adapted or reworked to do things that they expect will bring advantages to them in their struggles with political competitors, at home or on the international scene.
>
> (Skocpol 1992: 41–2)

At first sight, institutional statism appears to share something with the approach of the public choice theorists in emphasizing the importance of the independent influence of bureaucrats and other states' actors. But generally, advocates of institutional statism do not work within the neo-liberal variant of public choice. Rather, their work is directed towards historical accounts of the development of social institutions and practices which give due weight to the conduct of strategic state actors. Thus Skocpol's earliest empirical work, for example, was concerned to redress those accounts of the great revolutionary experiences (of France, Russia and China) which overemphasized the influence of societal forces at the expense of a detailed account of the frailties of the old state regimes. Later, writing with Margaret Weir, she sought to show how the differences in British and US responses to the economic depression of the 1930s could be explained in terms of the differing structures and capacities of the US and British treasuries (Weir and Skocpol 1985). More recently, she has focused upon the development of social policy in the USA (Skocpol 1992). In this context, she argues repeatedly that the directions of policy development, its legislative forms, its gendered consequences, its omissions, are all best explained in an account which gives due attention to the activism of policy-makers, to the context given by prior policy decisions and to the shaping influence of constitutional arrangements. There is, she argues, no straightforward relationship between societal structures and policy outcomes.

### State and society: feminist critique

In turning to feminist readings of the state–society relationship, we find accounts which, while internally diverse, share a sustained challenge to *all* of the ways in which we have seen this relationship appraised previously. For, however different these several earlier accounts may seem to be (and indeed upon their own terms may *really* be), feminist critics have characteristically seen them all as vitiated by a distinctive mis-vision – above all, a blindness to the constitutive political importance of gender – which has led them in turn to fail to grasp how the key relationships in the now-problematized categories of 'state' and 'society' should be understood.

This is perhaps least true of what has often been called the 'liberal feminist' approach (see, for example, Randall 1987; Knutilla and Kubik 2000; Steans 1998). In essence, this approach has involved taking the claims of liberal-democratic societies (and states) seriously – and then holding them to account for their failure to deliver. The legitimacy of liberal-democratic regimes is seen to rest upon the claim that, within its jurisdiction, all citizens are equal and that offices and opportunities are open to all categories of citizens without discrimination. The liberal feminist critique involves exposing the failure of liberal democracies to meet these criteria (so far as women are concerned) and in seeking appropriate reform (in both state and society). The discrimination exposed may be either explicit (unequal voting rights or pension entitlements, for example) or concealed (for example, where equal opportunity legis-lation fails to deliver substantive improvements in the status of working women). The agency of redress may be either the state (in both its legal and administrative manifestations) or society (for example, in pressure upon political parties to adopt more women candidates or campaigns to attract more young women into scientific training). This view suggests that there is plenty wrong in both state *and* society in terms of discrimination against women but also plenty that can be done (again in both spheres). It is, above all, a question of inclusion and participation.

The political agenda of liberal feminism is not *necessarily* reformist. The anti-discrimination agenda has been radicalized, for example, by black feminists both through their political activism (for example, the Southall Black Sisters) and at a theoretical level (on the latter, see Collins 2000). But it certainly allows that both state and society should *and* can be changed and that, with sufficient will and purpose, the mechanisms already exist that make such change possible. Liberal feminism of this kind is long established (in many ways, it is coterminous with the liberal-democratic claims it seeks both to critique and redress). Liberal feminists might also (perhaps legitimately) claim that it is their mobilization, often around an anti-discrimination agenda, that has furnished the most important political gains for women in the spheres of both state and society.

Other feminisms have always been around (including utopian visions of worlds without men or heterosexuality), but it is probably right to suggest that something like this liberal vision was 'dominant' (dominant, that is, within a deeply marginalized community) between the eighteenth and mid-twentieth centuries (on feminist utopianism, see Sargisson 1996). To some extent, in 'official' political discourse, it still is. But the last thirty years have seen an extraordinary outpouring of new feminist thinking (and practice) which leaves a field rich in ideas but of bewildering complexity. Here we can focus (however selectively) upon the ways in which this varied literature (and experience) has helped to recast the ways in which state and society and their interaction can be understood.

Although the social origins of the second wave of feminism (conventionally dated from the 1960s) are necessarily complex, a key source was a dissatisfaction with what an 'anti-discrimination' agenda had and could achieve. Even where important reforms, sometimes leading to 'formal' equality, had been achieved, the lived experience of women was still of a society dominated by, and run for, men. Although the liberal reform programme was still quite partially achieved, there was a sense that this was not only 'not enough' but also, at least in part, the wrong agenda. This rethinking of the feminist agenda was (and is) multifaceted. It certainly involved the belief that the state under liberal democracy was patriarchal. Thus, in one of the most influential statements of this position, Catherine Mackinnon insists that 'the state is male in the feminist sense: the law sees and treats women the way men see and treat women . . ., the way the male point of view frames an experience is the way it is framed by state policy' (Mackinnon 1989: 161, 167). Mackinnon sets out to substantiate this claim by considering the structure of law in a number of discrete areas – on rape, abortion, pornography and sex equality – showing how the state privileges a patriarchal world-view and distinctively male interests. Law under patriarchy may be *procedurally* neutral, because it is not primarily in the discriminatory *enactment* of the law but in the prior *construction* of the liberal state that patriarchal power is entrenched. Thus, 'in the liberal state, the rule of law – neutral, abstract, elevated, pervasive – both institutionalises the power of men over women and institutionalises power in its male form.' By the same token, '*abstract* rights authoritize the male experience of the world' (Mackinnon 1989: 238, 248; emphasis added). In this sense, liberal democracy is patriarchal not only in its *content*, but also in its *form*.

At the same time, very much more than law and the agency of the state were involved in the oppression of women. Male domination was inscribed not just in public institutions but also deep in the fabric of day-to-day life – in the organization of households and family life, in the field of 'private' sexual relationships, in the world-views of science and technology, even in the structures of everyday language. Both state and society (embracing not only social and legal relationships but also culture, language and even forms of knowledge) were profoundly patriarchal. This insight required, in its turn, a quite different view of the relationship between state and society and a quite different account of what politics meant. In some ways, the radical feminist approach belongs among those who see society as the dominant term in its association with the state. What *really* matters, in answering the question 'who exercises power?', are social and societal relationships rather than (or, at least, conceptually prior to) control of the key apparatuses of law-making and govern-mental power. But this does not mean that the distribution of power at the level of the state can, in any sense, be 'read off' from a series of independent relationships in society (as some of the simpler versions of both pluralism and Marxism have seemed to suppose).

Indeed, for feminists, the conceptual division of state and society is itself a part of the problem to be addressed. A division between state and society, and between public and private, is at the very core of modern liberalism. But it is this way of understanding the world, in particular the attempt to confine what counts as politics to the public sphere, and to privilege this as the area within which men act, that feminists have wanted to criticize. Marxists have criticized their liberal opponents for wishing to draw the boundaries of politics at the limits of the state, while allowing what goes on beyond these borders, within the formal economy, wholly (and wholly unacknowledged) to determine what happens in the formally political world. But feminists see this critique as much too conservative. However it has been understood (and the answer is, of course, 'variously'), the classical radical feminist slogan that 'the personal is political' captures the sense that power (and with it politics) is ubiquitous. Wherever power is exercised – in parliament, in the factory, in the household or in defining the limits of rationality – there is politics and, with it, the need to act (and to criticize) politically.

This has made some feminists profoundly sceptical of the value of speaking of 'the state' at all – as an abstraction from the lived experience of power and powerlessness that tends to serve the interest of patriarchal forces (see, for example, Allen 1990). A similar scepticism now attaches to the (unreflexive) use of the term 'society'. Given the central concern with the construction (and deconstruction) of knowledge and language and the ways in which unacknowledged powers are slipped into the interstices of texts (written or otherwise), it is perhaps understandable that radical feminism has been strongly influenced by (and has in its turn had a decisive impact upon) the several contemporary manifestations of poststructuralist and postmodern thought. Foucault, with his emphases upon the ubiquity of power, the importance of disciplinary practices and the centrality of 'bringing the body back in', alongside his scepticism about the notion of the sovereign state, has been an especially influential thinker (see, for example, Foucault 1994). It would be impossible here to capture the subtlety, complexity and sheer diversity of much of this contemporary feminist writing on the state–society relationship (for representative examples and surveys, see Connell 1990; Phillips 1998; Butler and Scott 1992). What we can say with confidence is that radical feminism problematizes or indeed ruptures many of the commonplace assumptions about the nature of state and society that have been dominant since the rise of modern liberalism. As well as disclosing the many unseen ways in which masculine power is inscribed in the banalities of everyday life, it demands of us that we think reflexively about the ways in which we use 'state' and 'society'. 'State' and 'society' are not just the terms we use to describe political phenomena but are themselves a part of what it is we need to try to explain.

## State and society: Foucault

One final response to this continuing challenge – and one which, as we have just seen, has had a profound impact upon radical feminists, among others – emerges from the later work of Michel Foucault (especially Foucault 1994). For Foucault, a significant difficulty in making sense of the state and the state–society relationship arises from the fact that we are asking the wrong question or, at the very least, looking for answers in the wrong place. Since its inception, so Foucault argues, modern political theory has been overwhelmingly concerned with issues of state, sovereignty, legitimacy and consent (as we saw in Chapter 1). But this is certainly not what *government* (in Foucault's very broad and particular sense) has really been about. Sovereignty is not the special and defining quality of the state and governing is not something that belongs uniquely to the state. In Foucault's account, governing is centrally about the effective and productive management of populations. Its ambition is to secure the optimum well-being, usefulness and collective strength of its members. Government began with the father's management of the domestic household (the 'economy' of classical usage). It was about the oversight, care and custody of the particular needs, interests and capacities of the members of the household. Governing could also be applied by the individual to him- or herself but, in a complex process, and with the decline of feudalism, it came increasingly to be the business of the state. In this context, the 'art' of government is about maximizing the strength of the state. It is about organizing a productive economy (here again evoking the classical origins of the term 'economy' as management of the domestic household). In its turn, this involves not so much coercion and extraction but rather a 'pastoral' approach, managed by the state's agencies of 'police' (where 'police' is given the somewhat archaic and continental sense of activities undertaken to secure the overall welfare of the population). It follows that the business of the state is not characteristically and straightforwardly to exercise domination over its constituent population. Rather governing is about managing 'the conduct of conduct', that is, working upon the ways in which individuals regulate their *own* behaviour to ensure this is consonant with the interests of the state. Thus, according to Foucault (1994: 322), 'the aim of the modern art of government, or state rationality', is 'to develop those elements constitutive of individuals' lives in such a way that their development also fosters the strength of the state.'

This does not mean that the agencies of the state are universally benign and citizen-friendly. An important part of Foucault's work was to show that the 'humane' interventions of the state could be highly disciplinary and coercive. But it does help to explain why the modern state is concerned (perhaps above all) with the economy (in its fully modern sense). The basis of the strong state is its economy. But a productive economy cannot be built directly by the agencies of the state or (as the powers of the former Soviet Union discovered) by the coercion of its population. Rather must the population be led to behave (both as producers and consumers) in ways which maximize economic growth.

These several ideas are perhaps best captured in Foucault's own term 'govern-mentality', that is:

the ensemble formed by the institutions, procedures, analyses, and reflections, the calculations and tactics that allow the exercise of this very specific albeit complex form of power, which has as its target population, as its principal forms of knowledge political economy, and as its essential technical means apparatuses of security.

(Foucault 1994: 219–20)

Thus, it seems that, for Foucault, what is most important in explaining modernity is not so much the 'statization of society' as the '"governmentalization" of the state', that is, the process through which the state comes increasingly to be the focus of those forms of government which aim (through both highly general and very specific interventions) at the overall well-being of the population (in the interests of the state or those who govern).

## Conclusion

One hundred years on from Hintze, the state–society relationship is still controversial and not a little obscure. But amid the seemingly ever greater diversity of explanations of this relationship, some commonalities may be dimly perceived. In fact, while these explanations have, in one sense, become more disparate, at the same time there has been a certain convergence among a range of authors starting from very different theoretical positions. Thus, we have seen, for example, Marxists affording some explanatory autonomy to the state, while pluralists begin to acknowledge that the state may exercise certain powers over society. Marxists come to recognize that social forces other than class may have a determining effect on the state's conduct, while some pluralists concede that business has a uniquely privileged position in its access to state actors. States are not all place or structure or agency, but a complex mixture of all three. These points of convergence in contemporary thinking on the state–society relationship are neatly captured by Dave Marsh (Marsh and Stoker 1995). He identifies the following points of commonality:

1   *Structured privilege*: Certain groups enjoy privileged access to the state because of their structural position.
2   *The role of agency*: States are the sites of intentional and strategic action by various groups of social actors.
3   *Limited number of structural bases of privilege*: There are a limited number of bases of structured inequality and privilege. Of these the most important are:

   a   economic/property resources
   b   gender
   c   political resources
   d   knowledge.

4   *Taking the state seriously*: Particularly among the more society-minded explanations (of pluralists and Marxists) there is a growing recognition that the state has to be taken seriously as an independent source of social power.

5   *Contingency*: There is a growing recognition that the outcomes of struggles over state and society are in part contingent and open-ended. Not all outcomes are possible, but no one outcome can be said to be pre-given.

6   *The primacy of politics?*: There is a growing recognition that state and societal structures are not given by some underlying characteristic of society, but are forged through political struggles within and between state and society.

There are above all, I think, two notable trends in this recent state theory. First, there is a much greater emphasis upon the uniqueness and contingency of particular state–society formations (a greater historical sensitivity) and, second, a self-conscious blurring of the lines that divide state from society and an awareness of their complex interaction (a self-awareness which in the case of some poststructuralist feminists amounts effectively to an abandonment of this terminology altogether). In keeping with this trend, Mitchell argues that the proper object of our critical attention should not be either state or society, but rather the ways in which their shifting division is defined:

> The state should not be taken as a free-standing entity, whether as agent, instrument, organization or structure, located apart from and opposed to another entity called society. The distinction between state and society should nevertheless be taken seriously, as the defining characteristic of the modern political order. [But] *the essence of modern politics is* not policies formed on one side of this division being applied to or shaped by the other, but *the producing and reproducing of this line of division.*
>
> (Mitchell 1991: 95; emphasis added)

## Further reading

Foucault, M. (1994) *Power*. New York: New Press.

Hayek, F. (1982) *Law, Legislation, and Liberty*, 3 vols. London: Routledge & Kegan Paul.

Jessop, B. (1990) *State Theory: Putting Capitalist States in their Place*. Cambridge: Polity.

Keane, J. (2003) *Global Civil Society?* Cambridge: Cambridge University Press.

Marx, K. (1998) *The Marx Reader*, ed. C. Pierson. Cambridge: Polity.

Nordlinger, F. A. (1981) *On the Autonomy of the Democratic State*. Cambridge, MA: Harvard University Press.

# 4  State and economy

Masterminding Bill Clinton's successful presidential campaign back in 1992 was George Stephanopoulos. Above his desk, as a constant reminder of the *key* issue of this (or any other) presidential contest, was a sign that read: 'It's the Economy, stupid!' At the start of the twenty-first century, almost everyone realizes the importance of the economy not just in deciding elections but also in shaping the more general processes of government. Indeed, some commentators claim that we are now living in an age of 'pocket-book politics', in which, with the decline of traditional political ideologies, narrowly conceived economic self-interest is the overwhelming driving force of the political process. Voters may have other concerns, such as health and education, but the anticipated competence of a government in economic management is seen to 'trump' all these other issues. Of course, state and government are about very much more than the winning and losing of elections. The day-to-day business of the state is, among other things, about the making and implementing of policy, the management of consent, the waging of wars, the processing of societal pressures, the provision of welfare services, the maintenance of law and order and so on. All of these activities have an economic dimension. They cost money which the state has to raise (through user charges, taxes or the sale of public debt), and the ways in which these monies are raised will itself have an effect upon the forms and levels of economic activity. The modern state is, as we have seen Schumpeter (1954) observe, a 'tax state'. In the last instance, it is dependent upon the health of the wider economy to fund its own activity.

Differing attitudes to the question of state and economy have also helped to define what is probably the single most important cleavage in political opinion of the past two hundred years. On one side there have been those, now best represented by the neo-liberals, who have argued for a minimal state and the greatest possible autonomy for an economy founded upon the private ownership of economic resources. We have seen in Chapter 3 how Hayek argued that the best economic outcomes could be guaranteed by trusting to the institutions of the free market. Given private proprietorship of their economic assets, self-interest would direct asset-holders towards the most efficient use of society's productive resources in an arrangement that was consistent with the greatest possible levels of individual freedom. In the neo-liberal view, the state's functions should ideally be limited to the provision of a 'neutral' framework for law and order and the maintenance of contract plus the provision of a very small number of genuinely public goods. On the other side have been those 'traditional' socialists (not all of them Marxists) who have seen private ownership in a market economy not as a solution, but as the core problem which the state has a duty to address. We have already seen that Marxists (and indeed socialists more generally) have diverse views on the desirable character and functions of the state. But there is certainly a very widely held view in traditional socialist accounts that a society which is to deliver on equality and liberty must be one in which the state (as representative of the people) owns and controls at least 'the commanding heights of the economy'. In this traditional socialist view, the economy is the site of society's most fundamental powers and individuals' most deep-seated interests. Under a market capitalist economy, these powers are expropriated by the owners of private capital at the expense of the great majority of working people. Economic power can only be reclaimed by the mass of the people by instituting the collective or common ownership of the economy, and this, in many accounts, is most effectively done through state ownership and control of all large-scale property.

Something like the latter argument was used to justify the massive state owner-ship that characterized the economies of the former Soviet states of the USSR and Eastern Europe. It was also one of the principal justifications for the process of *nationalization* through which productive assets in Western Europe were brought under state ownership. The argument of the neo-liberals, by contrast, has been used to justify the wholesale withdrawal of the state from immediate involvement in the economy, especially in the virtually world-wide process of *privatization* (moving state-owned economic assets into the private sector) which has been one of the most important political developments in the years since 1980. It has also been used to justify a whole series of reforms *within* the state apparatus which have sought to mimic market disciplines and incentives in the public sector (see below, pp. 84–6). Although the issue of capitalism versus socialism has receded, disagreement about the state–economy relationship continues to be at the heart of divided opinions about the general character of the modern state and its legitimate functions.

While most people would agree that the state–economy relationship is extremely important, in trying to explain it we face what is by now a familiar problem. How do we establish the boundaries between state and economy and, still more importantly, what is the flow of causation between the two? Do states shape economies, or do economies shape states? As might be expected following our discussion of the parallel problem of states and societies, neither question yields a straightforward answer. Indeed, there is a problem with posing the question in quite this way. There is an ever present danger that we may *reify* both terms, arguing as if 'state' and 'economy' were neatly demarcated *things* in the external environment which could act and react upon each other. Without entering into the arcane debate about what sorts of things there are in the world and how we might know about them, it is clear that 'the state' and 'the economy' are not observable social actors, but parts of a generally convenient (though sometimes quite misleading) shorthand with which we try to make sense of our surroundings. We saw in the opening pages of Chapter 1 how some critics insist that talk of 'the state' actually leads us to misunderstand the nature of the exercise of power. Similarly, feminist critics, for example, have long argued that the way in which 'the economy' is conventionally understood (as the sphere of paid labour performed outside the household) has systematically disprivileged women (McIntosh 1978). Defining 'the economy' is an inherently political task.

In this chapter, I try to make sense of the complex relationship between state and economy first by considering in some detail the various ways in which states have been seen to generate economic effects and then, rather more briefly, by outlining the ways in which economies may be said to shape states. I develop this latter position by focusing upon the ways in which states are 'inserted' in the economy and considering the specific context of change in the state–economy relationship since the 1960s. In reading these sections, it is always important to remember that the shorthand categories of 'state' and 'economy' are far from unproblematic.

## States acting in the economy

For the purposes of our analysis, the economic activity of the state may be divided into two. First, there are those areas in which the state is directly involved as an *economic actor*. A second field of activity is defined by those instruments of *policy* through which the state seeks to influence the economic process. This second category may itself be further divided between those state policies which are directly addressed to the economy (such as industrial and monetary policy) and those which have a profound but *indirect* impact on economic activity (above all, the government's social policy). Of course, in the real world these several areas of state activity almost always overlap and feed back upon each other. All are addressed in the coming sections.

### *The state as owner*

Perhaps the most obvious way in which the state has an impact as an economic actor is in its role as the owner of both land and capital. Modern states, at both the national and local level, are often society's largest landowners. Many have significant (sometimes controlling) shareholdings in what are formally private corporations. Much of a nation's underdeveloped or common land will be in the ownership of the state, and states' property also generally includes large numbers of valuable public buildings – government offices, schools, hospitals, universities, army establishments and so on – often in prime-site locations. In the UK, for example, the post-war state held title to as much as one-fifth of the nation's land and, despite the wholesale sell-offs of the 1980s and 1990s, it still owns something like 3 million private dwellings (Scott 1991; CSO 1995; www.housing.adpm.gov.uk/information/keyfigures/ #stock). Technically, in Britain, the Crown is the only fully legitimate owner of land (Cahill 2001).

In fact, ownership is not a single, simple principle, but rather, it is conventionally argued, a 'bundle of rights and claims', not all of which will be in the hands of a single legal entity (Honoré 1961). Once we recognize ownership as constituting a bundle of rights we can see that the actual pattern of state ownership is likely to be under-reported. The rights of private property-holders are actually qualified by certain powers which the state characteristically retains to itself (in the form of planning laws, environmental laws, the right to compulsory purchase and so on). Matters of dispute over ownership are generally adjudicated and then upheld by the state's judicial and police apparatus. Furthermore, in the last instance, most states, in claiming to be sovereign, retain certain special rights of ownership throughout their jurisdiction, which they may evoke in times of national emergency.

### *The state as owner–producer*

Generally more prominent in discussions of the state's economic role has been its function as the owner of public enterprises. In the state-socialist societies of East-Central Europe and the Soviet Union, state ownership was the preponderant (though not normally the exclusive) form of ownership within the formal economy. Disposing of these state assets in ways which are fair, efficient and lawful has been acutely problematic (Earle *et al.* 1993). In the societies of the developed West with which we are principally concerned, private ownership has always remained the predominant form. But, especially in the period after 1945, most of these countries developed a public enterprise sector of varying proportions, leading them to be described as 'mixed economies'. In the mid-1970s, public corporations across a range of these mixed economies (excluding the USA) accounted for some 13.5 per cent of capital formation, nearly 10 per cent of GDP and about 6–8 per cent of employment. By 1980, 54 of the 500 largest firms outside the USA were public enterprises. In the UK, at the end of the 1970s, the state sector accounted for about 11.5 per cent of GDP and had a workforce of close to 2 million (Parris *et al.* 1987; Mulgan 1993).

State ownership tended to be strongly focused upon the public utilities, that is, in providing basic services which were essential to everyone (gas, electricity, water, etc.), and whose supply was often seen to constitute a 'natural monopoly'. But public ownership was also extended more generally into larger corporations in particular key industries (energy supply, banking) and/or industries that faced particular competitive difficulties (e.g. the car industry in France and the UK). This reflected the fact that state ownership was initiated not solely, nor indeed primarily, to transfer rights of ownership to the public (the ideological grounds for public owner-ship). Rather, it was variously argued that the absence of effective competition required that these industries be publicly managed, that private management had failed to deliver services efficiently and effectively or that particular strategic industries should not be available for foreign ownership. At times, nationalization could also be an instrument of regional policy (encouraging industrial activity in underdeveloped regions), of employment policy (maintaining employment levels by subsidizing large but non-competitive enterprises) and of industrial policy (helping to subsidize firms in the private sector by providing inputs below cost price). It also seemed at one time that no self-respecting state could possibly be without its own flag-carrying national airline, from the globe-spanning British Airways to the rather more modest Air Malta!

In fact, levels of public ownership within the 'mixed economies' were always quite variable. Interestingly, the USA and Sweden, whose political complexion is quite different, have both had comparatively low levels of social ownership. In France, Italy and the UK, public ownership was much more extensive, peaking in the late 1970s (in the UK) or the early 1980s (in France and Italy). But the remarkable feature of the past twenty years has been the way in which states, led by the UK, have divested themselves of ownership of their formerly nationalized industries. By 1991, most of the UK utilities – telecommunications, gas, airports, water and electricity – plus those large corporations in which the state had exercised a controlling interest – BP, Cable and Wireless, Jaguar, etc. – had been privatized. The major sell-offs between 1984 (British Telecom) and 1990 (the electricity companies) raised some £37 billion for the British exchequer, though even supporters of privatization seem to agree that this figure did not reflect the true value of the assets disposed of by the British state (Bishop *et al.* 1994: 2). The last great sell-off – and certainly the most disastrous – was the rail industry. In France, the wave of nationalizations that came with Mitterand's election to the presidency in 1982 were almost immediately countermanded by the privatizations inaugurated in 1986. In two years, the French government sold off ten public companies, raising FF77 billion (around £8 billion). Of course, privatization was even more important as the watchword of economic reform in the economies of the former Soviet bloc after 1989. In fact, it has been a world-wide phenomenon. Over the 1990s, total privatization assets came close to US$1000 billion (OECD 2001). Although much of this activity was focused upon OECD countries, the late 1990s saw increasing levels of privatization in developing countries, coming close, proportionately, to the levels of public disinvestment seen in the countries of the former Soviet Union at the other end of the 1990s (United Nations 2002). An enthusiastic admirer of the British privatizations described them as effecting 'the largest transfer of property since the dissolution of the monasteries' (Pirie 1985: 21).

A number of political objectives lay behind the privatization programme. In the UK, there was the expectation that privatized companies would encourage greater competition and economic efficiency, that funding for new investment could be raised in the private money markets, that the sale of assets would generate much-needed revenue for the government, that the power of public-sector trades unions would be curbed and share ownership extended. More generally, the rush towards privatization was said to arise from 'the need to reduce budgetary deficits, attract investment, improve corporate efficiency and liberalis[e] markets in sectors such as energy and telecommunications' (OECD 2001: 43). However one judges the success or otherwise of these ambitions, it is clear that the economic role of the state as an owner–producer has been drastically reduced by the sale of these major industrial concerns. However, we must guard against exaggerating the nature of these changes. Privatization may have peaked in the late 1990s (after all, the more that is sold off, the less there remains still to sell) and the popular appeal of selling off public utilities may also be waning (as governments in both Australia and the UK have discovered at different times). And while the state's role as a producer has been radically reduced within the industrial sphere, if we broaden our remit to consider the production of other services, especially welfare services, the state continues to be an extremely important (and, in some contexts, almost a monopoly) supplier. As we shall see below, though, this is another area in which the nature of the state's activity has changed significantly in the last decade.

We may not instantly think of the state's welfare activities as economic. Clearly, they are not solely economic, and many critics insist that rights to certain forms of welfare provision are an aspect of our shared *citizenship* and should not be subject to the logic of the market. Also, some economic elements in the state's welfare activity are not best seen as arising from its function as an owner–producer. Thus, for example, state provision for income maintenance and pensions is generally best understood as a part of its *redistributive* function, even though parallel forms of provision may be purchased in the private insurance market (by those who can afford the premiums). Yet, as we saw in Chapter 2, throughout the twentieth century states took on an enormous role in the production of welfare services. Indeed, the rather incremental pattern of welfare state growth should not conceal from us the fact that this was one of the most remarkable social transformations of the twentieth-century world.

Institutional arrangements for the provision of welfare services vary from state to state. Some states have sought to discharge their welfare responsibilities principally through the transfer of resources to those in need, others through the state's purchase or subsidy of services from private suppliers, others again through the direct provision of services to their populations. A good example of the last was the 'traditional' or pre-reform NHS in the UK. Under the old system, the state both funded and provided the full range of health-care services to its population. There was a small private health-care market, but for the vast bulk of the population, health care came through a system that was funded, managed and delivered by the state. By the end of the 1980s, the NHS was the single largest employer in Western Europe, with a workforce in excess of 1 million, and by 2002 the annual budget had risen to £66 billion, projected to rise above £100 billion in 2007/8 (Hogwood 1992; www.offical-documents.co.uk/document/deps/hc). Taken together, the two areas in which the state has operated most clearly as a producer of welfare services – health and education – account for more than one-quarter of all public expenditure in the UK, by 2003 a sum in excess of £100 billion a year (www.official-documents.co.uk/document/deps/hc). Across the globe, governments spend on average about 7 per cent of GDP on health and education, a figure which rises to about 11.5 per cent in higher income countries (World Bank 2001: 80).

In recent years, however, this state production of welfare services has also been subjected to far-reaching reform. For parties of all persuasions in all developed states, the cost of welfare provision has been a perennial concern at least since the early 1970s. Naturally enough, neo-liberals, driven by the conviction that markets are almost always more efficient than states, that public-sector workers shielded from effective competition will always conspire against consumers and that overall levels of taxation are too high, have sought to address the problem of cost by extending market disciplines to state welfare activity. Some of the more committed neo-liberals have followed through this logic to the point where they propose, for example, that state health care should be abolished and replaced with some form of (compulsory) health insurance. But the major reform initiatives of the last decade have been less about the privatization of state welfare services than about the reform of modes of delivery within a more mixed welfare regime (that includes, alongside private and voluntary provision, various forms of public–private partnership).

At its simplest, this strategy of reform – often referred to as the *new public management* – has meant the introduction of private-sector management, organization and labour market practices into the public sector in the expectation that the sector can thus be made to deliver the sorts of service and efficiency that it is supposed the private sector (and its competitive environment) has already realized. Under these arrangements, the state remains responsible for funding services and for ensuring that they are generally available and provide an adequate level of service. Thus, for example, in the UK health reforms, the government retains its commitment that 'NHS services are available to all, paid for mainly out of general taxation; and mostly free at the point of use.' But delivery may not come through the traditional mechanism of the state-funded public service. The reformers' aspiration is neatly caught in a characteristic statement of intent from the UK Treasury:

> The Government's public service reforms aim to deliver efficient, responsive public services, with high standards achieved across the country, through:
>
> • clear, long-term, outcome-focused goals, set by the Government;
> • devolution of responsibility to public service providers themselves, with maximum local flexibility and discretion to innovate and incentives to ensure that the needs of local communities are met;
> • independent and effective arrangements for audit and inspection to improve accountability; and transparency about what is being achieved, with better information about performance both locally and nationally.
>
> (www.official-documents.co.uk/document/deps/hc)

In part, this is about the introduction of 'internal markets' within the domain of public provision. Under such reforms, public funding is retained but steps are taken to increase the powers of the consumers of public services over against their providers. The intention is that individual units (schools, colleges or health-care trusts) should compete for consumers of their services. The purchasers of these services (parents, students, patients or their surrogates) should be able to transfer their custom between providers with relative ease – and public resources should follow these choices. Greater information (examination results, waiting-list times, proportion of successful procedures, prices) should make it possible for consumers to make effective choices. At the same time, providers can be held to account for the level and standard of service delivered. Although this is primarily a system for delivering greater accountability and efficiency within the public sector (or so it is hoped), the reform agenda does involve the transfer of some activities outside the state sector, in some cases to voluntary or not-for-profit concerns but in others to fully commercial operators, as in the case of the Private Finance Initiative (see Regan

2003). In the USA, this reorientation was a part of the celebrated agenda for *Reinventing Government* which the Clinton administration took up with such enthusiasm (Osborne and Gaebler 1992). In the UK, it has been seen as a definitive part of the otherwise rather elusive politics of 'the Third Way' (see Giddens 1998).

In many European countries, these sorts of reforms have been accompanied by a decentralization of provision to local state level. In the UK, experience is more ambivalent. One of the key reforms of the first Blair government was to introduce devolved government in Scotland and, to a lesser extent, Wales. At times, this has made a real difference to policy outcomes (in relation to student fees and the financial support of the elderly, for example). At the same time, some reforms have seen a further *centralization* of political power, with traditional local authority functions reallocated by central government to a range of non-elected authorities appointed by ministers. These organizations are commonly described as 'quangos' (quasi-non-governmental organizations), though some commentators prefer to characterize them, confusingly but perhaps more accurately, as quasi-governmental organizations. In education, for example, functions traditionally discharged by the Department of Education or local education authorities have been reallocated to bodies including the School Curriculum and Assessment Authority, the Higher Education Funding Councils, the Council for the Accreditation of Teacher Education, the Funding Agency for Schools and OFSTED. Some observers see in the growth of the 'quango state' a new (and unelected) shadow apparatus of public administration.

Where the government has not found it possible to devolve its activity into independent bodies, it has recast its own internal organization. Thus, since the late 1980s, the British civil service has been substantially reconstituted with a small number of senior policy-makers remaining within Whitehall, while the implementation of policy is transferred to a series of partially autonomous executive agencies (the Benefits Agency, the Employment Agency, the Passport Agency, etc.). These agencies operate under a chief executive and are run along quasi-commercial lines, seeking to meet target criteria for the delivery of services to their 'customers'. Similar governmental reforms have been effected elsewhere (in Australia and New Zealand, for example). Indeed, in New Zealand, the 'retreat from the state' has gone still further than in the UK (Kelsey 1995).

Does all this mean that the role of the state as owner–producer of (welfare) services has been drastically reduced? In some ways, clearly, it does. Certainly, representatives of the UK government have consistently denied that their intention in these areas is to 'privatize' welfare provision in the fashion of the public utilities. In the long years of opposition the Labour Party in Britain repeatedly claimed that the Tories were set upon privatizing the NHS. Meanwhile Labour in power has found itself repeatedly under fire from both trades unions and its own backbenchers, who have claimed that various initiatives – the plan to offer further autonomy to 'foundation' NHS trusts or their willingness to replace schools and hospitals through the leasing of facilities built by the private sector, for example – represent moves to 'privatize' the existing welfare state. At times, this has become confused with criticism of the undermining of a public service ethic (for example, the belief that schools should not be forced to compete for student numbers) or simply the judgement that the new regime of permanent accountability is perverse (leading, for example, to a depleted curriculum and an obsession with results that undermine the breadth and depth of the educational experience). However we choose to describe this new public order, it is clear that the nature of the state as the producer of welfare services has changed. In some areas, the state has encouraged a transfer towards private-sector forms of provision (as, for example, in the UK's policy of selling off the public-sector housing stock to its present occupiers or in its on-going reform of a much-troubled pension sector). In others, it has introduced a much more explicitly 'contractual' relationship with those charged with delivering services (in terms of targets, penalties *and* incentives, as for example with the introduction of performance-related pay). Given all these changes, it is important to remember just how large (and in many cases near-monopolistic) are the services provided by government. In the next few years, health and education (which account for about a quarter of all government expenditure) are both set to rise as a proportion of a national income which is itself projected to grow. Health and education are together still smaller than the state budget for social security, most of which takes the form of transfers with quite limited scope for these sorts of service-delivery reforms.

### The state as employer

The huge growth of the public sector throughout the twentieth century, but more especially since 1945, led naturally enough to a comparable increase in public-sector employment. We have already seen that employment within the states' industrial sector had risen by the 1970s to somewhere on average between 6 and 8 per cent. In Italy, more than a quarter of the workforce in larger enterprises (of more than 2,000 employees) was in the state sector. In France, the proportion of public-sector workers in larger-scale enterprises leapt in 1982 to over 40 per cent, with a total of more than 2.3 million workers (Parris *et al.* 1987: 28–35). Even more significant in employment terms, however, was the expansion of employment within the welfare state. Not only did welfare budgets grow strongly through much of the twentieth century, but the nature of the services delivered meant that a large proportion of these budgets was devoted to wages, salaries and pension costs. In fact, within a more general shift in employment after 1945 from manufacturing to the service sector of the economy, state welfare has had a peculiarly prominent role. Studying changes in employment patterns in West Germany, Sweden, the USA and the UK, Rein found that, by the 1980s, the 'social welfare industry' accounted for between 11 per cent (West Germany) and 26 per cent (Sweden) of overall employment, and social welfare jobs accounted for between 20 and 40 per cent of all employment in the service sector (Rein 1985: 39–40). OECD figures compiled in the mid-1980s suggested that everywhere the gap between employment in manufacturing and government services had significantly narrowed since the early 1970s (OECD 1989: 123). Not only was the scale of state employment transformed in the twentieth century, but so was its composition. At some point in the nineteenth century, civilian state employment overtook employment in the armed forces in most developed states. By the 1980s, the numbers of military personnel were dwarfed by the size of civilian state employment. In the UK, in a public sector employing about 5 million workers, fewer than 300,000 were in the armed forces (CSO 1995: 168).

The reforms of the 1980s have certainly had an impact upon levels of public-sector employment. Privatization led to a dramatic decline in employment within nationalized industries, with the number of workers in this sector in the UK falling from 1.85 million in 1979 to less than half a million in 1992 (CSO 1995: 169). The decline in numbers in the civil service has been substantial if a little less dramatic. Between 1987 and 1993, there was a reduction of some 7 per cent in the numbers of civil servants in the UK (to 554,212). The ambition to reduce the size of the civil service was repeated in most European countries, though to date the impact has been rather limited (see Wright 1994: 137). In the UK, overall levels of general government employment fell through the 1980s by about 10 per cent, but this still left the government employing about one in every five workers (Wright 1994: 137; Hogwood 1992: 149).

Of course, these absolute levels of employment do not tell the whole story. A part of the increase in NHS employment through the 1980s was a product of the *reduction* in the standard working week from 40 to 37.5 hours. At the same time, the contractual basis of public-sector employment has changed. Traditionally, civil servants enjoyed tenure of office, ensuring, under normal circumstances, a 'job for life'. In the 'sub-contracted' state, however, terms and conditions are generally much less favourable, and recent years have seen the introduction of performance-related pay, personal contracts and many more fixed-term appointments. In France, for example, the number of officials on short-term contracts tripled through the 1980s (Wright 1994: 114).

In judging the economic role of the state as an employer, the following generalizations seem to be in order. To a quite varying degree (contrast say Japan and Sweden), the state grew throughout the twentieth century to become a major employer. Average public-sector employment in the OECD now stands at something close to 20 per cent. Across the globe, it is close to 30 per cent. Again, in a rather varying pattern, levels of public-sector employment tended to stabilize in the period after 1980 and then to decline (either in absolute terms or at least relative to a growth in private-sector employment) after 1990. In North America, East Asia, Australia and New Zealand, most of the growth in employment has been concentrated in the private sector. High levels of public-sector employment (but also the most rapid rates of decline) are found in the transition economies of the former Soviet Union and Eastern Europe. Levels of public-sector employment in developing states vary enormously (from 5 per cent in the Philippines to 50 per cent in Egypt), but only in Botswana and China did public-sector employment outstrip growth in the private sector during the 1990s (though using baselines of 1995 and 1996 respectively). Government employment has become more concentrated (especially within the most developed economies) upon the service sector. Despite all the changes of the last decade, and a real rebalancing of patterns of employment in the public and private sectors, government remains a major employer in all sorts of societies and a significant source of employment opportunities, especially for women (see Hammouya 1999).

## The state as regulator

One of the most keenly felt ironies of the 'withdrawal' of the state from its role as a direct producer of goods and services has been the mushrooming of the apparatus of 'regulation' through which it seeks to exercise a continuing control over its divested functions. In a broad sense, regulation may be taken to describe all those ways in which the state intervenes administratively or legislatively to control the behaviour of market actors. In this sense, states have always regulated markets, all the way back to the time when royal charters were granted to enable cities to hold markets and fairs at duly described times and in duly designated places. The state still forbids or itself controls markets in all sorts of goods and services (certified drugs, firearms, body parts, endangered species, sexual services, etc.). It sets the overall framework of ownership, contract, exchange and tort without which a market economy could not operate. It provides legal tender, controls the rates of interest at which money may be lent, sets hours of opening for shops, sets limits on the age of workers and on the hours that may be worked by prescribed groups. It registers certain forms of employment – e.g. nursing and midwifery – prohibiting work by unregistered persons and placing certain statutory obligations upon those who practise these professions. It legislates for the protection of consumers, controls the provision of credit by financial institutions, protects the quality of foodstuffs, establishes controls upon environmental pollution. It exercises powerful constraints over the use of private land and, in the areas of greatest architectural sensitivity, even prohibits private householders from replacing their window frames or trimming their trees without the written permission of the state! Recent years have also seen a wholesale expansion of legislation relating to health and safety provision at work and anti-discrimination measures to protect persons with disabilities. The list of examples of such state regulation could be multiplied many times over.

From time to time, politicians court popularity by promising to do away with 'red tape', 'freeing citizens to make their own choices' and putting the match to 'a bonfire of regulations'. But just one year of the most enthusiastic deregulating regime in the UK (1990) saw the passage of the Broadcasting Act, the Courts and Legal Services Act, the Environmental Protection Act, the Food Safety Act, the Human Fertilization and Embryology Act, the Town and Country Planning Act and Statutory Instruments including the Quick-Frozen Foodstuffs Regulations and the Scotch Whisky Order! These last two were squeezed between the Low Voltage Electrical Equipment (Safety) Regulations of 1989 and the Pencils and Graphic Instruments (Safety) Regulations of 1991. All had regulatory consequences. And this is before we begin to consider those statutory regulations which arose from Directives of the European Community (Ogus 1994).

That the state is so intimately and ubiquitously involved in regulating the minutiae of the market economy is of central importance. More than fifty years ago, Polanyi (1944) pointed out that markets require states and that the idea of a self-regulating market is a historical myth. There is, however, a rather more limited or technical sense of regulation, derived from US experience, which has become increasingly prominent in Europe with the reforms of recent years. In this rather narrower sense, regulation refers to 'sustained and focused control exercised by a public agency over activities that are generally regarded as desirable to society' (Majone, 1990: 1). In some accounts, regulation in this more technical sense presumes not just a framework of public law, but also designated public authorities with a statutory responsibility to see that the regulations are upheld. For all the rhetoric of deregulation of recent years, such regulatory regimes are almost certainly on the increase, and this, in part, is because of the state's abdication of its *direct* control of economic processes.

This points us towards one of the frequently reported ironies of recent experience. One of the principal ambitions of the state reforms of the past twenty years has been to *deregulate* the economy: to give greater power to markets and competition and to lessen the jurisdiction of states and their presumed monopoly. Yet, in many of those areas from which the state has withdrawn – especially in the welfare arena and the public utilities – the consequence has been the inauguration of a new regulatory regime in order to control what are now non-state functions. In the UK, for example, the newly privatized utilities generally found their prices set, not so much by the markets and competition, but rather by regulators appointed by the government. Prices are administered by a series of regulatory agencies (OFTEL, OFGAS, OFFER, OFWAT) which seek to strike a balance between the interests of consumers and shareholders. The administrative nature of these decisions has meant that they continue to be intensely *politicized* and increasingly the object of intense public discontent. Of course, this new regime is quite different from that which prevailed under the nationalized industries, but it cannot be read straightforwardly as an abandonment of control by the state in favour of markets and competition.

This points us towards a more general conclusion, which is that this changing state-economy regime adds up less to a policy of straightforward *deregulation* than to one of *re-regulation*. Thus, for example, it is widely argued that the attempt to 'free up' financial markets in the 1980s led to a wholesale *increase* in the ways in which these financial markets were regulated by the state, including the institution of new regulatory agencies. An example drawn from elsewhere in the reform agenda is the ambition to deregulate the labour market. Here, the aspiration was to move away from wages and conditions that were controlled administratively (e.g. by incomes policies or wages councils) and, so it was suggested, held above 'real' market levels by the actions of trades unions. But deregulating the labour market has meant an unprecedented level of state intervention in the internal administration of trades unions and a tighter proscription of their lawful actions. It has meant an ever tighter regulatory regime for those who are unemployed and/or in receipt of state benefits. It has meant introducing a much stronger statutory framework into the management of government training programmes. At the same time, it has run up against a process of regulation of welfare and the labour market at the European level which is often pulling in the opposite direction.

Furthermore, whether the state has retained or devolved the provision of services, newer forms of public management have tended to involve a much closer scrutiny of the performance of public duties. Where once the state provided resources and then left institutions 'to get on with it', there is now an elaborate structure of performance indicators, accountability and auditing. Whatever one makes of such reforms, no one working in a British university, for example, could possibly describe the experience of the last decade as one of state deregulation. In a context in which it seems likely that states will make increasing use of devolution of tasks, of 'contracting out' and 'agencification', it seems certain that the scale of its economic-regulatory functions will continue to increase.

### The state as redistributor

To tax is to redistribute. We have seen already that the modern state is a tax state and the process of taxing and spending is one in which governments redistribute wealth. Governments' tax and spending behaviour may be progressive (taking from the rich to give to the poor) or regressive (taking from the poor to give to the rich). It may shift resources between other groups, from men to women, from those in work to the unemployed, from those of working age to those who are retired, from adults to children. But however it chooses to direct these flows of resources, the consequence will be a redistribution. In modern times, the scale of governments' taxing and spending activity – and therefore of the redistribution of resources – has been enormous. According to the World Bank (2001: 236–7) at the end of the 1990s, general government outlays as a percentage of GDP ranged from under 8 per cent in Myanmar to over 50 per cent in Kuwait and Lesotho. UK government expenditure stood at 37 per cent, well above the global average (28 per cent) but a little below average in the EU (40 per cent). In the UK, a comparatively modest spender in EU terms, by 2003 annual general government expenditure had risen to £418 billion, representing 39.2 per cent of GDP. Spending on social security alone exceeds £100 billion (www.official-documents.co.uk/document/deps/hc).

These sorts of levels of expenditure require governments to raise a great deal of money. At the end of the 1990s, the average global tax take was around 26.5 per cent, an increase of 4 per cent over the decade, and ranging from 1.6 in the United Arab Emirates to 44 per cent in Belgium and the Netherlands and 45 per cent in Croatia (World Bank 2001: 234–6). Despite at least a decade's talk of tax-cutting, tax revenue has remained remarkably robust. Only in the Netherlands are tax ratios currently below their 1975 level (though still among the world's highest). Some countries have managed to curb the very high levels of ten to fifteen years ago (including Ireland, New Zealand and Sweden). But in the UK, for example, where levels fell to around 33 per cent of GDP in 1994, levels have returned to around 37 per cent and are projected to rise above 38 per cent by 2008–9. There has, however, been some significant redistribution of the tax burden in recent years. In general, corporation tax and income tax rates have been reduced (especially for higher income earners) and social security taxes have increased, as has the burden of indirect/consumption taxes (especially VAT or Goods and Services Tax). This has a real distributional impact (since indirect taxes tend to be less progressive than taxes on income). In the UK, social security contributions now raise almost two-thirds as much revenue as income tax, VAT more than half as much (www.official-documents.co.uk/document/deps/hc). Governments are also big borrowers. In

1998, global government indebtedness was running at about 1.5 per cent of GDP, although levels tended to be higher in the less developed countries. Perhaps more crucial are the levels of accumulated indebtedness and the burden this places upon government finances. Although this is not exclusively a problem for poor states, several countries in South Asia and sub-Saharan Africa have levels of debt well in excess of their GDP and/or levels of interest payments well in excess of 30 per cent of current revenues (World Bank 2001).

By almost any criteria, then, governments are 'big' economic actors. They are big spenders, big taxers and big borrowers. They are, as we have already seen, big employers and, we should add, big consumers. For governments not only buy labour, they also fund major capital projects and pay for road-building and other infrastructural work. They buy every sort of consumable, from paper clips to battle-ships. The less the state does things for itself, the more it enters the market to buy goods and services from suppliers in the private sector, and for some private corporations – especially those in defence-related industries – states may be their only customers.

But it is not just the scale of states' economic activity that is important. It is also the redistributive effects. All citizens pay some forms of taxation and virtually all are the beneficiaries of some state services. Significant sections of the population, particularly those who are unable to generate an income from other sources, may be almost wholly reliant upon the state for financial support. Generally, in societies with market economies, the effect of state policies (of tax-raising and service provision) is to make the *final* distribution of incomes less unequal than *original* market-generated incomes. The chain of state redistribution is more or less that described in Figure 4.1. To *original income* (from market transactions) is added the sum of state cash benefits. This yields *gross income*. From this the state extracts income tax and social security contributions to give *disposable income*. If we deduct from this the sum of indirect taxes (VAT and so on) we have *post-tax income*. Adding to this benefits in kind (educational provision, health services, etc.) gives us a figure for *final income*. Thus, we have a number of stages (and media) through which the state impacts upon its citizens' incomes.

Broadly speaking, the consequence of these several interventions is to narrow the range of income inequality. In the UK in 1998, for example, the income share of the bottom fifth was more or less doubled (to around 6 per cent of disposable income) as a result of taxes and benefits. While the *original* income of the top fifth of households was a little over 50 per cent, this was reduced by the impact of taxes and benefits to a little over 40 per cent. Heady, Mitrakos and Tsakloglou (1999) estimate that, across the EU, social transfers lead to a reduction in income inequality of around a third. The distribution of income in the UK is still radically unequal. The income of the top 10 per cent of households is around ten times that of the poorest 10 per cent of households (World Bank 2001). But the extent of this inequality and the pattern of its distribution has been profoundly shaped by the actions of the state.

Throughout much of the post-war period (and across most advanced industrial societies), income inequalities tended to narrow (though this left very different overall levels of inequality in, for example, the USA and Scandinavian countries). In

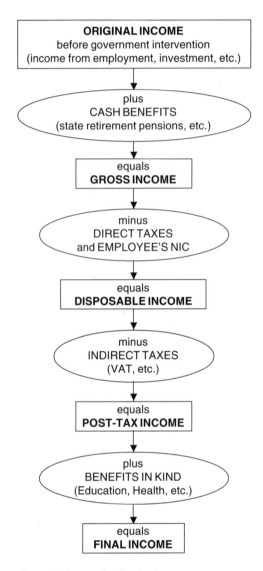

*Figure 4.1* Stages of redistribution.

many countries, however, the last twenty years have seen this process reversed, with income inequalities actually increasing. This growing income inequality has many causes (not least changes in the international division of labour), but in part it can be explained by changes in the states' tax and spending regimes. Virtually all states (the states of the European Union above all) have found it extremely difficult to reduce overall levels of taxation through the 1980s, not least because of the huge costs of running an economy with persistently high levels of unemployment. But many states (like the UK) did attempt to restructure the burden of taxation in various ways. Thus, they restricted the growth of taxation on corporations, reduced the progressivity of income tax (by lowering the higher rates and bringing more people into the income tax net) and, above all, increased the proportion of revenue raised through indirect taxes (especially VAT). In the UK, for example, the highest rate of income tax was cut to 40 per cent and the standard rate cut from 33 per cent to 22 per cent, while the rate of VAT was doubled and its range of application extended. In fact, the overall tax take in the economy is higher now than in 1979 and the pattern has been much more one of redistributing the tax burden than of cutting it. But indirect taxes (such as VAT) are much less redistributive in their consequences than is the tiered taxation of personal incomes. This led to a position in which, in the UK in 1993, the bottom fifth of households were paying 31 per cent of their disposable incomes in indirect taxation compared with 16 per cent for the top fifth. Overall, *Economic Trends* suggested in 1993 that the poorest tenth of households were paying 43 per cent of their income in tax, compared to 32 per cent among the most affluent tenth (CSO 1993). At the same time, most regimes have sought to rein in expenditure. Since social security is the single largest item in most states' budgets, the most effective way to control expenditure is to constrain growth in benefits. In the UK, this has been done by attaching increases in benefits to the rise in prices rather than (the more rapid) rise in incomes for those in work. Thus, over the past decade, in a context of more unequal original incomes, many (though by no means all) states' tax and spending regimes have become less redistributive, and consequently these have become societies of greater overall economic inequality.

As the figures for the UK suggest, the fiscal activity of the state is still important in reducing the levels of inequality that arise from original market outcomes. It generates 70 per cent of the income of the poorest fifth of households in the UK. But there is evidence across a range of industrialized countries that this redistributive effect has been lessened over the past fifteen years. States are now generally doing rather less to reduce inequality in a global economy in which original market incomes have themselves become increasingly unequal (Gardiner 1993). Why their role has changed in this period is something to which we will return in the closing pages of this chapter.

### The state as economic policy-maker

We have seen that, despite the recent substantial reduction in the state's function as a direct producer of economic goods and services, states are still massively present in the immediate processes of production, distribution and exchange. But the state also has an extremely important role as an *economic policy-maker*. In recent years, governments have (with some good reason) become rather less confident about their capacity to 'manage' the economy, not least because of a rather indifferent record of policy 'successes'. But this experience has not generally persuaded them to stop trying and, given that some commentators suggest that delivering economic growth may now be *the* key to governments' re-election, this is perhaps understandable (Sanders 1990). In the post-war world, governments set themselves a series of economic targets – to maximize economic growth, to maintain full employment, to secure price stability, to maintain a favourable balance of payments on international trade – and they pursued a series of policies which they believed would deliver these *desiderata*. Circumstances and priorities have changed. But governments still generally strive for maximum levels of overall economic growth, consistent with reasonable price stability.

We know that, *within their own jurisdiction*, states have certain powers of compulsion (in the last instance backed by force) and they use these particularly in raising revenue. But historically, forcible extraction has not proven an especially effective or efficient vehicle for sustained economic growth and, since in a market economy the principal factors of production are in private hands, states have generally to try to *induce* economic actors to do the things that governments believe will enhance economic growth. Much of this involves states in establishing the appropriate background conditions under which investment will take place. We have already touched on the state's *taxation policy* as this relates to redistribution, but such policy is just as much, perhaps even more importantly, oriented around other economic objectives. If we consider the changes of recent years, governments have reduced levels of corporation tax so as to encourage inward investment. They have reduced higher rates of personal taxation so as to encourage 'entrepreneurial' activity. In the UK, there have been a number of tax inducements to encourage long-term personal saving, personal pension provision and investment in British and European corporations. Taxation is not just about covering government expenditure or redistributing original income. It is also about encouraging specific forms of economic activity.

Governments make similar use of *monetary policy* to encourage particular forms of economic behaviour. Interest rates on borrowing (the cost of money) are varied so as (to attempt) to slow down or to speed up levels of general economic activity. In the early 1980s, the first Thatcher administration attempted (not very successfully) to control the supply of money in the economy in the expectation that this would control the level of inflation. From time to time, states devalue their currencies (marking down the rate of exchange with other currencies) in part to generate a competitive advantage for their own economies. Governments have also set the terms and conditions upon which banks and other financial institutions may lend to private borrowers (e.g. stipulating a particular ratio between an institution's overall assets and its quantity of lending).

A number of states under a variety of circumstances have also sought to uphold more or less legally binding *incomes policies*. One ambition of such policies (certainly as they were pursued over a long period, as in Sweden) was to achieve greater equality of wage-earners' incomes (Korpi 1983; Esping-Andersen 1985). More generally, however, incomes policies have been used to constrain present wages and that portion of the economic product going to labour, in the expectation that such controls would promote higher levels of profitability, higher levels of investment and thus more rapid economic growth.

As well as setting the broad parameters of economic activity so as to induce particular patterns of economic behaviour, states have made more particularistic policy interventions in the economy. Much of this activity is summed up under the general rubric of *industrial policy*. In Bardach's account (1984), the major instruments of this general policy field are:

- protectionism in the form of tariffs and non-tariff barriers, and export subsidies (trade policy);
- programmes to improve the human capital and level of labour skills of the workforce; financial assistance and reskilling for displaced workers in declining industries (employment and training policies);
- subsidies and other support for research and development; support in developing the capital infrastructure (research and development policy);
- anti-trust policy;
- tax inducements to stimulate capital investment (taxation policy);
- the provision of direct loans and loan guarantees to industry to share the risks of investment (including joint private–public ventures);
- government procurement policy (buying home-produced goods).

Almost everybody's favourite example of a state with a successful industrial policy is (or was) Japan. The extraordinary rise of the Japanese economy in the post-war period was certainly based upon markets, but markets which were extensively managed or 'rigged' by state institutions, including, above all, the hugely influential Ministry of International Trade and Industry (MITI). In the period of its most rapid development, Japanese industry enjoyed not only a favourable financial environment but also

> the extensive use, narrow targeting and timely revision of tax incentives; the use of indicative plans to set goals and guidelines for the entire economy; the creation of numerous, formal and continuously operating forums for exchanging views, reviewing policies, obtaining feedback and resolving differences; the assignment of some governmental functions to various private and semi-private associations; . . . an extensive reliance on public corporations . . . to implement policy in high-risk [areas]; the creation and use by government of an unconsolidated 'investment budget' separate from and not funded by the general account budget; the orientation of anti-trust policy to developmental and international competitive goals rather than strictly to the maintenance of domestic competition; governmental-conducted or government-sponsored research (the computer industry); and the use of the government's licensing and approval authority to achieve developmental goals.
>
> (Johnson 1982: 318)

Nobody pretends that the entirety of the success of the Japanese economy (or its more recent problems) can be explained in terms of its government's industrial policy. On the other hand, few would seriously question the input that the state made, under Japanese circumstances, to enhanced economic development. Interestingly, although there are important variations in the experience of the subsequently successful economies of the Far East, they have generally been characterized by comparatively high levels of state involvement (Vartiainen 1995; Wade 1995).

Almost as frequently cited at the other end of the scale of successful developmental states is the UK. Although there are a multitude of explanations of the UK's long-standing comparative economic decline, there is a measure of consensus that, broadly speaking, industrial policy in the British state has been, by turns, unsuccessful and non-existent. When intermittently it has appeared, it has been underfunded, unsystematic and undermined by the archaic structure of the British state (Gamble 1985; Marquand 1988).

### *The economic consequences of the state as non-economic policy-maker*

Despite a great deal of international variation, we find (even in the most reluctantly interventionist states) a whole range of governmental economic policies – monetary policy, fiscal policy, employment policy, trade policy, etc. – that have a profound effect upon the nature of the economy and upon the forms and levels of economic activity. Almost as important are the economic effects of governmental policies which are *not* directly addressed to the economy, yet whose indirect impact may be considerable. Of course, in one sense this is true because *all* government policies involve the spending of money, and these costs have to be allocated to someone. But we can also isolate areas of policy-making whose effects upon economic activity are almost as direct as those we have already addressed. Increasingly, states themselves have come to recognize that what were once regarded principally as 'non-economic' spheres of their activity have now to be recast in terms of their economic impact.

We can see this, for example, in the government's *transport policy*. Historically, states have taken an extremely active part in the provision of transport infrastructure. In part, this is because such infrastructure may constitute a public good or else (so it has until recently been generally supposed) because market mechanisms would not yield an efficient transport network. States have also had geo-political reasons for taking such an interest in transport – from the building of military roads into the rebellious Scottish highlands to the laying down of the German system of railways and motorways. Yet quite clearly, the nature of state transport policy – its provision of highways of differing kinds, its subsidization of urban public transport, its underwriting of the car economy – has a directly economic effect. Similarly, the state's *environmental policy* – e.g. setting limits to noxious emissions or upholding certain standards of water purity – impacts directly upon industrial producers and their customers. But possibly the most economically significant of the state's so-called non-economic policies is defined by the broad area of *social policy* – and here the change of focus is one about which state actors have themselves been quite explicit.

A brief and institutional definition of social policy would identify it with the main areas of activity of the welfare state: education, health, housing, income maintenance (social security) and personal social services. As we have seen, the state appears increasingly as a regulator–funder of these activities, a little less frequently as a producer. Its interventions in this area have a directly economic effect in their redistribution of resources and opportunities. But they also have an *indirect* economic effect which is almost as important. Thus, the education system is the principal mechanism through which a multi-skilled and value-adding workforce can be generated. Patterns of housing tenure may encourage or deter labour mobility (see Pierson 1994). Above all, governments have come to recognize the impact that the social security system (in terms of both benefits and charges) has upon patterns of employment. In this respect, Europe (with comparatively generous levels of social protection and correspondingly high social security charges) has been contrasted with the USA (low benefits and lower costs). In Britain, New Labour put an 'employment-based social policy' at the heart of its reform agenda after 1997. The several New Deals that it developed, alongside its adoption of the previous Conservative regimes' newspeak of 'jobseekers' rather than the unemployed, signalled a conviction that the social security regime should privilege employment – a regime of 'work for those who can; security for those who cannot' (on Labour's new social policy, see Ellison and Pierson 2003). Elsewhere, reforms embodied many of the same assumptions (for the evidence on Australia, see Pierson 2002, 2003). Whatever the disagreements about the most desirable kinds of social policy reforms and their objectives, almost no one now denies this intimate link between *social* provision and overall *economic* performance.

## Economies shaping states?

Overall, we might judge that, for all the important changes in the nature of the state's activity in recent years, there is still plenty of evidence of its continuing centrality as an economic actor, in terms of both direct expenditure and policy-making. Nonetheless, it is possible that we are actually seeing the state–economy relationship 'the wrong way around'. Perhaps in the interaction of state and economy, it is the economy that is really determinant.

Such a possibility was extensively discussed in the last chapter, especially in the context of Marxist commentaries on the state–society relationship. In the more *instrumentalist* Marxist accounts, this relationship was seen above all as one in which members of the economically ascendant class directed the activity of the state. Although, in its most vulgar form, this argument is not especially convincing, it is certainly not without value. Authors such as Miliband and Scott in the UK and Domhoff in the USA have gone into considerable detail in tracing the inter-connections between elites in business and government. In recent years in the UK, there has been growing public concern about the 'revolving door' through which former ministers and senior civil servants move into lucrative posts in private-sector corporations with whose regulation or, in the case of the newly privatized utilities, even creation they have until very recently been directly concerned. In New Zealand, the process of state restructuring, corporatization and privatization shows the most intimate connections between state reformers and corporate elites (Kelsey 1995). The strange political status of central banks – perhaps, above all, of the Bank of England – as part private, part public, institutions, exercising political authority while acting, at least to some degree, as representatives of private financial interests, also points towards the quite exceptional power of the largest private financial institutions.

Perhaps more compelling as a general account of the ways in which economic forces shape states is the *structuralist* Marxist explanation which focuses upon the location of the state within a wider (capitalist) political economy. We saw in the previous chapter that exponents of this view understood the state less as 'captured' by the interests of private capital than as 'constrained' by the imperatives of an economy premised upon private investment decisions. Of course, the structuralist Marxists give this relationship a particular political 'spin', and some have seen capital as strongly determinant, albeit in a notoriously obscure 'final instance'. But a rather weaker premise of 'structural constraint' can be found well beyond the limits of Marxian explanations. In his study *Politics and Markets*, Lindblom (1977), for example, adjusts his earlier endorsement of the pluralist model of representative democratic governance by arguing that, given its strategic importance to industrial performance (and thus to governments' income and re-electability), business has a 'privileged position' in the politics of liberal democracy, a sort of 'veto power' over what democratically elected governments can and cannot do. As early as 1918, Schumpeter had written of the fiscal limits to the capitalist state:

> The state has its definite limits [and these are] limits to its fiscal potential. . . . [In] bourgeois society . . ., the state lives as an economic parasite. [It] must not demand from the people so much that they lose financial interest in production.
> (Schumpeter 1954: 20–2)

Upon such an account, for economic forces to constrain the state requires no capitalist conspiracy or 'banker's ramp'. The Labour prime minister Harold Wilson is supposed famously to have complained of his economic policy being blown off course by the activities of the financier 'gnomes of Zurich'. But the limits to democratic states' actions may be set not by the ill-will of a tightly organized group of powerful financiers, but rather, in classic neo-liberal fashion, by the unintended consequences of millions of individually inconsequential financial decisions in international markets. A graphic example is given by recent attempts to sustain across a range of European Union states the integrity of the Exchange Rate Mechanism of the European Monetary System. The Asian financial crisis of 1997 or the secular decline of stock market values in 2003 may have been influenced by certain key players (not least, in the latter case, by the fraudulent behaviour of leading executives in the USA) but it would be hard to portray these 'disasters' as products of the intentional action of economic élites. Indeed, the lack of control over these sorts of processes is one of the key features of the logic of *globalization* to which we turn in the closing pages of this chapter.

## States and a changing international political economy: the impact of globalization

Traditionally, the relationship between state and society (and state and economy) has been discussed as if this were a relationship which was at its core *domestic* – that is, principally constituted and determined within given national boundaries. Of course, this has never been seen to exhaust the limits of the relationship between state and society, especially for those societies which were subordinated to some external state authority. But whether state, economy or society was seen to be the principal term, their interrelationship has typically been modelled as if this were best understood within a particular *national* context, with the international environment acting as a largely exogenous influence. In recent years, this account has come under sustained challenge above all by those who wish to recast the relationship between state and society (or, more narrowly, between state and economy) under the logic of *globalization*. At its simplest, it is argued that the limits of states' capacities are now increasingly set by an international or, more properly, a global social and political environment. Generally, it is argued further that this changing context has seen a shift in power away from states and towards international social forces (above all, to various global markets or simply 'the global economy'). In this account, a contrast is typically drawn between an emergent new order whose origins are retraceable to the early 1970s and the period of greater stability (and state power) which is seen to have preceded it in the twenty-five years following the Second World War. The interventionist state of the post-war period, with its characteristic commitment to full employment, macroeconomic demand management and a growth-funded expansion of public welfare, is seen to have been appropriate to the forms of economy that dominated internationally from the end of the Second World War until the late 1960s. However, the crisis of this economic order which developed in the early 1970s is seen at the same time (and, for some commentators, above all) to be a crisis of the interventionist state. It is suggested that the present transition towards a new type of global economy built upon 'flexibility' and transnationalism is bringing with it a transformation in the nature of the state. While few have argued that state intervention in the economy is going to 'disappear', there is widespread support for the view that under a new regime the character of the state's interventions will be quite different and that increasingly the state will find itself not a 'policy-maker', but a 'policy-taker' forced to respond to an external environment over which it has very limited control (Strange 1995).

## The rise and fall of the Keynesian Welfare State

First, it would be helpful to identify the characteristics of the form of state and international economy it is presumed we have lost. In fact, there is a good deal of disagreement about how best to characterize the international political economy that prevailed in the quarter-century between the end of the Second World War and the turn of the 1970s. There is, however, some measure of consensus about the institutional features that were most typical of this period. In terms of the economy, this was an era of unprecedented growth, based upon the dominance of mass production and mass consumption (especially of consumer goods) and massified, semi-skilled labour. It saw an enhanced status for the collective bargaining of wages and conditions (increasingly upon a national basis), and a correspondingly increased role for large-scale capital, organized labour and a mediating state. At the international level, it was built upon a commitment to 'free markets' and stable exchange rates, both under US military and economic leadership. Domestically, the new order was secured around:

1    Keynesian economic policies through which the state sought to sustain demand, to secure full employment and to promote economic growth;
2    the development of a more or less 'institutional' welfare state to deal with the dysfunctions arising from the market economy, 'to establish a minimum wage, to generalize mass consumption norms, and to coordinate the capital and consumer goods sectors'; and
3    broad-based agreement between left and right, and between capital and labour, over these basic social institutions (a managed market economy and a welfare state) and the accommodation of their (legitimately) competing interests through elite-level negotiation.

(Jessop 1988: 5)

A number of commentators refer to the state formation characteristic of this period as the *Keynesian Welfare State* (or KWS). This Keynesian Welfare State was shaped by both the accumulation needs of capital and the defensive strength of the organized working class. It provided not only the class basis for mobilization behind the welfare state (the massification of labour) but also the corporate basis (in the rise of organized labour and organized capital) and the institutional basis (with the rise of the interventionist state) (Pierson 1994).

There is also fairly widespread agreement about the circumstances under which this epoch drew to a close. Almost everyone could see that the downturn in the economy from the late 1960s onwards posed difficulties for the interventionist state. Many on right and left went further and argued that these economic difficulties were themselves a product of the cumulative rigidities built into the KWS regime. Thus, those very same arrangements which had secured the stability which made renewed capital accumulation possible in the period after 1945 had now grown 'sclerotic' and become a fetter upon continued economic growth. The economic consequences of 'rigidity' could be seen in the deployment of both capital and labour. On the one hand, there was increasing difficulty in finding new opportunities for the profitable investment of capital. At the same time, there was a range of corresponding problems with the supply of labour. In Nielsen's paraphrase of the new economic orthodoxy of the 1970s,

Wages were seen as too high and too rigid, wage differentials as too small, and legally based labour rights, employment protection schemes, and social security systems as taken too far. The consequences were seen to be that workers priced themselves out of jobs; labour mobility, and thus structural adjustment, was hindered; and hiring of workers was discouraged while voluntary unemployment was encouraged. . . . Inflexibilities in capital markets and government regulations were said to discourage risk-taking and implied a bias against the small entrepreneur and venture capitalist who had difficulty obtaining funds.

(Nielsen 1991: 4)

The KWS was seen to be deeply implicated in this crisis. First, there was the burden of funding a constantly expanding welfare budget. Social expenditure grew rapidly in the post-war period, rising across the OECD countries from 12.3 per cent of GDP in 1960 to 21.9 per cent in 1975. Increasingly, this expenditure (especially in the case of social security and pension payments) was regarded not as an investment in 'social capital' or the meeting of a social obligation, but as an 'unproductive' cost, which diverted resources away from the (shrinking) productive sectors of the economy. Rapidly rising levels of social expenditure were seen not as a way of generating 'human capital' or sustaining demand, but as an economic disincentive to both capital and labour. High marginal taxation rates, bureaucratic regulation of business and the growth of public-sector employment were seen to be 'squeezing out' productive private investment. Meanwhile, the commitment to full employment and to a rising 'social wage' strengthened the defensive power of the organized working class, driving up wage costs beyond corresponding rises in productivity, hampering the process of 'structural adjustment' and consolidating the veto powers of organized labour. As economic growth faltered, the costs of the entitlement programmes of the welfare state grew, while the revenues out of which these could be funded declined, generating the much discussed 'fiscal crisis' of the mid-1970s (O'Connor 1973; Pierson 1998). At the same time, the institutions of corporatist intermediation which had been established to reconcile the interests of state, capital and labour became increasingly an obstruction to economic reorganization. Thus, the institutions of the KWS, which had once secured the grounds for capital accumulation by sustaining effective demand and managing the relations between capital and labour, had under new circumstances become a barrier to further economic growth. Governments' attempts to meet this crisis with traditional Keynesian solutions simply intensified their difficulties.

## Globalization

Initially, this challenge to the institutional logic of the interventionist state was understood principally in terms of the impact of domestic social and economic forces (a general loss of political deference, over-powerful trades unions, changes in class structure and the fiscal overloading of welfare budgets). Increasingly, in the late 1980s and 1990s, attention shifted towards the international or global impediments to interventionist state regimes (the heightened international mobility of capital, the intensification of international trade, the requirements of 'competitiveness'). Now the context for understanding the limits of states' action is seen to be set, above all, by the dynamics of international or globalized economic forces.

The idea of globalization has been called upon to do an extraordinary amount of work in accounts of recent social and political change and, as such, it has generated a vast literature and a great deal of disagreement. At one extreme are those who believe that nation-states are increasingly losing their powers, as ever more perfectly integrated international markets articulate the sovereignty of the global consumer across what is rapidly becoming a 'borderless world' (Ohmae 1990). Sceptics, by contrast, doubt that there really is a new phenomenon of 'globalization', insisting that nation-states have always faced powerful transnational forces and that, in spite of these, they retain significant governing capacities and policy discretion (Hirst and Thompson 1995). Unremarkably, the truth probably lies somewhere between these two perspectives (Perraton *et al.* 1997).

Globalization is clearly a multifaceted phenomenon – an 'open-ended process' rather than a given 'end state' in the treatment by Perraton *et al.* (1997). Its most significant impact upon modern states arises from two sources. First, at least since the 1960s, there has been the emergence of a 'new international division of labour' which has seen the transfer of manufacturing activity (and the semi-skilled jobs that go with it) from the developed economies of the North to newly industrialized countries (NICs), especially in the Pacific Rim. With new developments in transport and communication technologies, newly industrializing economies are able to offer a low-wage, low-tax environment which draws investment away from traditional developed economies, presenting these economies with the twin potential problems of rising unemployment and a fiscal shortfall (see Martin 1997). A second difficulty lies in the consequences of a seemingly exponential growth in transnational economic activity: increasing trade, rising foreign direct investment (FDI) and, perhaps above all, a rapid intensification in international financial movements. In Robert Cox's account:

> The two principal aspects of [economic] globalization are (1) global organizations of production (complex transnational networks of production which source the various components of the product in places offering the most advantage on costs, markets, taxes, and access to suitable labour, and also the advantages of political security and predictability); and (2) global finance (a very largely unregulated system of transactions in money, credit, and equities). These developments together constitute a *global economy*, i.e. an economic space transcending all country borders, which co-exists still with an *international economy* based on transactions across country borders and which is regulated by inter-state agreements and practices.
>
> (Cox 1993: 259–60)

This process has affected different states in differing ways. But generally, 'economic globalization has placed constraints upon the autonomy of states' and, increasingly, 'states must become the instruments for adjusting national economic activities to the exigencies of the global economy' (Cox 1993: 262, 260, respectively). In a context in which it makes increasingly little sense to talk of distinct 'national economies', it is less and less possible for individual states to regulate the economic activity that goes on within and across their borders. Rather, states find themselves involved in a permanent competition to attract footloose capital to their shores by creating an attractive environment for inward investors. Under these circumstances, the international markets and currency exchanges function as a 'permanent referendum' upon governments' capacity to pursue a sound economic policy.

For some commentators, these changes herald the coming 'end of the nation-state'. According to McGrew (1992b), 'globalization is compromising the authority, the autonomy, the nature and the competence of the modern nation-state'. He identifies four specific challenges:

1   *The challenge to the competence of the state*   Increasingly, the most basic interests and well being of a nation's institutions and its individual citizens are shaped by forces beyond the physical boundaries and the policy reach of the individual nation-state. The state is decreasingly able to determine the fate of its own citizens.
2   *The challenge to the form of the state*   Changes in the transnational context mean that even domestic states are increasingly '*internationalized*'; that is, even domestic bureaucracies and ministries become oriented around the growing number of international fora in which transgovernmental policies are shaped.
3   *The challenge to the autonomy of the state*   In the economic field above all, globalization severely restrains the policy options available to state managers. With the decline of truly 'national' economies, the state finds that it is no longer 'in control' of the economic processes that go on within its jurisdiction. It is increasingly a 'policy-taker' rather than a 'policy-maker'.
4   *The challenge to the authority of the state*   'Very succinctly, the thesis is that, because globalization undermines the competence and autonomy of the nation-state, it reduces the effectiveness of government which, in turn, undermines the legitimacy and authority of the state.'

(McGrew 1992b: 87–92)

This greater subservience to global markets does not, however, necessarily mean a decline in a state's activity. Ironically, creating a more favourable climate for investment may require states to increase their involvement in certain policy fields. Thus, for example, deregulation of the UK labour market required the government to intervene to an unprecedented extent in the internal organization of British trades unions (Marsh 1992). It is not so much the volume as the character of state interventions that has changed. In this context, Jessop writes of a 'fundamental strategic reorientation' of state intervention away from the traditional policies associated with a Keynesian welfare state towards what he calls a 'Schumpeterian workfare state'. The strategic goals of the Schumpeterian workfare state are:

to promote product, process, organizational, and market innovation in open economies in order to strengthen as far as possible the structural competitive-ness of the national economy by intervening on the supply side; and to subordinate social policy to the needs of labour market flexibility and/or to the constraints of international competition.

(Jessop 1994: 24)

It is important that we do not exaggerate the scale of these changes. A number of dissenting voices (Gordon 1988; Panitch 1994: Cable 1995) have challenged the claim that globalization is in any real sense subverting the power of individual states. Mann (1993b) is among those who caution against the belief that a change in the international circumstances in which states operate is part of a process whose end-point will be 'the death of the nation-state'. It is one of the many paradoxes of the age of globalization that it is, at the same time, an age of revived nationalist sentiment. Nonetheless, it is hard to deny that transnationalism and globalization have profoundly altered the parameters for states' action.

I return to some of the consequences for the modern states' system of this changing international political economy in Chapter 6. The parameters of globalization are explored further in Chapter 7.

## Conclusion

The state–economy relationship is quite crucial to any understanding of the modern state. States in modernity have always been centrally concerned with the generation of economic resources, not least because they wanted a share of them. Indeed, we saw in Chapter 1 that the raising of revenue (to fight external wars) was one of the original 'causes' of the rise of the modern state (see above, pp. 24–5). In those states which have had basically 'privately owned' economies, this relationship has always been complex but also intimate and continuous. In this chapter, we have had an opportunity to consider just what substantial economic actors modern states have become – in terms of ownership, production, employment, regulation and redistribution. We have also seen the range of policy domains – on taxation, incomes, money supply, the regions, industry, the environment, health, housing, social provision, transport – in which state effects on the economy are generated. We have also seen how, contrastingly, economic forces, partly constituted by and partly constructed against the state, set parameters within which all state actors have to operate. (There is a long-standing Marxist argument that in a capitalist economy the institutional separation of economic and political powers is a systematic curb upon the repertoire of interventions available to state actors.) I have reported a growing consensus that recent years have seen power shifting away from states and towards transnational economic forces to a point at which, in some accounts, states are powerless in the face of global economic imperatives. We shall return to this issue of states in a changing international political economy in Chapter 6. For now, it will be enough to sound a cautionary note about the declining powers of the nation-state. Certainly, states have lost many of the capacities which at least the more successful and powerful enjoyed during the heyday of the Keynesian Welfare State. But in most of the developed world, the state remains the single largest and most decisive economic actor. Much taxable activity (especially outside the corporate sector) is still resolutely national (since we all have to live, shop and work *somewhere*). States still command and dispose of vast economic resources, and, generally, the state has not responded to external economic challenges to its power simply by *retreating*, but quite as much by *restructuring* the ways in which it intervenes in a society over which it still exercises formidable powers (Cable 1995; Hirst and Thompson 1995). This is especially clear in big spending areas such as social security and education, where the story is much less one of 'cuts' in expenditure and much more a rewriting of the terms and conditions under which public money is spent.

# Further reading

Chang, H.-J. and Rowthorn, R. (eds) *The Role of the State in Economic Change.* Oxford: Oxford University Press.

Held, D. and McGrew, A. (eds) (2002) *Governing Globalization.* Cambridge: Polity.

Held, D. and McGrew, A. (eds) (2003) *Global Transformations Reader.* Cambridge: Polity.

Pierson, C. (2001) *Hard Choices: Social Democracy in the Twenty-First Century.* Cambridge: Polity.

Stubbs, R. and Underhill, G. (eds) (1994) *Political Economy and the Changing Global Order.* London: Macmillan.

World Bank (2003) *World Development Indicators.* New York: World Bank.

# 5   States and citizens

The idea of citizenship as a key element in the structure of modern states was raised briefly in Chapter 1. There we saw that the invocation of the citizen as the constituting subject–object of state activity could be seen as one of the defining aspects of modernity, and the idea of citizenship has been especially important for those who have sought to establish a *normative* defence of the state (i.e. for those who have tried to *justify* the nature of modern state institutions). A number of commentators (Turner 1990; Oldfield 1990; Lister 1993; Kymlicka and Norman 1994; Stewart 1995) have also observed that, with the waning of some of the defining ideologies of the modern age (above all, those built around state-administered forms of socialism), the idea of citizenship is taking on a renewed lease of life. Of course, the idea of citizenship is not new. The Greeks certainly had a word for it and, in his historical survey of the citizenship idea, Heater identifies 'five distinct contexts' in which citizenship has been developed over the past two and a half millennia: 'the Greek city-state, the Roman Republic and Empire, the medieval and Renaissance city, the nation-state and the idea of the cosmopolis' (Heater 1990: 161). While citizenship has been an important principle in each of these contexts, our attention here will be focused upon the fourth category: citizenship as a constituting principle of the modern nation-state.

Like democracy, citizenship has suffered from the twin qualities of being almost universally admired – hardly anyone thinks it's bad to be a good citizen – and yet imprecisely defined – what exactly is it? Rather like the state itself, citizenship embodies a 'cluster of meanings'. In Heater's discussion (1990: 163) these are identified as: 'a defined legal or social status, a means of political identity, a focus of loyalty, a requirement of duties, an expectation of right and a yardstick of good social behaviour.' Writing of the distinctively modern form of citizenship, Brubaker (1992: 35) identifies the following defining features:

> the formal delimitation of the citizenry; the establishment of civil equality, entailing shared rights and shared obligations; the institutionalization of political rights; the legal rationalization and ideological accentuation of the distinction between citizens and foreigners; the articulation of the doctrine of national sovereignty and of the link between citizenship and nationhood; the substitution of immediate, direct relations between the citizen and the state for the mediated, indirect relations characteristic of the *ancien régime*.

For Brubaker, all these qualities of modern citizenship were crystallized in the experience of the French Revolution: 'The Revolution, in short, invented both the nation-state and the modern institution and ideology of national citizenship.'

## The characteristics of modern citizenship

In the pages that follow, I want to develop a rather fuller account of the nature of modern citizenship and its relationship to the modern state around a series of widely shared features.

### Citizenship as membership

Membership is perhaps the broadest and most generic quality of citizenship. To be a citizen is to be a member of a political community. In the ancient world, to be a citizen was to be a full member of the *polis*, with others (including women, slaves and foreigners) reduced to a subordinate status. Typically (though not exclusively), in the modern world, the political community within which such citizenship has been enjoyed is the nation-state. Certainly over the last two hundred years, citizenship and nationhood have become inextricably entwined. Both are related in their turn to the enhanced claims of sovereignty made by modern states. Characteristically, as we shall see in the coming sections, citizenship entails certain rights or privileges and an attendant set of duties and obligations. Like membership of any club, it may also be an important source of personal identity and of self-worth. For many commentators (e.g. Held 1989b), membership also entails an element of *participation*, but this proves to be one of the most variable qualities of differing accounts of citizenship, ranging from the most token involvement (amounting to little more than tacit consent) to almost full-time engagement in the business of self-government.

Quite central to citizenship as membership are the criteria according to which members and non-members are to be defined. Clearly, there cannot be privileges attached to citizenship without some population that is disprivileged by exclusion from membership. Upon some accounts (Marshall is a good example, see pp. 112–13), the history of liberal democracy over the past two centuries can largely be redescribed as a struggle to expand the numbers of the population entitled to full rights of citizen participation, most graphically the extension of the right to vote. For some, 'universalization' of the franchise represents the happy completion of this historical struggle to realize popular democracy and full citizenship. But, more broadly conceived, citizenship has always served as a form of 'social closure', establishing a particular population to whom the benefits of citizenship should apply.

Of course, assumptions about citizenship as membership of a political community do not prescribe a particular size for that community. Some forms of political association, not least the classical Greek *polis*, were comparatively small. On the other hand, Heater (1990: 8–15) raises the prospect of a *cosmopolitan* conception of citizenship in which, at the limits, we are all citizens of Planet Earth, and Held (1995) has also turned his attention to cosmopolitan forms of democratic participation. In fact, scale has long been recognized to be hugely consequential for the possibilities of active citizenship. Few commentators have argued that, even with the benefits of new interactive information technologies, a fully participative and direct democracy is possible in communities that have more than a few thousand citizens. And while we undoubtedly share quite vital common interests as the citizens of our one world, we certainly as yet lack the institutions through which to make binding and effective decisions within this biggest of all clubs. In practice, in modernity the nation-state has been the peculiarly privileged site of citizen membership. Nation-states have differed profoundly in size and character, but we have already seen how they became the seemingly ubiquitous form of political association in the modern world.

Interestingly, the exclusivity of nation-state citizenship is now coming under challenge not so much at a global as at a *regional* level. Meehan's (1993) advocacy of a European citizenship built around the state-like institutions of the European Union is an interesting example. It may, as she suggests, be a very long time before the visitor arriving in the Far East from Germany, France or the UK would describe herself as 'a European citizen'. Nonetheless, the inhabitants of the European Union already exercise some of the rights and discharge some of the duties of citizenship at the level of the European Union. To this extent, we may already have become, in practice if not in sentiment, European citizens. It remains as yet unclear whether this formative European citizenship is really a product of an emergent European statehood.

The European example also raises the issue of whether our citizenship must be exclusively enjoyed in one particular political community. One might quite intelligibly claim to be a citizen of the County of Santa Barbara, the State of California and the USA, and one might act as a citizen – e.g. paying taxes and casting one's vote – at each of these levels. Yet many states see membership of their own club as exclusive in the sense that they will not allow individuals to hold forms of dual or multiple citizenship with other states. Citizens in the USA, for example, may not hold dual citizenship with some other state, nor may they vote in elections in another jurisdiction without forfeiting their US citizenship. This demand may, in its turn, be related to the sorts of claims to a *monopoly* of authority within a given physical space which we have seen to be characteristic of the modern state.

For all the interesting possibilities opened up by global or European citizenship, overwhelmingly the experience of the two hundred years since the French Revolution has been one of citizenship at the level of the nation-state. And it is overwhelmingly at this level that the privileging of citizenship and the practice of social closure against outsiders has been observed. This relationship is neatly captured by Brubaker:

> In global perspective, citizenship is a powerful instrument of social closure, shielding prosperous states from the migrant poor. Citizenship is also an instrument of closure *within* states. Every state establishes a conceptual, legal, and ideological boundary between citizens and resident foreigners. Every state discriminates between citizens and resident foreigners, reserving certain rights and benefits, as well as certain obligations, for citizens. Every state claims to be the state of, and for, a particular bounded citizenry, usually conceived as a nation.
>
> (Brubaker 1992: x)

In the modern nation-state, *formal* membership of the citizen body is not now normally restricted on the basis of gender, employment status or religious affiliation (though the issue of the status of children and their rights is much more of a problem than the usual disclaimers about their exclusion would allow). But discrimination on the basis of ethnicity or country of origin is still quite commonplace. Of course, it is clear why we might wish to exclude tourists, whose vacation happens to coincide with a general election, from helping to shape the political destiny of the nation. It is perhaps a little less clear why long-standing residents (perhaps even of a second or third generation) who are subject to the same duties as citizens (e.g. the duty to pay taxes or to abide by locally promulgated laws) should be excluded from participation in political decision-making. But all states seek, albeit in varying ways, to exercise discrimination about those who may hold political and civil rights within their jurisdiction. In most states, there is some category of resident adults who do not enjoy full rights of political participation, and those states which do allow for the acquisition of citizen status by outsiders usually establish a fairly complex and extended set of procedures which aspirant citizens must satisfy before they come to enjoy the status which the indigenous population possesses by accident of birth.

There are a number of ways we might seek to explain these formal mechanisms of membership and social closure in the modern nation-state. In part, there is a fear among more affluent nations that an influx of migrants from less prosperous regions (so-called economic migrants) might dilute their wealth. Often, this fear is rather poorly distinguished from a more general cultural and ethnic prejudice against varyingly defined 'outsiders'. It may be that, historically, citizenship rights have been acquired as a 'reward' for the (especially military) endeavours of a particular population. Certainly, it points towards an association between citizenship and the idea of a political community with a particular national identity and national consciousness, however 'imaginary' this sense of nationality may be. It can also be related to the claim that states characteristically make to be the final arbiters of what should or should not happen within a particular territory. Deciding who shall be allowed to cross the border into and out of the national territory is one of the most jealously guarded rights of sovereign nation-states.

In recent years, the issues of statelessness, refugees and asylum-seekers have moved rapidly up the political agenda, especially in Western Europe. In circumstances of civil strife, depriving populations of their citizenship is a widely deployed tactic. Increasing numbers of asylum applications in the 1990s, driven by regime change in Eastern Europe and population displacement in the war-torn Balkans, have led politicians in a number of European countries to attempt to place further restrictions upon those seeking to acquire citizenship. It has led to a number of inter-state disputes, as countries have tried to pass on the responsibility for displaced persons, and to attempts to impose new eligibility tests for those seeking new national homes. In a context of continuing civil strife in many regions of the world and the enormous disparity in economic status between those in the richest and poorest parts of the planet, the pressure to migrate (and the corresponding pressure to resist migration) is likely to continue unabated. (For data on asylum applications, see Home Office 2003; for data on the international denial of citizenship, see

Human Rights Watch 2003.) It remains extraordinarily unattractive to be a 'stateless' person.

### Citizenship as status

Some of the peculiarities of citizenship as membership may also be explained in terms of its special character as a type of *status*. The coming of modernity has sometimes been summarized as a general transition 'from status to contract' (Maine 1890: 170). In this account, the rigid hierarchies and established orders of feudalism are seen to have given way to more socially mobile and fluid societies in which contractual relations (above all, those of the marketplace) are dominant. Yet, paradoxically, modern citizenship is a form of *status* relationship. Citizenship is conventionally an *ascribed* quality, usually given to us at birth. It is neither earned nor voluntarily acquired. It is normally premised upon where we are born and/or upon the citizenship and nationality status of our parents. Within one tradition, at least, citizenship is seen as following a particular line of descent, identifying political citizenship with ethnic identity and marrying citizenship not just to the nation but also to the idea of the 'imagined community' of nationalism (Brubaker 1992: 52; Anderson 1991). In this way, an association is developed between, for example, German citizenship and what it means to be German or between British citizenship and what it means to be British. Disputes about the legal status of citizenship (as, for example, in the British example, with the changing rights of inhabitants of the former colonies to take up British citizenship and residence) become disputes about what it is to 'belong' to a given nation. In this context, citizenship status is an important component of individual identity (who I am).

As something ascribed rather than acquired, citizenship is not normally something which we think of as 'tradeable'. In practice, wealth has a great deal to do with the possibilities of acquiring a new citizenship status, but most naturalization regimes will impose some requirement for residency and extract some token of political commitment, even if it is little more than a mumbling familiarity with the essentials of the US constitution. While the financial criteria for acquiring citizenship may place an insurmountable hurdle in the face of poorer aspirants, it is not *formally* the case that citizenship can simply be bought or indeed 'sold on' in any but the most degenerate regimes. In other contexts, as with Norman Tebbit's notorious 'cricket test', 'proper' citizenship is identified with loyalty to one's acquired national status. Those whose ethnic origins lay in the Asian subcontinent or in the Caribbean could demonstrate their full 'British-ness', in Tebbit's half-serious test, by supporting England in her generally rather unhappy sporting confrontations with the former colonies. The 'cricket test' is one illustration of the extent to which national citizenship may be perceived not so much as a set of legal rights, but rather as a badge of national identity.

At the same time, citizenship status, so 'naturally' acquired by 'indigenous' populations, so struggled for by 'incomers', is not easily abandoned. Banishment has always been one of the severest sanctions which states have been ready to impose upon their citizens, and a characteristic response to law-breaking is to suspend an offender's citizenship rights (e.g. the right to vote or to hold public office). But citizenship is not easily renounced. If I declare that, upon mature reflection, while I wish to remain domiciled in Britain, I no longer wish to be counted a citizen of the UK, I shall find my position impossible to sustain. Opting out of the nation-state is not possible for individual citizens (or, indeed, for dissenting groups). And this observation goes to the heart of one of the more remarkable features of the modern state and its membership – a problem which greatly troubled the major figures of early modern political theory: the terms of political association. I have never consented to the arrangements under which I am taxed, governed, coerced and conscripted by the state (to mention only some of the more genteel things which states do to their citizens in Proudhon's account). Democratization may give me some control (pooled with millions of others) over who is to exercise the state's rule over me, but it does not give me the opportunity to defect from the set of arrangements for ruling to which I am subject. It was this that motivated the (generally pretty fruitless) quest among early modern political theorists for some original contractual basis for the modern state. To suggest that I have actively consented to the existing state simply by casting my vote, paying my taxes or even 'walking down the Queen's highway' looks like a piece of fairly gross sophistry. At least in part, we might suggest, citizenship has the quality of a *status* because there is no possibility of establishing an appropriate *contractual* relationship between state and subject.

Article 13 of the United Nations' Universal Declaration of Human Rights (Brownlie 1992: 20) indicates that citizens should have the right to leave a particular jurisdiction. There is, however, no corresponding and general right to take up residence anywhere else. The threat of becoming a 'stateless' person in a world exclusively divided up between nation-states may make one's present citizen status almost always the lesser of two evils. But the expectation that the privileges of citizenship (including the enjoyment of general social order) make the citizen's tutelage to the state comparatively advantageous can hardly be said to make it freely chosen.

### Citizenship as a set of rights

For all its intimations of personal and ethnic identity, citizenship is, above all, a positive *legal* status; i.e. it is attached to a set of justiciable rights and duties. Citizenship in the French revolutionary tradition is in its origins a discourse replete with appeals to the 'Rights of Man and the Citizen' (Brownlie 1971: 8–11). In this revolutionary tradition, to be a citizen is to be the bearer of a set of fundamental rights (and subject to certain republican duties). In many countries (the USA is a good example), the rights of the citizen are written down in a state-founding document or constitution. In the UK, by contrast, citizenship is much more frequently portrayed as an emergent quality, as a set of piecemeal rights gradually accumulated over a number of centuries.

In fact, modern citizenship and its attendant rights and duties have always taken varying forms in different historical and national contexts. Some indication of this is given by Turner (1990), who outlines a useful fourfold typology of these differing types of citizenship. The two axes which he employs turn upon two questions: 'Was citizenship principally the outcome of radical pressure from below or gradual concessions from above?' and, second, 'Was citizenship conceived primarily as a mechanism promoting active public involvement or a means of protecting the privacy of the individual from the intrusive interventions of the state?' This yields the ideal–typical possibilities seen in Table 5.1. According to Turner, these four ideal types of citizenship development correspond (again quite approximately) to the generalized historical experiences in Table 5.2. Upon Turner's own admission, these are highly stylized descriptions. Obviously, there was a good deal of 'bottom-up' in the quest for British citizenship and plenty of 'top-down' in the French experience! Yet it is important to observe (as with Brubaker's more detailed comparison of French and German traditions) that, while manifesting certain elements in common, citizenship in the modern world has taken a variety of distinctive national forms.

Here, I want to focus on the British experience of citizenship rights, and in this context, the definitive source is the work of T. H. Marshall, especially his seminal essay on 'Citizenship and social class' (Marshall 1964). Addressing the specifically British experience, Marshall characterizes the process of modernization over the past three hundred years as one of the general expansion of citizenship. It is a history both of the repeated expansion of rights of the citizen and of a growth in the numbers of those entitled to citizen status.

Marshall identifies three species of citizenship rights (see Table 5.3) – civil, political and social – each with its own 'typical' historical epoch, which have been cumulatively secured over the last three hundred years. The macro-history of the period in the UK since the Glorious Revolution of 1688 is seen as one of progress from the securing of a body of civil rights – the rights of the freely contracting

*Table 5.1* Sources of citizenship

|  | *Citizenship* | |
|  | *From below* | *From above* |
|---|---|---|
| Public involvement | Revolutionary context | Passive democracy |
| Private space | Liberal pluralism | Plebiscitary authoritarianism |

Source: Turner (1990).

*Table 5.2* Citizenship: national experience

|  | *Citizenship* | |
|  | *From below* | *From above* |
|---|---|---|
| Public involvement | Revolutionary French tradition | English case |
| Private space | American liberalism | German fascism |

Source: Turner (1990).

*Table 5.3* The growth of citizenship

|  | Civil rights | Political rights | Social rights |
|---|---|---|---|
| *Characteristic period* | 18th century | 19th century | 20th century |
| *Defining principle* | Individual freedom | Political freedom | Social welfare |
| *Typical measures* | Habeas corpus, freedom of speech, thought and faith; freedom to enter into legal contracts | Right to vote, parliamentary reform, payment for MPs | Free education, pensions, health care (the welfare state) |
|  | ——————————→ Cumulative —————————→ | | |

Source: Marshall (1964: 70).

individual, sometimes identified with the structure of a capitalist market economy – which, in turn, made possible the expansion of political rights (principally, the expansion of voting rights), which meant in its turn the enfranchisement of the working class and the rise of mass democratic parties. The winning of civil rights (in the eighteenth century) and of political rights (in the nineteenth century) made possible the securing in the twentieth century of an epoch of social rights. Such rights, which Marshall describes as embracing 'the whole range from the right to a modicum of economic welfare and security to the right to share to the full in the social heritage and to live the life of a civilised being according to the standards prevailing in the society', have frequently been identified with the broad parameters of the post-war welfare state. Upon this account, the welfare state is the culmination of a centuries' long and progressive history of expanding citizenship.

In the UK, Marshall's account has been hugely influential though widely criticized. Critics have tended to see his explanation as Anglocentric (focusing exclusively upon the rather unusual pattern of citizenship development in the UK), as too evolutionary (describing a pattern of cumulative, if contested, growth in differing types of rights) and as historicist (seeing the addition of social rights in the immediate post-war period as 'completing' the apparatus of British citizenship). Some critics have challenged the plausibility of Marshall's threefold division of rights (offering their own alternatives) or else they have seen the three strands of citizenship as mutually inconsistent and the rights themselves as much more 'reversible' than Marshall supposed. Some have argued more generally that social and economic rights cannot be seen as rights of the same kind as those which entrench our civil and political liberties.

The fact is that Marshall has not always been well served by secondary accounts of his ideas, and brief sketches of his views on citizenship (like mine!) fail to do justice to the subtlety of his account. Many of the charges levelled against Marshall (of evolutionary optimism, of the neglect of social struggle and citizens' inequality) have to be severely qualified in the light of the detail in his arguments. Nonetheless, it is fair to suggest that Marshall's is a very partial and particular understanding of the nature of citizenship. Here, I confine myself to commenting on three aspects of this partiality. First, there is a signal disadvantage in focusing so closely on British experience since, on the question of citizenship at least, the UK does not really look like a 'properly' modern state at all. In fact, Britons are almost uniquely *not citizens* in a way that we would recognize this status in most other developed liberal democracies. According to Turner,

> the constitutional settlement of 1688 created the British citizen as the British subject, that is a legal personality whose indelible social rights are constituted by a monarch sitting in parliament. The notion of *citizen-as-subject* indicates clearly the relatively extensive notion of social rights but also the passive character of British civil institutions.
>
> (Turner 1990: 207; emphasis added)

Of course, having a formal framework of rights is no guarantee that these rights will be upheld. The Soviet constitution of 1936, for example, embodied an impressive array of civil and political liberties, virtually none of which were respected (Brownlie 1971: 25–8). But in the absence of such formal rights, the integrity of the subjects of the British state has rested upon conventions of restraint exercised by a sovereign crown-in-parliament. In recent years, the traditional restraints which made the British settlement 'work' have been increasingly abandoned, with the subject left constitutionally defenceless in the face of the will of the state. Some limited progress towards formal citizenship has been made at the level of EU institutions and under the provisions of the Human Rights Act of 1998, but almost no advance has been made in establishing an appropriately 'modern' relationship between state and citizen in the British polity.

A second source of difficulty with Marshall's account lies with the nature of those rights which he chooses to identify with the completion of citizenship. A number of commentators draw attention to the rather passive character of Marshall's list of 'social rights' or see his civil-economic rights as mis-specified (Giddens 1982). Others, like King (1987: 177), call for specific additional rights: 'the right to full employment through an active labour market policy; and women's rights, which require a significant change in existing values in society as well as in the way social citizenship rights have been conceptualised.' Perhaps the boldest and most original attempt to redefine the sphere of the rights of the citizen has come in the recent work of David Held. He insists that

> a democracy would be fully worth its name if citizens had the actual power to be active as citizens; that is to say, if citizens were able to enjoy a bundle of rights which allowed them to command democratic participation and to treat it as an entitlement. Such a bundle of rights . . . should be seen as entailed by . . . the very notion of democratic rule itself. If one chooses democracy, one must choose to operationalize a structural system of empowering rights and obligations, for such a system constitutes the interrelated space in which the principle of autonomy can be pursued – and enacted.
>
> (Held 1994: 53–4)

This persuades Held that a satisfactory basis for democratic autonomy could be secured only with a much more elaborate and broadly based apparatus of citizenship rights, extending to sets of health, social, cultural, civil, economic, pacific and political rights (Held 1994: 54–5). Held's is an explicitly *normative* list (these are the rights we would have to guarantee if we were to secure an appropriate form of democratic autonomy), rather than one describing the rights that any state's population presently enjoys. But his arguments do suggest that Marshall's own conception of the 'completion' of citizenship may be too narrowly conceived.

This connects to a third area of difficulty in Marshall's work: the nature of his account of social citizenship. To some extent, and in line with Held's comments, this is a criticism from the left insisting that Marshall's social rights have been too closely identified with the institutional apparatus of established welfare states. It has also been argued (Pierson 1998: 32–4) that Marshall is too ready to identify the practice of actual welfare states, which may bring together quite differing political intentions and forces, as an embodiment of the aspiration to social citizenship. There has also been an argument that Marshall's social rights connote a form of citizenship which is too *passive*, fostering a clientelistic relationship between the state and its welfare beneficiaries. This is an objection that has been raised from both left and right, but it is undoubtedly the right-wing variant of this criticism that has been the most politically influential in recent years.

In essence, the argument from the right has been that the citizens of welfare states have become too ready to press their *entitlement* to particular forms of welfare benefit (especially income maintenance) without recognizing that they have corresponding duties to state and society (e.g. finding work and paying taxes). In part, this is an argument that social rights are categorically different from civil and political rights. The latter are the proper and necessary basis of a liberal-democratic society, while the former are a peculiarly non-negotiable way of pressing the case for the preferential treatment of particular groups of citizens at the expense of others. It is, at the same time, an argument that the apparatus of social rights has become fatally detached from a system of corresponding *duties*. Thus:

> Whereas Marshall had argued that social rights enable the disadvantaged to enter the mainstream of society and effectively exercise their civil and political rights, the New Right argues that the welfare state has promoted passivity among the poor, without actually improving their life chances, and created a culture of dependency. Far from being the solution, the welfare state has itself perpetuated the problem by reducing citizens to passive dependants who are under bureaucratic tutelage.
>
> (Kymlicka and Norman 1994: 355–6)

The right's preferred solution has been to reduce the range and generosity of social provision, to increase the salience of markets as allocators of welfare and to reinforce the element of obligation upon those who find themselves dependent upon the state.

### Citizenship as a set of duties

Duty was certainly an important component of the classical conception of citizenship. Indeed, it is widely argued that the ancient world lacked a conception of 'rights' in anything like its modern sense. Citizenship in such a context was an amalgam of 'ruling and being ruled in turn' (Aristotle 1946: 134). In recent years, following the influential advocacy of Amitai Etzioni and fellow 'new communitarians' in the USA, there has been a widespread rehearsal of the need for a *balanced* citizenship which entails both rights *and* duties.

This is not so new. Tom Marshall was clear that, while rights had multiplied in modern societies, so had duties. If we look at a core constituent of political citizenship, voting, we find that it is often regarded as both a right *and* a duty: either a civic duty, i.e. something the good citizen ought to do, or else a legal duty, something which the citizen is required to do by law. It is, in fact, rather unusual to find a form of citizenship which is entirely exhausted by an account of the citizens' rights without the specification of any accompanying duties.

Often, the duty that citizens have been liable to perform is a military one. Goran Therborn (1977), for example, relates the development of the universal franchise in Western Europe to the military mobilization of the population in the early twentieth century. In this sense, citizenship may be seen as a reward for discharging the duty to defend the state. For long, the supposed inability of women to perform military duties was taken to justify their exclusion from the citizenry. In the USA, the extensive range of social rights exclusively enjoyed by veterans might also be said to correspond to this logic. But there are other forms of duty to which citizenship entitlement might be seen to correspond. Beveridge's (1942) outline of social rights in the post-war UK, for example, is often seen to have attached welfare rights for women to their responsibilities as mothers, providing the state with its most basic resource, people. We can see this same logic applied in the pro-natalist policies of other European states (on France, see Ashford 1986). Of course, motherhood has just as frequently been used as a reason to *exclude* women from citizenship altogether, on the basis that theirs were essentially private responsibilities (for husband and family) which did not merit inclusion in the public sphere of citizenship. When citizenship was conceded, it was often on formally less advantageous terms than those enjoyed by men, as the Beveridgean model attests. (For a fuller discussion of women and citizenship, see below, pp. 120–3.) The duty of the citizen might also include the duty to work. This was especially clear under the Soviet constitution (Brownlie 1971: 25–8), but it was also an aspect of Marshall's model (Marshall 1964: 129–31). Those who were to be the beneficiaries of the new rights of citizenship (including social insurance) had also to recognize an obligation to enter into gainful employment when they were able to do so. Thus, the right to unemployment benefit, for example, was always attached to a 'work test', which required that the recipient of benefits had to be 'genuinely seeking work'. Citizenship has nearly always involved an obligation to pay taxes, a principle that found peculiarly direct expression in the UK's experience under the poll tax (Butler *et al.* 1994).

These comments point us towards a broader issue about citizenship, duty and the state. We have already seen how difficult yet central to the legitimacy of the state is the question of citizens' obligation. Upon some accounts, the citizen is owed at least a subsistence level of income and the most basic health, education and housing provision, as a part of the deal in which he or she agrees to be subject to the state's jurisdiction. One might give this a contractarian spin and suggest, first, that it cannot be assumed that citizens would have consented to membership of the state in default of these basic guarantees of their well-being and, second, that the failure to uphold these guarantees weakens the liability of the individual citizen to obey the state, placing greater weight upon prudential arguments about avoiding the threat of state violence or something worse. Yet, in fact, the coincidence of the state with a market economy complicates this relationship considerably. The state has established as a condition of many citizenship rights (e.g. for those not specifically excluded by being too young or too old) a requirement to work not for the state but within the market economy. But this duty must, in its turn, rest upon the existence of appropriate opportunities within the labour market which the state does not directly control. In part, this explains the commitment of post-war governments down to the 1970s to supporting full employment. Beveridge, among others, argued that imposing a work test where there was no work to be had was impossible and unreasonable. In recent years, the terms of this 'deal' between state and citizen have become increasingly unattractive for many less skilled or less employable citizens. Should the state still impose the 'work test' for citizenship when it is quite unable to guarantee work opportunities for many millions of its citizens? Should citizens be obliged to take work of whatever kind and however poorly paid to avoid exclusion from full citizenship?

Some have argued that the background economic conditions and opportunities for citizenship are now so transformed, that citizenship and the guarantee of basic economic security should be disconnected from labour market participation. This is, in essence, the position of those who call for citizenship to be recast under the rubric of a guaranteed basic income, i.e. the *unconditional* payment by the state to all citizens of an income sufficient to keep them in modest economic security. Whatever the particular merits of such a proposal (and these are fiercely debated), the argument for a basic income illustrates the difficulties in a system of social rights premised upon the duty to work without, in many cases, a corresponding right or even opportunity to enter gainful employment.

This in its turn points us towards a more general problem in the peculiar relationship between state, market and citizenship. The core of the problem is this: relationships within markets, including the labour market, are contractual and the rights and duties attendant upon it are those contractually undertaken. But the relationship between state and citizen is not contractual. The rights and duties of citizenship arise not from a contract but according to an ascribed status. It is not possible to make status as a citizen dependent upon contingent opportunities in the marketplace. It might be thought that I have rights expectations and corresponding duties in a contractual relationship which does not arise from duress (though this is itself a difficult area). But what about a situation in which I have not entered into such a contract? If I do not have rights against the state (as some on the New Right argue), what is the corresponding duty (rather than fear of force) that I have to the state, and how might I 'exit' from a relationship with whose terms I am no longer satisfied?

### Citizenship as (universal) equality, I

A powerful source of the rhetorical appeal of citizenship is that it bestows a status which is said to be equal and universal. We have already seen that there are some important reservations to be voiced about these claims of universality. Citizenship may seem to be universal to those who are admitted to it. It may in principle be available to us on the basis of our shared humanity, rather than according to some less general criterion (such as our gender or religious affiliation). But it has never, as we have seen, been a status extended to all competent adults living within the appropriate jurisdiction. Furthermore, we tend to enjoy citizenship not as members of the human race, but rather as the members of particular nation-states. When we cross a national border, we must expect to give up at least temporarily many of the rights of citizenship which we would enjoy on home soil. Nonetheless, the partially realized expectation that all competent adults should enjoy the same formal status does mark off modern citizenship from those earlier periods in which to be a citizen was to enjoy a privilege from which most people were excluded. Premodern states explicitly recognized that not all inhabitants were or could expect to become full citizens. Modern states may not actually universalize citizenship, but they certainly claim to do so. The idea of universality carries with it a presumption about equality, itself one of the most powerful devices of modern politics. If everyone was entitled to claim citizenship, then all must be equal at least in this one sense of being a citizen. In modernity, there could not be differing forms and places of representation or different systems of justice for differing classes of persons. There could not be, as formally there was under feudalism, for example, one law for the rich, another law for the poor and something else again for those in holy orders!

Even those who are the keenest advocates of citizenship as a definitive expression of political equality within modern liberal democracies might concede that, in practice, universal equality of citizenship is unevenly realized. But there have always been those who have argued that even the perfect realization of equal citizenship would fail to embody any worthwhile sense of universal human equality. Indeed, it has sometimes been argued that *formal* equality of citizenship is itself the very basis upon which a much more deep-seated and *substantive* social inequality has been built. This is the essence of the Marxist critique of citizenship rights, and it is a claim that is worth considering in some detail.

The Marxist critique of citizenship and its rights structure can actually be retraced all the way to Marx's own very earliest writings and to his confrontation with Hegel's account of the modern state as exemplified by the experience of the French Revolution (Marx 1975). The confrontation between these two great luminaries of the German intellectual tradition does not make for easy reading (even in translation!), but we can distil from Marx's commentary the essentials of a powerful critique of the idea of citizenship rights. In line with Marx's own supposition that, when it came to revolution, the French did it and the Germans thought about it,

Marx confronted Hegel in terms of the latter's idealized account of the structure of modern society. Marx held Hegel to have been broadly right in supposing that the transition from feudalism to modern society was marked by an increasingly clear institutional division between the state (or political society) and civil society. He also argued that Hegel was right in seeing this division as the expression of an underlying societal contradiction. Hegel was wrong, though, so Marx supposed, when he claimed that this contradiction was reconciled or at least effectively managed through the state's acting as the highest expression of society's universal interest. Echoing his own general claim (discussed in Chapter 3) that the existence of a state distinct from society is in itself an expression of the failure to overcome societal contradictions, Marx insisted that the division into political and civil society signalled the irreconcilable contradictions of the modern social order (what he was soon to come to call capitalism).

In describing the relationship between state and civil society, Hegel had been mistaken about which was the primary and determining sphere. In Marx's account, it is not the state which determines what goes on in society, but rather relationships in civil society (above all in a marketized economy) which determine what goes on within the state. The French Revolution, as the harbinger of modern society, certainly established a new realm of political equality – the sphere of equal citizenship. But it did so only upon the basis of a new and deeper inequality in civil society – the realm of economic needs and the market economy. Marx insisted that the more profound inequalities which divided civil society constantly undermine the largely formal equalities inscribed in the constitutional structures of the state. In this way, Marx argued, the individual in the modern world leads a double life. In the political sphere, the modern individual emerges as free and autonomous, vested with a series of shared rights of citizenship. But this shared and equal status is constantly belied by the underlying reality of profound inequality and coercion in the war of all against all that is the market economy.

Nor was this all. For Marx argued that, in fact, the emergence of a society of 'independent individuals who are related by law' – a part of the citizenship form – was actually essential to the development of a fully marketized economy. Only formally free individuals could enter into those contractual exchanges between the private owners of commodities (including labour power) which made capitalism work. In Marx's account, workers had to be free in two senses for capitalism to develop – legally free (from feudal villeinage) to enter into labour contracts and 'free' of any other means of supporting themselves. So the modern social order required a citizenry that was free to enter into legally binding contractual relationships, but not free in the existential sense of controlling their own self-development and certainly not free (in the case of propertyless workers, at least) in the sense of being able to avoid entering into an exploitative wage–labour relationship with a capitalist employer. Furthermore, the 'real' inequalities of economic well-being in civil society kept on creeping back in to determine action at the level of the state. In Marx's view, citizenship does not eliminate inequalities at the level of the state, it simply denies them any formal political status. To take Marx's own example, the modern state 'annuls' private property when it eliminates the property restriction upon voting rights. But this does not alter the fact that those who command substantial economic resources will always be much more effective in lobbying the state than those who have only their votes to trade. Thus, private property is denied formal political status, but it continues to do its work of favouring the political interests of the wealthy just the same.

Given the subsequent history of Marxism, it should be stressed that Marx was not hostile to the winning of political rights or the universalization of the franchise. If he was generally sceptical about what parliaments could actually do, he was not hostile to the struggle for conventionally conceived rights of citizenship (for a discussion, see Pierson 1986: 14–16). He was, however, keen to stress the quite partial nature of the purely political emancipation which he held that citizenship represented.

As the more mature Marx 'discovered' historical materialism, the labour theory of value and the capitalist mode of production, his attention was drawn away from a direct consideration of these issues of citizenship. He was, perhaps, more persuaded (as many second-generation orthodox Marxists were to be) that citizenship rights were little more than the legal form required for capitalism to function. But three points in the early Marxian critique are of continuing importance. First, the construction of citizenship as a possession of legally constituted rights-exercising individuals does at least correspond to the legal and contractual necessities of a marketized economy and society. There was some historical coincidence between the development of capitalism and the kinds of civil and political rights identified with citizenship. Second, equality is a powerful ideological device, and Marx was certainly on to something when he stressed that the formal equality of citizenship was in marked contrast to a much greater *substantive* inequality in wealth and life chances. To describe the citizens of liberal democracies as 'free and equal' requires us to put a very particular slant on these words. Marx also directs our attention to the somewhat puzzling fact that citizenship as a right of participation tends to be confined to a limited range of deliberative institutions (councils, parliaments, etc.). It does not generally extend into the economy (where private property rights trump collective decision-taking rights) or even into the less public spaces of the state (the military, quangos, etc.). It is surely important to recognize that the winning of citizenship, democratization and political emancipation are quite partial achievements.

### Citizenship as (universal) equality, II: the feminist critique

An even more fundamental challenge to the claim that citizenship is a status characterized by universality and equality can be found in much recent feminist writing. In this case, it is argued that the supposed universality of citizenship has always been (or at least has always promised to become) universal equality *for men*. Liberal feminists reflecting on this experience have tended to press a political agenda which seeks to make citizenship live up in practice to what it promises in principle. They have generally endorsed the normative case for universal individual rights and freedoms, but have pressed for these freedoms to be extended to women on the same basis as they are thought to be enjoyed by men. They do not doubt that such a change may be politically difficult to accomplish, but they do believe that, to some extent, women's exclusion from full citizenship is contingent, if systematic. Upon this account, there is not too much wrong with citizenship, except that women do not have it!

Radical feminists share with these liberal critics the view that women have been effectively excluded from full citizenship, but they are much more sceptical about the general claims made for citizenship, especially as this idea is presently constituted. Here, the argument is that citizenship is *systematically* rather than contingently patriarchal and that, if citizenship is to be fully enjoyed by women, the character of citizenship itself must be changed. It is worth considering this argument in some detail.

This radical view of citizenship is built upon (at least) two insights which have become commonplaces of virtually all contemporary feminist political thought. First, there is the insistence that almost all *malestream* political thought has misconstructed the division in society between the public sphere (formal, law-governed, politicized and male) and the private sphere (informal, affective, non-political and feminized). Politics and citizenship have been seen overwhelmingly to belong in a public domain which has been populated predominantly by men. Thus, citizenship may be (at least in aspiration) a quality which is enjoyed universally and equally by all those who are active in the public sphere, but those eligible for this status have tended quite disproportionately to be men. Indeed, the individual with which classical liberal theory has concerned itself is already gendered (Pateman 1988a). The second element in the radical feminist critique has been the centrality of marriage and 'traditional' forms of the family in articulating relations between men and women. In Vogel's account, 'the peculiar constraints upon women's citizenship have derived, above all, from the fact that as a consequence of marriage they lost the basic entitlements to citizen status' (Vogel 1991: 62). In practice, these two criticisms are entwined. For the ways in which women have been defined out of the public sphere have a great deal to do with the ways in which gendered relationships within the family have been conceived. Thus, 'the public character of civil society/state is constructed and gains its meaning through what it excludes – the private association of the family' (Pateman 1988b: 236).

These two elements were certainly combined in what has been the most traditional defence of the exclusion of women from citizenship – i.e. the argument that women were 'virtually' represented by their husbands or fathers. Since women had an especial responsibility for the home and the raising of children, they had fewer interests in the public sphere and could confidently leave the promotion of their more limited concerns in this area to their male protectors. In the republican tradition, as Vogel (1991) observes, the right to citizenship was often seen to derive from the capacity militarily to defend the state. Since it was frequently assumed that this was a competence which belonged, as it were, *biologically* to men, it followed that it was to them alone that citizenship might apply. The legal exclusion of women from active military service seemed like a self-fulfilling vindication of this 'natural' supposition. Even where motherhood was seen as a surrogate form of 'service to the state' which might merit the extension of citizenship to women, this was citizenship under a differing rubric and upon a particular account of what it was that women did that was of value to the community.

Under more contemporary forms of social citizenship, so Pateman argues, a similar logic of exclusion obtains. She argues that, in societies based on market economies, 'paid employment has become the key to citizenship' (Pateman 1988b: 237). Access to the more generous system of contributory social rights, as well as self-esteem, seem to turn upon one's record in employment. But the work that counts towards citizenship is paid work in the public sphere of the formal economy. Under the Beveridgean welfare state in the UK, for example, women were quite explicitly given a secondary status and welfare rights which derived from their presumed marriage to a male breadwinner. Beveridge (1942: 53) recognized that 'housewives as mothers have vital work to do' – but it would largely be as unpaid carers and mothers in the home. Even in an economy which looks less and less the way that Beveridge imagined it to be, women's practical experience of welfare citizenship (because of differing patterns of employment, lower lifetime earnings, greater responsibility for dependants and so on) is different from that of men (Pierson 1998; Lister 1993). According to Pateman, 'if an individual can gain recognition from other citizens as an equally worthy citizen only through participation in the capitalist market, if self-respect and respect as a citizen are "achieved" in the public world of the employment society, then *women still lack the means to be recognised as worthy citizens*' (Pateman 1988b: 246–7; emphasis added).

According to Vogel, we may draw the following conclusions:

> First, the main traditions of European political thought (if we exempt feminist projects) do not offer any genuinely universal conceptions of citizenship. Second, women are not simply omitted or forgotten about. Even the most egalitarian formulations of political rights are predicated upon the gender division between citizens and non-citizens. Third, this means that the barriers against gender equality have been substantive rather than formal, qualitative rather than quantitative. . . . Fourth, not the only but the main constraint upon women's citizenship had been the institution of marriage and the mechanism of ownership and rule associated with it. Finally, it is not feminism that has carried politics into the private sphere of personal relations . . . marriage has always been subjected to political imperatives and the legal enforcement of inequality.
>
> (Vogel 1991: 78)

This commentary poses the issue of citizenship and universality in a quite new way. The problem is not (as the advocates of enhanced citizenship have so frequently supposed) ensuring that existing rights of citizenship are universally acquired. For citizenship, so it is argued, is not universal in the way that its keenest advocates have supposed. Citizenship is already constituted in a gender-specific way. Women can only enjoy 'full citizenship', as this is presently conceived, upon men's terms. In Pateman's view, 'women cannot be full citizens in the present meaning of the term; at best, citizenship can be extended to women only as lesser men' (1988b: 252–3). Does this mean that there must somehow be a 'women's citizenship' alongside (and one suspects in danger of being permanently a little beneath) 'men's citizenship', or should it be possible to recast a truly 'universal' citizenship that is 'non-gendered'? Certainly, a number of feminist writers have been sceptical about whether a *universal* citizenship (or indeed any 'universal' political status) is really what we need. They have been a party to the view that, in circumstances where universalism will in practice *always* be exclusionary in its effects, we are better off looking to ways of securing and protecting difference.

It is not easy to see how this dilemma might be resolved. But it is an argument that should make us think again about the apparently unproblematic aspiration to universality and generality of citizenship. As Hall and Held suppose, 'difference' really is 'the joker in the citizenship pack' (Hall and Held 1989: 177). Citizenship defines a status that is abstracted from the particularities of those individuals who enjoy it. But what if the citizenship so defined is itself particularistic in certain ways? And do we act justly if, in abstracting from the particular qualities of individuals with systematically differing experiences and opportunities, we treat them all as 'the same'? It should be clear that the same sorts of issues are raised by the Marxian critique of citizenship. They must, at the very least, cause us to pause before endorsing citizenship as a substantive embodiment of universality and equality.

### Citizenship as active participation

This brings us finally to what some have always regarded as the first virtue of citizenship – that is, the commitment to active participation in the community of the state. This can be seen above all in the reinvigoration of a *civic republican* approach to citizenship, which invokes an ancient (Greek and Roman) tradition of active participation in political life as a desirable model under modern circumstances. Its advocates suggest that individuals in modern states have become increasingly consumed by their own private interests and their private well-being. They have abandoned that concern with the general good of the whole community which should be the first consideration of the good citizen. They have come to take a purely instrumental view of both the political process and their own citizenship. In this context, Kymlicka and Norman (1994: 353) draw a useful distinction between two core conceptions of citizenship: '*citizenship-as-legal-status*, that is, as full membership in a particular political community and *citizenship-as-desirable-activity*, where the extent and quality of one's citizenship is a function of one's participation in that community.' It is with this second, more active and more public-spirited conception of citizenship that we are principally concerned in this section.

A number of commentators (Stewart 1995; Oldfield 1990; Kymlicka and Norman 1994) have drawn attention to the recent renewal of interest among mainstream party politicians in this idea of a more active citizenry. Having fallen into abeyance for half a century or more, invocations of active citizenship now pepper the more grandiose speeches of contemporary politicians on both right and left. In the UK, it has even found its way into the schools' National Curriculum! Some have seen this renewed interest in active participation as a response to a perceived collapse of traditional forms of civic activism. Some argue that it is a response to a 'moral panic' about growing *incivility* – ranging from a decline in public manners to an escalation of violent crime. Others see it as an attempt to address growing public disenchantment with the day-to-day business of political life. The more cynical have seen it as a way of legitimating a shift in the burden of social provision from an overstretched state to the more or less freely provided services of ordinary citizens. Whatever occasioned this renewed interest, we can certainly find politicians on both right and left arguing that the relationship between the rights and the *duties* of citizenship has become skewed to the almost wholesale neglect of the latter.

Perhaps, as ordinary subjects, we are entitled to feel a little sceptical about our rulers' new-found concern with the quality of our citizenship. Advocating 'good citizenship' and a greater sensitivity to the needs of the 'community' sounds states-manlike, responsible and unobjectionable. So long as it only involves exhorting people to volunteer to do more good, it is uncontroversial if rather vacuous – and it does not cost anything! But, in its most rigorous and thoroughgoing form, the civic republican ideal of active citizenship is actually profoundly controversial. In this uncompromising form, it confronts some of the most deep-seated assumptions of virtually all modern Western political thought.

First, civic republicans give a quite unmodern priority to the political activity of the citizen and to the importance of *public* rather than *private* life. Modern political theory and practice has tended to give precedence to the private wants and needs of individuals. Liberal-democratic politics has characteristically been seen as the (sometimes collective) means of realizing individuals' private aspirations or prevent-ing governments from interfering in them. By contrast, civic republicans insist (in the manner of the ancients) that participation in public, political life is the highest form of human good. Civil republicans regret the ways in which modern political life has been invaded by social and economic issues and interests to the neglect of the principal political virtue of reasoning our way to realizing the greatest public good. In Barber's view, we should be seeking to create 'a political community capable of transforming dependent, private individuals into free citizens and partial and private interests into public good' (Barber 1984: 132). Participation in public decision-making should be the central life activity.

Second, for many civic republicans, our nature as citizens places upon us quite onerous duties. These duties to the community are not discretionary. Thus, citizen-ship is not simply permissive. It does not simply afford us the opportunity to be involved *if we so wish*. It obliges us to conduct ourselves as active citizens. In Oldfield's account,

> individuals have no sovereign or overriding moral priority. Claims may legitimately be made on their time, their resources, and sometimes even on their lives, for it is only if the community is sustained in being that the practice of citizenship is ensured continuity in time, and the identity of individuals as citizens is preserved.

Engaging in the practice of citizenship is not a 'lifestyle' choice: 'the term "private citizen" is . . . an oxymoron' (Oldfield 1990: 181).

Third, the purpose of political education is not to generate, at maturity, a morally free agent capable of choosing his or her own destiny. Rather, the individual must be educated into the traditions of his or her own particular political community:

Civic republicanism holds out the possibility of a level of moral agency, a form of human consciousness, being, and living, that is simply not catered for in liberal individualism. It is also a constant theme in civic republicanism that human beings will not choose this level of agency and form of consciousness unless they are educated into it, but that they would choose it if they could know, which they never can, everything in advance.

(Oldfield 1990: 185)

Upon this view, the political community does not exist to service the needs of individuals. The community is prior to the individuals within it. The community has claims to make which are prior to the individual rights of its citizens, and the citizen–community relationship and the obligations of citizenship are not contractual. 'Citizenship is not a status, but a practice or an activity, which is underpinned by an attitude of mind' (Oldfield 1990: 181).

Of course, this is not the only way of conceiving of a more active citizenship. Indeed, it is a peculiarly severe way of recasting this relationship. There is really no reason to think that joining the local school board or lobbying for a local community swimming pool means abandoning our identities in some greater public purpose! Active citizenship is clearly a spectrum, at the near end of which things would look not very different from the way they are now (give or take the odd Neighbourhood Watch). Nonetheless, raising the possibility of greater civic involvement in this rather 'extreme' form does highlight some more general difficulties in the field of active citizenship. One is the issue of duties. We have seen that citizenship does already entail significant duties (including military service, the payment of taxation, abiding by locally generated laws), but many of these duties are rather passive. We do not, for example, have to go very far out of our way to pay taxes! We have also seen how, in the post-war period, *social* citizenship came to be perceived preponderantly in terms of *entitlements*, whose corresponding duties were much more diffuse. A greater civic activism means taking duties much more seriously. For some, perhaps above all for party politicians, these expanded duties are seen as *morally desirable* and, to this extent, for specific individuals, discretionary. It would be *good* to be more active and helpful, but there can be no legal requirement to be so. Kymlicka and Norman (1994: 353) pose this issue succinctly:

We should expect a theory of the good citizen to be relatively independent of the legal question of what it is to be a citizen, just as the theory of the good person is distinct from the metaphysical (or legal) question of what it is to be a person.

At the limits, however, this is a stipulation which some versions of civic republicanism do not accept. To some extent, the *authentic* citizen is the *good* citizen, and fulfilment of an extended set of duties of citizenship is not discretionary. Civic republicanism poses the question of compulsory duties in a way which is quite uncomfortable for contemporary political sensibilities. This leads us to a second major issue. For if we even begin to accept this much stronger account of our civic duties, we have to reconsider the terms of political association which would bind the citizen to fulfilling these greater obligations. No commitment to this much stronger account of citizens' duties could be possible without a reconsideration of the terms and conditions of our membership of the political community. The civic republican position on active citizenship raises in a peculiarly direct and stark way questions about both our obligation to the state (why should I have these obligations to this political community?) and about existing democratic practices (since it is clear that our more active citizenship could not be satisfied under the existing and vastly impoverished institutional arrangements of liberal representative democracy). Thus, a more active citizenship might bring not only unwelcome obligations but also an undermining of the entire apparatus of representative democracy under which we now operate.

## Conclusion

Citizenship has long been a key term for those who want to describe the state as a political community or as a solution to the problem of political association. Those who can speak state and democracy in the same breath often present citizenship as the linking term that makes this a legitimate connection. Yet for all its positive associations – citizenship is almost universally regarded as a 'good thing' – it proves upon close examination to be surrounded with problems. These stretch from the question of who is a citizen and what is an appropriate political community, through the balancing of citizens' rights and duties, to the question of what 'universality' really means. It is right to see citizenship as a central term in 'the state debate'. The many problems that it generates are perhaps less a reflection of inadequacies in existing conceptions of citizenship than an indication of more deep-seated problems in existing conceptions of the state and its relation to its constituting and legitimating base. One of the clearest manifestations of this right is the insufficiency of trans-national conceptions of citizenship. In a world of increasing transnational activity and in which nation-states decreasingly constitute a definable 'community of fate', how can citizenship be reconstituted? Indeed, how generally should we understand the character of the state and its citizens in an increasingly global social and political order? It is to questions of the supra-national political order that I turn in the next chapter.

## Further reading

Brubaker, R. (1992) *Citizenship and Nationhood in France and Germany*. Cambridge, MA: Harvard University Press.

Heater, D. (1990) *Citizenship: The Civic Ideal in World History, Politics and Education*. London: Longman.

Kymlicka, W. and Norman, W. (1994) 'Return of the citizen: a survey of recent work on citizenship theory', *Ethics* 104, 352–81.

Oldfield, A. (1990) 'Citizenship: an unnatural practice?', *Political Quarterly* 61, 177–87.

Pateman, C. (1988) *The Sexual Contract*. Cambridge: Polity.

Vogel, U. and Mann, M. (eds) (1991) *The Frontiers of Citizenship*. London: Macmillan.

# 6    States and the international order

Throughout this book, I have insisted upon studying not *the* state in majestic isolation, but states varyingly placed in an international order of unequal and competing states. In this context, we should not suppose that, at first, states developed endogenously and that it was only at some later point in their development (when they started 'bumping into each other') that inter-state relationships developed. Rather, modern states have always been part of a wider states' system. As Giddens insists,

> the sovereignty of the modern state from its beginnings depends upon a reflexively monitored set of relations between states . . . 'International relations' are not connections set up between pre-established states, which could maintain their sovereign power without them: they are the basis upon which the nation-state exists at all.
>
> (Giddens 1985: 263–4)

As was pointed out in earlier chapters, frontiers may mark the edge of the wilderness, but borders always abut another (sovereign) jurisdiction and, at least since the Peace of Westphalia (in 1648), leading states' actors have recognized the necessity of managing their mutual affairs in some more or less systematic way.

For some commentators, it has always been these *external* relationships *between* states that constitute the most important object of the political life of modern states. In Chapter 2, we saw that the key concept of sovereignty has both an internal and an external aspect. Modern political theorists have certainly devoted the greater part of their attention to the *internal* aspects of sovereignty, to questions of the state's claim legitimately to exercise exclusive control over the means of violence and the terms of political association through which citizens come to surrender or share their powers with the state. But historians and others more immediately concerned with the practicalities of states' conduct have often focused rather more upon the *external* aspect of state sovereignty. Characteristically, they have been concerned with the behaviour of a number of nation-states competing in a context where they recognize no higher or overarching international authority. Naturally enough, those who focus upon this conflicting relationship between competing sovereign states have tended to stress the centrality of warfare and 'armed peace'. In an 'anarchic' world order, armed might is seen as the most basic arbiter of inter-state relations. In the twentieth century, most extensively in the period since 1945, this perspective on the political process has given rise to its own sub-discipline – *international relations* (IR). At its simplest (and narrowest), IR can be understood as the study of 'the official relationships and diplomatic interactions between national governments, including relations between governments and intergovernmental organizations'. It is 'the domain of foreign and defence policy and the preserve of foreign ministries and diplomats' (McGrew 1992a: 5). In recent years, the field of IR, the objects of its attention and the methods through which these are studied, has become much more diverse (as we shall see in this chapter). But it is still probably fair to see it as concerned, above all, with the ways in which sovereign states interact.

While the (sub-)discipline is new, its concerns, clearly, are not. The interplay of war and peace is a ubiquitous aspect of the human condition. The literature of IR characteristically retraces the systematic intellectual concern with these questions to the Greek soldier–writer Thucydides (471–400 BC) and his *History of the Peloponnesian War* (Thucydides 1982). Thucydides' history of the war between Athens and Sparta in the fifth century BC is intended not just to give an account of the military struggle, but also to *explain* why war broke out and to draw general lessons about the circumstances that may give rise to inter-state conflict. Whatever the proximate causes of the conflict, Thucydides insists that 'what made war inevitable was the growth of Athenian power and the fear which this caused in Sparta.' And whatever morality might seem to require, in inter-state struggle, so Thucydides memorably insisted, 'the strong do what they have the power to do and the weak accept what they have to accept' (Thucydides 1982: 49, 402).

Moving forward two millennia, anticipations of the 'timeless' perspective that has come to typify IR can be found in the work of early modern political theorists – e.g. in Machiavelli and Hobbes. Though much misunderstood, Machiavelli's primer for prospective rulers, *The Prince*, sets out the preservation of the state as the ultimate political goal. To achieve this end, the prince 'should have no other object or thought, nor acquire skill in anything, except war, its organization, and its discipline': 'The art of war is all that is expected of a ruler. . . . The first way to lose your state is to neglect the art of war; the first way to win a state is to be skilled in the art of war' (Machiavelli 1961: 46).

Nor, in the pursuit of his state-making ambitions, should the prince feel bound by the common conventions of personal morality. He should be

> so prudent that he knows how to escape the evil reputation attached to those vices which could lose him his state, and how to avoid those vices which are not so dangerous if he possibly can; but, if he cannot, he need not worry so much about the latter.
>
> (Machiavelli 1961: 49)

At all times, he should be guided by the maxim that 'it is much safer to be feared than to be loved.' In general, men (and their word) are not to be trusted and, since 'men are wretched creatures who would not keep their word to you, you need not keep your word to them' (Machiavelli 1961: 52, 55).

Still more in Hobbes's *Leviathan* do we find a foreshadowing of themes that have become commonplace in the literature of IR. We have already seen (in Chapter 1) how Hobbes's political theory is informed by a profoundly pessimistic view of human nature and the human condition. The natural qualities of men [*sic*] are those of self-love, greed, vanity and deceitfulness. Their natural condition is one of comparative equality (at least so far as self-admiration and the capacity to inflict injury on others are concerned). Under these circumstances, 'without a common Power to keep them all in awe', Hobbes argues that men 'are in that condition which is called Warre; and such a warre, as is of every man, against every man.' Such a state of war, he insists, 'consisteth not in Battell onely, or the act of fighting . . ., but in the known disposition thereto, during all the time there is no assurance to the contrary' (Hobbes 1968: 185–6). Thus, for Hobbes, the core problem of social and political life is not the pursuit of warfare, but rather the maintenance of *security*. Within a particular jurisdiction, the security problem is overcome by the subjection of all citizens to an all-powerful Leviathan state. But since international society is *not* subject to such an overweening sovereign, it remains subject to all the threats and vices that arise from the natural human condition. Thus:

> In all times, Kings, and Persons of Soveraigne authority, because of their Independency, are in continuall jealousies, and in the state and posture of Gladiators; having their weapons pointing, and their eyes fixed on one another; that is, their Forts, Garrisons, and Guns upon the Frontiers of their Kingdomes; and continuall Spyes upon their neighbours; which is a posture of War.

Hobbes also furnishes an elementary statement (in terms of individual men rather than individual states) of that 'security dilemma' which leads even the most peace-loving of nations to arm themselves:

> There is no way for any man to secure himselfe, so reasonable, as Anticipation; that is by force, or wiles, to master the persons of all men he can, so long, till he see no other power great enough to endanger him. . . . Also because there be some, that taking pleasure in contemplating their own power in the acts of conquest, which they pursue farther than their security requires; if others, that otherwise would be glad to be at ease within modest bounds, should not by invasion increase their power, they would not be able, long time, by standing only on their own defence, to subsist.

Finally, Hobbes insists that, in the war of all against all, 'nothing can be Unjust': 'The notions of Right and Wrong, Justice and Injustice have there no place. Where there is no common Power, there is no Law; where no Law, no Injustice. Force, and Fraud, are in warre the two Cardinall vertues' (Hobbes 1968: 183–8).

## Idealism . . .

These classical themes – of an unchanging and untrustworthy human nature, of anarchy in the international order, of 'cold war' as a semi-permanent state, of amorality in international affairs, of the security dilemma for non-bellicose states – have dominated the agenda of IR as a distinct discipline. In its earliest development, between the two world wars, although these were the characteristic problems addressed, the solutions canvassed tended to be more optimistic. In this early period, the predominant view was shaped by the awful and seemingly pointless experience of the First World War. There was a strong presumption that the war had shown that military force could no longer achieve its objectives and that, indeed, the descent into war was in some sense an 'accident' in which all the belligerent powers had found themselves drawn into a contest which none of them really intended. This earliest writing in IR disclosed a powerful normative sense that the discipline and its policy offshoots should be about the generation of a more rational and less violent way of managing inter-state affairs. The belief that progress in this direction was possible led to this approach being described retrospectively (and sometimes rather patronizingly) as 'idealism'. Its mind-set is neatly captured by Hedley Bull:

> The distinctive character of these writers was their belief in progress: the belief, in particular, that the system of international relations that had given rise to the First World War was capable of being transformed into a fundamentally more peaceful and just world order; that under the impact of the awakening of democracy, the growth of the 'international mind', the development of the League of Nations, the good works of men of peace or the enlightenment spread by their own teachings, it was in fact being transformed; and that their responsibility as students of international relations was to assist this march of progress to overcome the ignorance, the prejudices, the ill-will, and the sinister interests that stood in its way.
>
> (Bull 1972: 34)

### . . . and realism

The experience of the 1930s – above all, the rise of fascism and the descent into a second world war – dealt a severe blow to this liberal-minded progressivism and made space for what was to become the dominant paradigm in IR: *realism* and its second-generation progeny, *neo-realism*. In its earliest manifestations (Carr 1939; Morgenthau 1978), the realist approach was set out in self-conscious contrast to idealism. Yet it has, no less than its forerunner, a strongly normative core. It furnishes, as Halliday observes (1987: 219), a conception of the state which 'is not merely an analytic abstraction, but also one replete with legal and value assumptions (i.e. that states are equal, that they control their territory, that they represent their peoples).' At the heart of the realist approach is the insistence that we study the political world 'as it actually is and as it ought to be in view of its intrinsic nature, rather than as people would like to see it' (Morgenthau 1978: 15). For realists, both human nature and the character of international politics to which this gives rise are, in their essentials, timeless and unchanging. The nature of the problems that our political leaders now face is little different in underlying substance (though much altered in its form) from that which confronted the leaders of Sparta and ancient Athens. Human nature is more or less as Machiavelli and Hobbes described it. The problem of national security and the predisposition to war are little changed from the world so graphically described by Thucydides. The possibility of peaceable change and the limits of state morality are set by these underlying constraints. In so far as IR is a policy science, its recommendations are said to be informed by a soberly 'realistic' appraisal of the world as it is and not by 'utopian' aspirations about what it should become. *Neo-realism* is the label frequently attached to that related approach (exemplified by Waltz 1979) which 'combines a micro-economic approach to the international system (individualism) with the Classical Realist emphasis on power and interest (materialism)' (Wendt 1999: 2).

As subsequent critics have argued, much of what is 'realistic' about 'realism' is in the eye of the beholder (or propagator), and the implicit claim that realism is 'scientific' and non-ideological is unsustainable. This has not prevented it from having a profound effect upon the ways in which relations between states have been understood, not just in the academy but also in a much wider world (in 'official' political life, in the media and in public opinion). Certainly, recent years have seen a growing challenge to the intellectual hegemony of realist approaches, and the (sub-)discipline of IR is now methodologically and epistemologically quite diverse. Of especial importance in this growing diversity has been the impact of varying forms of *social contructivism*. In the words of one of its key protagonists, social constructivism involves the claims '(1) that the structures of human association are determined primarily by shared values rather than materialist forces, and (2) that the identities and interests of purposive actors are constructed by these shared ideas rather than given by nature' (Wendt 1999: 1). In the rest of this chapter, I organize discussion of the IR of states (and other actors) around the claims of realism ('classical' and 'neo-') and the counter-claims of these critics.

## The essentials of realism

The underlying principles of realism are disarmingly straightforward. According to Keohane, 'the three most fundamental Realist assumptions' are these:

> that the most important actors in world politics are territorially organized entities (city-states or modern states); that state behaviour can be explained rationally; and that states seek power and calculate their interests in terms of power, relative to the nature of the international system that they face.
>
> (Keohane 1989: 38–9)

To these assumptions, Joseph Grieco adds the following:

> For realists, international anarchy fosters competition and conflict among states and inhibits their willingness to cooperate even when they share common interests. [It] argues that international institutions are unable to mitigate anarchy's constraining effects on inter-state cooperation. [It] presents a

pessimistic analysis of the prospects for international cooperation and of the capabilities of international institutions.

(Grieco 1988: 485)

We can develop these characteristic claims of realism in terms of the eight key propositions which follow.

### States are the major actors in world affairs

There is a simple but extremely deep-seated presumption that underlies the realist position – i.e. that the key strategic actors in world politics are *nation-states*. In Bull's account (1977: 8),

> the starting point of international relations is the existence of *states*, or independent political communities, each of which possesses a government and asserts sovereignty in relation to a particular portion of the earth's surface and a particular segment of the human population.

Similarly, in Robert Gilpin's opinion (1981: 18), 'the state is the principal actor in that the nature of the state and the pattern of relations among states are the most important determinants of the character of international relations at any given moment.' Non-state economic actors and supra-state international organizations are allowed some explanatory weight in realist explanations, but preponderantly it is states that are the motive force of international politics.

### States behave as unitary actors

Realists work under the assumption that states are essentially *unitary* actors. Although the making of external policy may involve differences of interest and opinion within individual nation-states, the presumption is that, once a policy is decided upon, it will be prosecuted uniformly and consistently by the state's external representatives. It is as if, in their external relations, all members of the state agree to be bound by a principle of *collective responsibility*. It is this presumption which justifies the realist convention (itself clearly a fiction) of speaking of nation-states – America, Russia, Germany, the UK and so on – *as if* they were unitary actors. It also underpins the further convention of reporting the discussions and decisions of diplomats and political leaders as if they were the embodiment of the nations they represent and attributing intentionality to the states themselves ('Britain is angry . . .', 'the United States promised . . .', and so on).

### States act rationally

It is further assumed that these state actors will behave *rationally*. Of course, the goals that states pursue may not themselves be reasonable (though there is a further presumption in much of the realist literature that states will actually tend to be utility-maximizers). But once the state's goals are established, there is a powerful assumption that the state will act rationally in seeking to realize them. Thus, states may be expected to consider the full range of feasible means of achieving their ambitions, assessing these within the constraints of their own capabilities and the limits imposed by the external environment. States are said to be 'sensitive to costs', recognizing that 'the international environment severely penalizes states if they fail to protect their vital interests or if they pursue objectives beyond their means' (Grieco 1988: 488). Of course, states can make mistakes both about where their 'real' interests lie and about their 'real' capabilities. They are especially prone to mistake the capabilities and strategic intentions of *other* state actors. The realists' presumption, however, is that states will generally behave as unitary actors and will pursue their objectives rationally (including a willingness to calculate costs and benefits). This is an extremely important presumption, for it underpins the realist belief that we can 'reconstruct' the conduct of state actors in terms of the criteria of strategic evaluation which any rational actor would apply. It also allows realists to model the likely *future* behaviour of political actors facing a given set of strategic choices and limitations.

### International anarchy is the principal force shaping the motives and actions of states

It is absolutely central to the realist position that the political context within which sovereign states interact is *anarchic*. Recall that the first principle of the Westphalian model (see above, p. 37) is this: that 'the world consists of . . . sovereign states which recognize no superior authority.' The context in which all international political actors must operate is one in which there is no higher authority and no overarching system of enforceable law to which inter-state disputes can be referred.

Ultimately, conflicts between states are resolved by force (either exercised or threatened). According to Waltz:

> Each state pursues its own interests, however defined, in ways it judges best. Force is a means of achieving the external ends of states because there exists no consistent, reliable process of reconciling the conflicts of interest that inevitably arise among similar units in a condition of anarchy.
>
> (Waltz 1959: 238)

It is just as important to see, however, that this does not commit realists to the view that anarchy must (as in its uncritical popular usage) mean disorder and chaos. The realists' usage is much closer to the Greek original *an-archos*, meaning the absence of rule, and they have been very much concerned with explaining the ways in which an anarchic world is nonetheless 'ordered'. Of course, relations between states may descend into unordered chaos, but this is not the *normal* state of affairs in IR. In more normal times, states have bilateral and multilateral relationships. They cooperate in certain collective endeavours, They maintain diplomatic relationships, enter into alliances and sponsor international trading links. The important proviso in the realist account is that states do all these things under the particular constraints and conditions that arise from the absence of any overarching international political authority. In the end, cooperation is always chronically *provisional*, because it lacks a convincing agency of enforcement. This makes international political life *qualitatively* different from the management of internal political affairs. It also encourages some realists to see the internal and external political business of the state as almost wholly *separate*.

### States in anarchy are preoccupied with issues of power and security

It is a commonplace of the realist literature that states struggle to exercise power. Indeed, realism has sometimes been redescribed as the 'power-politics' approach. In Morgenthau's words: 'International politics, like all politics, is a struggle for power. Whatever the ultimate aims of international politics, power is always the immediate aim.' At its simplest, international politics could be understood as 'interest defined in terms of power', and this, so Morgenthau argues, is 'an objective category which is universally valid' (Morgenthau 1978: 27, 5, 8, respectively).

Given the anarchic nature of the world system and the preponderance of 'power politics', states (as unitary actors) are seen to be chronically concerned with the protection of their own interests, and this means, above all, ensuring the integrity of their physical territory. Thus, realists conventionally perceive *national security* to be the first and preponderant interest of all states. This helps to explain the priority they give to military and strategic issues. In an anarchic world, states must look to their own military power to be able to protect their territory against the threat of invasion. Of course, states will also seek to deflect this threat through a range of political devices, including diplomacy and the attempt to forge reliable alliances. This helps to explain why so much attention has been devoted in realist writing to attempts to establish and maintain the international *balance of power* (in such a way that the penalties of invasion should always deter an aggressor from pursuing territorial aggrandizement). Morgenthau wrote of the balance of power as 'a perennial element of all pluralistic societies' (1978: 10). These characteristic concerns have persuaded some realist writers to draw a contrast between the 'high politics' of national security, military and diplomatic policy and the 'low politics' of international economic and social affairs, an inferior status which characteristically they share with the entirety of the state's domestic political activity!

### Morality is a radically qualified principle in international politics

A concern with the politics of effective power does not mean that morality is entirely absent from the international scene. Founding figures of realism, such as Carr and Morgenthau, insisted that there was a place for moral judgement in international political life and that what they rejected was the utopian optimism of those who felt that morality was more or less *exhaustive* of what should count as IR. But they also argued that it is as well to recognize that, in many circumstances, political leaders have acted without the least concern for the general moral consequences of their actions. Even in the most propitious of circumstances, the guardians of the state must allow their moral ambitions to be tempered by prudential considerations. Indeed, in Morgenthau's account, statespersons should *not* be moral absolutists: 'prudence – the weighing of the consequences of alternative political actions – [is] the supreme virtue in politics. Ethics in the abstract judges action by its conformity with the moral law; political ethics judges action by its political consequences' (Morgenthau 1978: 11). Both recognizing this and saying it is seen to be a part of what makes this position 'realist'.

### States are predisposed towards conflict and competition, and often fail to cooperate, even in the face of common interests

We have already seen that the idea of anarchy in the international order does not mean that states are engaged in permanent armed conflict. Yet, if states are not forever striking the 'posture of gladiators', they are nonetheless essentially rivalrous and competitive. As Hobbes observed, even the most peace-loving of states are drawn into the competitive military struggle, if only to protect themselves from those more belligerent states whose territorial ambitions know no bounds. Indeed, states tend to mimic the dispositions of Hobbes's natural men. They are not incapable of an occasional act of kindness, but for the most part we should expect the worst of them. Certainly, it would be ruinous not to prepare oneself in the expectation that they will behave badly. It is this that leads us towards the conditions for the non-cooperation of states, *even* in the face of their mutual interests. Within sovereign states, we have a structure of obligation and compliance which enables us to realize collective interests shared with other citizens, without the fear that they will abuse our willingness to cooperate. Thus, the state can provide certain collective public goods funded from a system of compulsory taxation of the general citizenry. Indeed, the capacity to organize such provision, and to oblige all citizens to contribute, is one of the principal justifications for having a state in the first place. But our anarchic world order lacks an over-riding sovereign authority which can bind individual states to a regime of cooperation. Under these circumstances, states lack the institutional structures for the delivery of collective goods, because of the expectation that some states would not be bound by collective decisions or would seek to 'free ride' on the contributions made by others. Thus, the absence of an overarching world authority means that states are unable and unwilling to cooperate even where such cooperation would be to every state's individual advantage. This logic may not just rule out the promotion of public goods, but it may actively foster public 'bads' – e.g. encouraging the escalation of military preparedness associated with an international arms race or a careless attitude to the despoliation of the global environment.

In the literature of realism (and beyond) these sorts of paradoxes are often developed in terms of *game theory*. In essence, game theory involves simulating real-world decision-making by generating model scenarios in which actors have to choose (rationally) from a limited range of options. By establishing what choice a rational actor would make under a set of clearly specified conditions and constraints, it is argued that we can model the sorts of choices that real actors (including states) would be most likely to make faced with a similar situation. Perhaps the best known and most frequently cited of these political decision-making 'games' is the Prisoner's Dilemma.

A typical scenario for the Prisoner's Dilemma is one in which two individuals, let us call them David and Victoria, are apprehended late at night outside a bank with a bag of safe-breaking tools. They are taken to a police station, placed in separate cells and each invited to make a full confession of their intended crime. In return for a confession which implicates the other, David and Victoria will receive a state pardon while their accomplice can expect a five-year sentence. If they both remain silent, both will be charged with possessing safe-breaking tools and face a one-year period of imprisonment. If both confess at the same time, both receive a three-year sentence for possessing the tools with the intention to rob a bank. David and Victoria have to decide how to respond to the bargain offered by the police, without knowing how the other is going to behave. Under the rational choice assumption that both David and Victoria are seeking to minimize their risks, both will confess. At worst, if they confess, they risk a three-year sentence. At best (if the other stays silent) they could go free. Choosing to remain silent would mean at best a one-year sentence and at worst (if the other confessed and received a pardon) a full five-year stretch. Thus, both confess and both receive a three-year sentence. Had they been able to trust each other, both could have remained silent and reduced their sentences to one year each. The moral question – whether they should tell the truth about what they did – is not considered to be relevant. The range of choices and consequences facing both parties to the Prisoner's Dilemma is represented in Figure 6.1.

The Prisoner's Dilemma (and other similar simulations) has been used to help to explain a wide variety of seemingly paradoxical political choices. In particular, it is taken to show that, where two or more participants are involved, rational actors

|  | VICTORIA'S CHOICES | |
|---|---|---|
| DAVID'S CHOICES | Stay silent | Confess |
| Stay silent | One, 1 | None, 5 |
| Confess | Five, 0 | Three, 3 |

*Figure 6.1* The Prisoner's Dilemma.

Source: after Dunleavy and O'Leary (1987: 79–80).

Note: a simple matrix showing the range of choices available to David and Victoria and their consequences. Outcomes (indicating length of prison sentence) are reported in words for Victoria and as numerals for David.

seeking to maximize utility will often generate collective outcomes which are sub-optimal because of the conditions under which choices must be made. Since no one state can be sure that others will not defect from any bargain that it strikes, there is a rational incentive not to enter into non-enforceable cooperative arrangements, even if cooperation could secure a greater gain for all those involved. Similar modelling is taken to show that resources which are collectively owned or 'held in common' will always be overexploited, because there is no incentive to husband resources which others may freely and rapaciously exploit. Game theory is also widely used in simulating the logic of military deterrence.

### *International organizations have a marginal effect upon these prospects for inter-state cooperation*

We have already reported that the realist view of international relations is 'state-centric' (Keohane 1989: 39–40). Although there is some recognition of the increasing role of international organizations of varying kinds (the United Nations, the World Bank, the European Union, etc.), the realists' insistence is that states' interests remain paramount and that often these new institutional orders constitute a new context in which fairly conventionally defined national interests may be pursued. Thus, rather than the United Nations being a new forum for world government, it is seen as another context in which the most powerful nation-states (above all, the USA) pursue their own national interests. Similarly, it has been suggested that the institutions of the European Union are not primarily about establishing a new and continental level of transnational government, but rather about providing an institutional framework within which individual states can continue to promote their national interests (Milward 1992). Whatever concessions realists are willing to make to the growth of transnational organizations, at the core remains their insistence that by far the most important international political actors are nation-states. The existence of supra-national organizations has a quite limited impact upon the ability of states to cooperate, especially where such cooperation would require the surrender of sovereign state authority to some other agency. Certainly, realists resist the suggestion that any of these transnational institutions is coming to constitute some sort of 'proto-state' with the capacity to overcome the collective choice problems of individual states by acting as an authoritative arbiter of national interests.

### The critics of realism

Although it has long been the dominant paradigm in IR, the claims of 'realists' have never gone unchallenged. Throughout the post-war period there have been several successive waves of criticism which have taken issue with just about all of the more important claims in the realist account of the state. Indeed, in the contemporary introductory literature on IR, it has become customary to contrast the dominant approach of the realists with two further and critical paradigms: the liberal-pluralist and the global-structural perspectives (Viotti and Kauppi 1993; Hollis and Smith

1991). In the period since the end of the Cold War, this diversity has flourished and the field of IR studies is now awash with varying 'schools' reflecting the differing approaches to study adopted in university towns scattered across the globe. Within the broad rubric of 'social constructivism' there have emerged distinctive (if internally diverse) feminist and 'postmodernist' critiques. (For excellent surveys, see Steans 1998 and Der Derian 1998.) In practice, the lines of division between these critical approaches have become increasingly blurred (Der Derian 2000). Here I want to order what these alternative IR perspectives have to tell us about the state around a number of characteristic criticisms made of the realist orthodoxy. I do this by discussing a set of characteristic claims which contrast explicitly with assumptions identified in the realist approach.

In adopting this approach, it is important to remember that the best researchers in all schools might be expected to have a much greater sensitivity to the provisional nature of these seemingly axiomatic claims.

### States are not the only major actors in world affairs

Critics of realism begin by challenging the assumption that states are the only *key* international players. This claim takes a variety of forms.

Typically, liberal-pluralists point to the rise of *transnationalism*, i.e. to the growth of intense and frequent contacts among a range of non-state actors sustained across national borders. These contacts may range from large public organizations (such as the World Health Organization or Oxfam, or large corporations, such as Unilever or IBM) through to interpersonal contacts on the Internet or the mass movements of individual tourists. Realism has tended to stress the 'timeless' qualities of inter-state relations, but critics insist that the modern world is qualitatively different from its historical forerunners, not least in the levels of interaction among individuals and institutions (other than states) that it promotes across the world. In a long-fashionable cliché, we are all now residents (though not as yet citizens) of 'the global village'. In the wake of 'the revolution in transport and communication technologies, modern societies display an incredible permeability to trans-national forces, as evidenced in the massive flows of goods, ideas, knowledge, people, capital, services, crime, cultural tastes, values, fashions, social movements and even social problems, which cut across or fail to respect national territorial boundaries' (McGrew 1992a: 7). This changed world has seen a phenomenal growth in *trans-governmental* relationships (with the number of official international governmental organizations more than doubling since 1945) and profound changes in the character of diplomacy. Still more significantly, so far as the critics of realism are concerned, there has been a burgeoning of *transnational non-state* organizations, which operate simultaneously in a number of states with little regard for national boundaries. McGrew estimates that the number of transnational bodies has quadrupled in the period since 1958 (McGrew 1992a: 7–8). Probably the best known of these organizations are multinational corporations, or MNCs (such as Shell, Ford and Nestlé), but almost every sphere of human endeavour (from mud-wrestling to macramé) seems now to have its own international organization. These organizations frequently interact with states, but just as frequently they bypass the formal governmental apparatus to establish direct transnational arrangements among organizations and individuals under separate jurisdictions.

Of peculiar importance has been the growth of those international organizations which have a clearly political or political–economic role: the World Bank, the International Monetary Fund, the United Nations and the European Union. Many liberal-pluralists would accept that these remain institutions through which, much of the time, individual nation-states continue to pursue their own narrowly conceived national interest. Yet, they would also argue (though to very varying degrees) that these organizations exercise an influence that is independent of the will of particular national governments. There has, for example, been a lively debate about whether the moves towards a European Union have been about burying the nation-state or saving it. But if the *de facto* power of nation-states may have been strengthened by their collective activity in the European Union, it is surely unarguable that a significant part of their sovereignty has been surrendered to European-level institutions, including the European courts. (This is a debate to which we return in Chapter 7.) It has become a commonplace of commentaries on less developed countries (especially in Africa) that their domestic social and economic policy is determined more by the resource-controlling officials of the World Bank than by indigenous political forces.

Some commentators argue that the trend towards transnationalization has reached such a pace in recent years that it is now more appropriate to think of IR in terms of the logic of *globalization*. At its simplest, globalization refers to the processes through which the world has become ever more closely and intensely interconnected: 'first, it suggests that political, economic and social activity is becoming world-wide in scope. And, secondly, it suggests that there has been an intensification of levels of interaction and interconnectedness within and among states and societies' (Held 1993: 39). More and more events and institutions are seen to have a world-wide significance and, at the same time, world-wide processes seem to impinge ever more intrusively upon our local and even intimate life. Drawing upon the work of Giddens, Held and McGrew write of globalization having two interrelated dimensions: 'scope (or "stretching") and intensity (or "deepening")':

> On the one hand, the concept of globalization defines a universal process or set of processes which generate a multiplicity of linkages and interconnections which transcend the states and societies which make up the modern world system: the concept therefore has a spatial connotation. Social, political and economic activities are becoming 'stretched' across the globe such that events, decisions and activities in one part of the world can come to have immediate significance for individuals and communities in quite distant parts of the global system. On the other hand, globalization also implies an intensification in the levels of interaction, interconnectedness or interdependence between the states and societies which constitute the modern world community. Accordingly, alongside this 'stretching' goes a 'deepening' such that even though '. . . everyone has a local life, phenomenal worlds for the most part are truly global'. Thus,

globalization involves a growing interpenetration of the 'global human condition' with the particularities of place and individuality.

(Held and McGrew 1993: 262–3)

What are the consequences of globalization for the integrity of the nation-state?
More specifically, does a growth in the importance of the global necessarily presage
a weakening of the nation-state? This issue has been fiercely debated. There are
some who argue that globalization, especially the emergence of a truly global
economy, is fatal to the effective power of individual states. For example, it is widely
held that national governments can no longer manage their domestic economies in
the way that they did for some thirty years after the Second World War because *all*
economies are now open to the forces that shape the international economy. No
government, it is said, can buck the *global* market. At the same time, there are good
grounds for believing that 'the decline of the nation-state' may easily be exaggerated.
Clearly, there were global constraints upon domestic economies before 1970, and
the discretion that governments could exercise in managing their domestic
economies before (and after) that date depended very heavily upon their location
within that wider international economy. There is also evidence that in the present
period the nation-state is not so much withdrawing as redirecting its attempts at
economic intervention – e.g. using the state to create a more welcoming environment for inward investment or patrolling the labour market so as to generate more
'internationally competitive' wage levels. It is clear, as well, that globalization will
have a very different impact upon states that are differently placed in the international economic and political order. Not every state is weakened by its insertion in
a global order. It may also be that the new context is one in which individual states
will have to act in concert with other states, but while this may compromise the
state's claims to *de jure* sovereignty, it may actually augment its *de facto* powers.
Finally, we do not yet see, even in rudimentary form, the sorts of political
institutions which might correspond at the global level to the nation-state (though
for a penetrating attempt to peer forwards through the mist, see Held 1995). It is one
of the ironies of present circumstances that the epoch of globalization has witnessed
an intensification of the aspiration to national self-determination and new statehoods
(Hobsbawm 1990).

On balance, globalization has probably attenuated the power of nation-states.
Trans-governmental arrangements have become more important and *some* transnational actors have seen their power enhanced. But in a game where *nobody* calls the
shots, the more powerful states are probably still the biggest players around, a claim
that seems vindicated in the light of the experience of the Second Gulf War in 2003.
We return to this issue in Chapter 7.

### *Anarchy is constrained by forms of international cooperation*

Consideration of transnationalism and globalization leads naturally enough to a
second set of criticisms of the realist position, those that are premised upon forms of
international cooperation. We have already seen that the realist presupposition of

anarchy means rulelessness rather than unlimited and chaotic violence. Nonetheless, realists have tended to see the encounters between states in the world order as confrontations between unitary, sovereign and discrete authorities. Sometimes this is described as the 'billiard ball' view of IR in which a number of more or less self-contained and self-sufficient units crash into each other with more or less violent results (Burton 1972). Liberal-pluralists, by contrast, focus upon the several ways in which states and societies in the international system have become enmeshed in a whole network of relationships (economic, political, social and cultural) at differing levels (national, sub-national and supra-national) which tend to promote forms of stable international cooperation. The central idea here is that of *interdependence*. In its earlier formulations, this view tended to be premised upon the expectation that the imperatives of economic growth would lead towards enhanced economic cooperation and that this would, in time, lead to greater cooperation at the political level. In the 1970s, Keohane and Nye recast the idea in terms of the logic of 'complex interdependence', envisaging 'a world in which actors other than states participate directly in world politics, in which a clear hierarchy of issues [with military security at its peak] does not exist, and in which force is an ineffective instrument of policy' (Keohane and Nye 1977: 24).

As Keohane and Nye make clear, interdependence is not necessarily a *benign* relationship. They do not assume that interdependency is something from which every partner gains. Under some circumstances, 'cooperation' may be imposed by a stronger partner. This 'down side' is still more explicit in the global-structuralist literature, in which *dependency* has been a key term in expressing the dynamic and conflictual relationship through which dominant states in the world capitalist order subjugate those that are less developed. The essence of interdependency is not then equality but *enmeshment*.

### Institutional arrangements may allow for much greater international cooperation than realism supposes

In some accounts of this process, interdependency may provide the basis for an *institutionalization* of inter-state relations which further diminishes the idea of anarchy. According to Keohane:

> International politics . . . is *institutionalized*. That is, much behavior is recognized by participants as reflecting established rules, norms, and conventions. . . . Such matters as diplomatic recognition, extraterritoriality, and the construction of agendas for multilateral organizations are all governed by formal or informal understandings; correctly interpreting diplomatic notes, the expulsion of an ambassador, or the movement of military force in a limited war all require an appreciation of the conventions that relate to these activities.
>
> (Keohane 1989: 1)

There may be no law-giver in the international order but, so Keohane argues, there may be institutions embodying conventions, rules and established practices which serve to stabilize inter-state relations. Sometimes these institutional orders are identified with the idea of systematic international *regimes* – where a regime is taken to describe a set of rules and institutions through which relations between states and their representatives are managed. Regimes need not be (indeed, they may normally not be) world-wide, but for those who participate, they bring a certain amount of order, predictability and rule-guidedness to international affairs. Sometimes it is suggested that an international regime can only be securely maintained in the presence of a single leading state power or *hegemon* – able to 'police' compliance with the regime's imperatives. Here, again, the assumption is not that the hegemonic power is necessarily benign. No one doubts that the UK used its hegemonic power in the nineteenth century to promote its national economic interests (so far as was possible) at the expense of everyone else. And there is a school of global-structuralist opinion which uses Marxist accounts of hegemony (derived from the Italian theorist Gramsci) to develop a more sophisticated account of patterns of power and dependency in the contemporary global capitalist economy. But if the hegemonic power is self-interested, it is said nonetheless to perform a 'public service' by maintaining the overall stability of the system and (eventually) paying a considerable cost for discharging its leading role (as several accounts of the rise and fall of hegemonic nations suggest). Thus, it has frequently been argued that the post-war international economic regime of 'embedded liberalism' was stable only during the period of US hegemony. The faltering of US economic leadership at the end of the 1960s is said to have heralded a period of much greater international economic instability. One view of the disorders of the present global economy is that it lacks (perhaps permanently) an effective hegemonic power – though this sits strangely with the overwhelming military superiority of the USA.

There are certainly problems with these accounts of hegemonic power. But these do not detract from the more general point about the consequences of institutionalization:

> In relatively non-institutionalized systems, the physical capabilities of states are most important . . . but in relatively institutionalized international systems, states may be able to exert influence by drawing on widespread diplomatic norms, on legally institutionalized transnational financial networks, and on those international institutions known as alliances.
>
> (Keohane 1989: 9)

The fundamental point here is that the logic of interdependence, institutionalization, international regimes and hegemonic powers argues fairly persuasively against the realist view of effective anarchy in inter-state relations.

### International organizations may have a significant effect upon the prospects for inter-state cooperation

From the logic of interdependence it follows that, for some liberal-pluralists at least, international organizations may be much more effective agencies of cooperation than the realists have supposed. This argument is not generally advanced in the fashion of the early liberal idealists who believed that international institutions could promote a greater understanding of humankind's collective interests in a way which would help to promote peaceful cooperation. Rather, a number of recent commentators have used a game-theoretic methodology to explain the circumstances in which cooperation can (and cannot) be expected to arise. There is a suggestion that the collective actor problems which states face – i.e. the difficulties of cooperating without an overarching authority – are exaggerated by realists. First, if military security is not always prioritized (e.g. because, within a particular international regime, military attack is not seen as an imminent danger), states may find it easier to reach compromises that underpin their collective economic interests. Again, the Prisoner's Dilemma will not generate the same incentives to defect from cooperation if the game is iterated (i.e. repeated several times). Axelrod (1984) is among those who have argued that, in an iterated Prisoner's Dilemma, states (or other actors) may 'learn' to cooperate by reacting to the (anticipated and actual) responses of other players. Others have pointed to the existence of transnational 'epistemic communities' – i.e. transnational groups of policy experts who see a collective problem in broadly the same way and who correspondingly advise their national governments in ways which tend to coincide. The existence of both international regimes and epistemic communities tends to promote inter-state cooperation because they 'reduce uncertainty, provide information, and facilitate negotiation' (Milner 1992: 479). Even if we do not allow that sovereign states will relinquish powers to transnational authorities, the fact that inter-state rivalries are played out within these contexts may give such organizations an unintended authority. International agencies develop their own personnel and their own agenda, which may help to fashion the ways in which the institutionalized confrontation of national interests is managed. Certainly, we might expect that the existence of international fora of this kind improves the possibilities for negotiating intergovernmental agreements. Once again, the argument is not that nation-states are giving way to supra-state organizations; rather, it is that international institutions, conventions and regimes moderate the extent to which inter-state relations can be conceived as genuinely and 'actively' anarchic. Some supra-state organizations, perhaps most graphically the agencies of the European Union, clearly have an impact upon the form and context of inter-state relationships.

### States are not solely preoccupied with issues of military security

It is something close to a first principle of the realist approach that states are preponderantly concerned with questions of military security and with the maximization of political power which is, in the last instance, supported by physical force. Opponents accept that the physical integrity of the state will always be a fundamental concern, but not, under normal circumstances, to the exclusion of everything else. Keohane and Nye are especially clear in this regard: 'The agenda of interstate relationships consists of multiple issues that are not arranged in a clear or consistent hierarchy. This *absence of hierarchy among issues* means, among other things, that military security does not consistently dominate the agenda' (Keohane and Nye 1977: 25).

The very uncertainty of the global order means that, at very short notice, military issues and options may force themselves to the top of the state's international agenda and the potential for violence is never very far away. Nonetheless, under conditions of complex interdependence, military force may in normal times occupy a quite 'minor role': 'particularly among industrialized, pluralist countries, the perceived margin of safety has widened; fears of attack in general have declined, and fears of attacks *by one another* are virtually nonexistent.' Furthermore, 'force is often not an appropriate way of achieving other goals (such as economic and ecological welfare) that are becoming more important' (Keohane and Nye 1977: 27–8). Thus:

> The key characteristic of complex interdependence is the well-founded expectation of the inefficacy of the use or threat of force among states – an expectation that helps create support for conventions or regimes, delegitimating threats of force. Western Europe, North America, and Japan form a zone of complex interdependence: power is an important element in relationships among these states (as well as between state and nonstate actors), but this power does not derive from the use or threat of force towards one another.
>
> (Keohane 1989: 9)

Where the military threat is not high, states may choose to focus upon other policy areas, and they may be willing to enter into arrangements with other states to promote these alternative policy goals. 'States concerned with self-preservation do not seek to maximize their power when they are not in danger. On the contrary, they recognize a trade-off between aggrandizement and self preservation' (Keohane 1989: 47).

### Increasingly, international relations are about economic power

Critics of realism have always insisted that the logic of 'power politics' systematically underestimates the importance of transnational *economic* relationships, both as an issue for the state and as an independent force in international relations. In nearly all its manifold forms (from functionalist integration theory, to neo-functionalist regional integration theory, to accounts of states' interdependence) the liberal-pluralist approach has emphasized the importance of economic forces. This is even more true of those who criticize realism from a global-structuralist (and generally Marxist) perspective. These critics have tended to argue that states have *never* been the principal determining power in world affairs, at least, not in the sense in which this process has normally been understood. At the heart of the global-structuralist approach is the assertion that it is, above all, the *economic* forces unleashed by a *capitalist* world economy that have determined the development of the international political order in modernity. In one of the most influential accounts, Immanuel Wallerstein argues that

> The capitalist world-economy has, and has had since its coming into existence [in the sixteenth century] boundaries far larger than that of any political unit.

Indeed, it seems to be one of the basic defining features of a capitalist world-economy that there exists no political entity with ultimate authority in all its zones.

This does not mean, however, that states are irrelevant or illusory.

Rather, the political superstructure of the capitalist world-economy is an interstate system within which and through which political structures called 'sovereign states' are legitimized and constrained. Far from meaning the total autonomy of decision-making, the term 'sovereignty' in reality implies a formal autonomy combined with real limitations on this autonomy, which are implemented both via the explicit and implicit rules of the interstate system and via the power of other states in the interstate system. No state in the interstate system, even the single most powerful one at any given time, is totally autonomous – but obviously some enjoy far greater autonomy than others.

(Wallerstein 1993: 502)

Wallerstein goes on to identify a tendency for activity in the world economy to become geographically divided into areas of core and periphery, with a semi-periphery lying between the two. It is correspondingly possible, 'for shorthand purposes', to refer to core states, peripheral states and semi-peripheral states. In certain economic phases, there may be a single dominant or *hegemonic* core state (the United Provinces between 1620 and 1650; the UK between 1815 and 1873; the USA between 1945 and 1967). In such periods, the hegemonic power enjoys an unusual degree of autonomy. But such phases are comparatively short-lived. Wallerstein argues that 'the drive of bourgeois for competitive advantage [the "logic of capitalism"] has led to increasing definition ("power") of states as political structures and increasing emphasis on their constraint by the interstate system' (Wallerstein 1993: 507). In that system, it is the 'core' states that have tended to exercise the greatest power, but the activities of these states have generally been 'in the interests of capital', in line with the traditional Marxist view of the capitalist state (see above, pp. 59–60). Thus, Wallerstein places very considerable emphasis upon the role of the state and the inter-state system. Unlike Marx and many nineteenth-century liberals, he does not think that a world economy means one (global) state or none. He does, however, argue that states acting in the inter-state system do so according to what is primarily an *economic* rather than a *political* logic.

In Wallerstein's account, we find the presumption that economic forces have *always* shaped the modern state system. Much more widespread is the belief that, under the twin imperatives of growing transnationalism and globalization, cross-border economic relationships have become the newly decisive element in the international system. Corresponding to this change of emphasis has been the growing prominence of IR's own sub-discipline of *international political economy* (IPE). At its simplest, IPE is concerned with 'the interaction of a trans-national market economy with a system of competitive states', where 'state and market are part of the same, integrated system of governance: a state-market condominium' (Stubbs and

Underhill 1994: 21; Underhill 2000: 808). Its focus is upon the ways in which international economic forces interact with the activities of nation-states.

Attention here has become focused upon the ways in which the international political economy, especially globalized production and world-wide financial markets, has become more and more evasive of individual states' control. The growth of transnational production, increasingly global marketplaces, new information technologies and, above all, increased capital mobility has generated a world economy in which states are seen to be increasingly 'disempowered' in the face of transnational economic forces or, more simply, 'the markets' (see Pierson 2001a, 2001b). The international financial deregulation of the 1980s has left huge sums of highly mobile capital chasing around the global economy in search of the best short-term rates of return and has contributed to an ever greater interdependence between a range of global and regional markets.

This process was extensively discussed in Chapter 4 (see pp. 101–4). Here it is worth adding that globalization may have an impact not only upon the *effectiveness* of states but also upon the pattern and forms of states' governance. Thus, Cox observes globalization 'generating a more complex multi-level world political system, which implicitly challenges the old Westphalian assumption that "a state is a state is a state"':

> Structures of authority comprise not one but at least three levels: the macro-regional level, the old state (or Westphalian) level, and the micro-regional level. All three levels are limited in their possibilities by a global economy which has means of exerting its pressure without formally authoritative political structures.
>
> (Cox 1993: 263)

Similarly, James Rosenau speaks of the emergence of 'two worlds of world politics'. Alongside the traditional inter-state system of national governments and nation states, there emerges 'a multicentric system of diverse types of other collectivities . . . a rival source of authority with actors that sometimes cooperate with, often compete with, and endlessly interact with the state-centric system' (Rosenau 2003: 225). States are still crucially important, 'but so many new collectivities and structures have emerged as equally important that keeping states exclusively at the epicentre tends to blind us to the underlying forces and processes that sustain the evolution of global politics' (Rosenau 2000: 187).

### There is no clear-cut division between domestic and international politics

Of course, few realists have ever suggested that there exists a watertight division between a state's domestic and foreign policy concerns. Nonetheless, they have from time to time ventured a contrast between 'high' and 'low' politics, which has placed the state's foreign policy somewhat above and aside from the mundane business of domestic politics. Transnationalists have always challenged this assumption, and those who now argue from the logic of globalization find this division even less convincing. The direct peacetime exposure of domestic populations to international forces, seen most clearly though not exclusively in the impact of global market forces, brings a transnational dimension into the most localized of political issues. At the same time, states can now often secure the domestic welfare of their inhabitants and their institutions only through (collaborative) action at the transnational level. As national boundaries become less important, so too does any division between a 'domestic' and an 'international' political sphere. In Stubbs and Underhill's account:

> As the economies of the market system . . . become increasingly international-ized . . . and thereby increasingly outside the direct control of individual states, the more it becomes necessary to understand the interaction of democratic and international levels of analysis. States remain the principal (and, indeed, the only legal) decision-makers in the anarchic international order, and they con-tinue to respond to essentially domestic political constituencies. But . . . with the transnationalization of economic decision-making, what were once essentially matters of domestic politics have now spilled over and become more conten-tious in relations among states and other actors in the international system.
>
> (Stubbs and Underhill 1994: 20)

Of course, political actors have always had to operate within parameters set by their external environment. What is different about the situation now is the extent to which states are forced to seek cooperative solutions to the problems posed by this external environment (exemplified by the economic summitry of the G8 countries and, in Europe, by the move towards a single currency) and the degree to which political decisions taken within international fora and institutions impinge upon the interests and well-being of domestic political forces.

Though less frequently observed, the interconnectedness of domestic and foreign policy issues may also run in the opposite direction. Milner (1992: 491–3), for example, explains the seemingly perverse outcome of international negotiations on the liberalization of international agricultural trade, in which states seem not to have sought to maximize their own 'national interest', in terms of the composition and power of *domestic* political lobbies. Milner argues that, in international negotiations during the 1980s, a number of European countries acted against what would appear to be in their 'national interest' by opposing liberalization. Her explanation is in terms of the privileged political position occupied by domestic agricultural lobbies in these several countries. 'Gains to agricultural producers count more than gains to consumers', she argues, and this domestic balance of forces then has an impact upon the way in which 'national interests' are conceived and pursued at the international level. No comprehensive explanation of international cooperation is possible, she concludes, without a prior consideration of the balance of domestic political forces:

> First, domestic politics tells us how preferences are aggregated and national interests constructed. . . . Second, domestic politics can help to explain the strategies states adopt to realize their goals. . . . Third, the final step in establish-

ing cooperative arrangements occurs when domestic actors agree to abide by the terms negotiated internationally.

(Milner 1992: 492–3)

In passing overall judgement on these changes, we need again to exercise some caution. It is not the case that political power has simply been 'transferred' from domestic to international political agencies. In part, it is that old forms of power, associated with more secure national boundaries, have simply disappeared. But at the same time, new powers may have been created. It is, for example, information technology (IT) that has, at least in part, made possible the new global financial order and to this extent contributed to a weakening of the powers of the state. On the other hand, IT has also delivered into the hands of governing authorities capacities for surveillance of its population that were unimaginable for even the most totalitarian of historical regimes. At the same time, the changing balance of domestic and international forces has led to a reconstruction of states internally, granting greater authority to the 'outward-turned' departments of state and giving every department an increasing interest in the transnational aspects of its remit. According to Cox:

> Power within the state becomes concentrated in those agencies in closest touch with the global economy – the offices of presidents and prime ministers, treasuries, central banks. The agencies more closely identified with domestic clients – ministries of industry, labour ministries, etc. – become subordinated.

(Cox 1994: 49)

This tendency can be seen in the way that ministries responsible for education have been frequently recast as a sub-branch of ministries for employment, which are themselves seen increasingly as adjuncts of national treasuries.

### States are not unitary-rational actors

Realists recommend that for most analytic purposes we can treat states as *unitary* and *rational* actors. That is, the shorthand of treating 'France', 'the UK', 'the USA' as unified actors is not just a time-saving convention but actually tells us something about the ways in which states really behave. Furthermore, we have seen that realists generally assume that states act rationally in pursuing a common goal that is defined as the maximization of effective power (variously defined). It should be clear from what has been said thus far that this position is not sustainable. First, states are not unitary. Certainly, there are contexts, above all in the claim to exercise sovereign power, in which the representatives of the state portray themselves as the vehicles of a single unified will. But, in fact, states and governments are complex organizations with their own internal divisions of interest, multiple goals and competing agendas. It is a long-standing commonplace of studies of the workings of (public) bureau-cracies that these organizations are riven by internal divisions of interest, that individual actors and groups within the bureaucracy will have goals other than the maximization of the explicit goals of the whole organization, and that bureaucratic procedures may chronically lead to sub-optimal and even irrational outcomes. Indeed, neo-liberal critics (e.g. Niskanen and Tullock) have used the conventions of rational choice (presuming that individual actors act rationally in terms of their own personal goals) to show that bureaucratic procedures will always yield sub-optimal and irrational outcomes at the level of the state. It is only at moments of crisis (e.g. in the Westland Affair in the UK in the mid-1980s) that the ever-present clashes of interest between differing government departments (in this case, between the Ministry of Defence and the Department of Trade and Industry) become public. In practice, state organizations have multiple points of interaction with both domestic and transnational actors, and these interactions are very far from disclosing a single and unified will. Graham Allison's celebrated investigation of US policy-making in the Cuban Missile Crisis (of 1962) seeks to show how organizational and bureau-cratic processes – and the fact that actual decision-makers operate under constraints of time and with imperfect information – explain government behaviour in a way that the assumptions of a unitary rational actor cannot (Allison 1971). Overall, it seems clear that:

1   sociologically speaking, states are not unitary actors;
2   not all actions of the state's agents are rational and goal-oriented (i.e. oriented around finding the most parsimonious way of realizing some clearly established goal);
3   those who represent the state may be pursuing quite different and, in some cases, contradictory policy goals.

Thus, an important element in the critique of realism is that its most basic working assumptions are not sustainable.

### *Morality may have a place in international relationships*

Of course, it is not true that realists deny *any* space to morality in the conduct of international affairs. Both Morgenthau and Carr raise the moral dimension, and upon a charitable reading even Machiavelli had a place for conventional morality. After all, he did recommend that we should try to avoid those vices which didn't in some way serve our interests! And the realist position was set out in self-conscious contradistinction to those 'idealist' accounts which saw morality as a compelling force in IR (in the face of a considerable weight of contrary evidence). Nonetheless, some contemporary critics do suggest that the realists go too far in squeezing moral considerations out of the practical life of IR. Without underestimating the cynicism with which politicians invoke morality (to serve their own ends), critics argue that there are transnational institutions which do at least exercise some constraint upon the morally outrageous conduct of states and that, in a world of instantly transmittable information, the moral concern of a transnational public opinion does carry at least some weight.

This development is perhaps clearest in the field of international law. In a world order which is so widely regarded as anarchic, international law has always had a strange status. It seems of the essence of law-like relations that there should be a (sovereign) power which is able to enact what the law dictates (although down at least to the early modern period, the rubric of a God-given natural law was held to be effective without any this-worldly enforcer). This has never really been the case with modern international law. Yet, as Held shows, particularly in the period since 1945, international law entrenching certain basic humanitarian values (sometimes couched as 'human rights') has been significantly strengthened.

> The development of international law has placed individuals, governments and nongovernmental organizations under new systems of legal regulation. International law has recognized powers and constraints, and rights and duties, which transcend the claims of nation-states and which, while they may not be backed by institutions with coercive power of enforcement, none the less have far-reaching consequences.
>
> (Held 1995: 101)

As Held points out, international law is not any longer seen as simply a law between states. Now individuals have certain rights in international law. They also have obligations which, in some circumstances, over-ride their duty of obedience to the nation-state. Some of the traditional mainstays of national sovereignty – recognizing that within the limits of its jurisdiction no other authority may controvert the will of the state – have been challenged both by international conventions on human rights and by a willingness to try miscreant political leaders under another jurisdiction. In the case of the European Convention on Human Rights, individuals are empowered to bring actions against their own governments.

It would be quite wrong to overestimate the impact of morality in the conduct of IR. All too easily, 'human rights' and 'the defence of democracy' become appropriated as part of the arsenal with which politicians pursue their all too grubbily realist ambitions in international affairs. But nor can this moral agenda be too readily dismissed as just a 'pious wish-list'. The discourse of human rights and the availability of an appeal to international law and conventions may give the disempowered a point of access to the political process. Transnational organizations such as Amnesty International are undoubtedly strengthened in their work by the authority that derives from shared understandings of human rights and international humanitarian conventions. At some point, moral outrage may have economic (and thence political) consequences, as the clear but contested process of change in South Africa would suggest. The kernel of truth in the realist position, sadly, is that the imposition of these moral criteria upon reluctant states (whether by the United Nations or any other agency) remains fairly feeble.

### Women are systematically excluded from the 'international relations' picture

Feminists have had an increasingly significant impact upon the understanding of international politics over the past two decades by posing the disarmingly simple question: Where are the women? (Enloe 1989: 7). As Steans (1998: 46) has it, 'International Relations is a *gendered* discourse.' In raising this issue, feminists are carrying into the international arena what has long been their principal challenge to the canons of *malestream* political science and political theory. At its simplest, this approach asks why women are so under-represented in political life and why this under-representation should have seemed so unremarkable to political commentators. In the more general treatment of this issue, attention has focused upon the ways in which 'the political' is (narrowly) defined, the ways in which the public/ private division in social life is constructed and the fact that the disembodied individual at the heart of liberal-democratic political thinking, while presented as ungendered, has in fact represented not everybody but 'Everyman'. Gendered assumptions have been sneaked into political argument as unconsidered premises or as 'non-political' and thus 'irrelevant' (Pateman 1988a). These criticisms seem still more compelling when applied to IR. Typically, realists have focused upon security issues, warfare and the (diplomatic) conduct of political élites. Where discussion has expanded to take in economic issues, this has generally been in terms of the 'big players' (states, multinational companies, the World Bank and so on). This is very largely a man's world. Within individual nation-states, feminists have struggled to draw issues that had been seen as 'domestic', 'private' and thus 'non-political' – including the ways in which masculinity and femininity were constructed – on to the overtly political agenda. Feminists in IR seek similarly to draw supposedly 'non-political' issues on to the agenda of international politics. The aspiration is to extend the classical feminist insight that 'the personal is political' beyond the national level, to insist that 'the personal is international' and that 'politics is not shaped merely by what happens in legislative debates, voting booths or war rooms' (Enloe 1989: 195). As Sylvester has it (1994: 7), 'there are nation-states but there are no households in realist IR'. In Enloe's view, 'if we employ only the conventional ungendered compass to chart international politics, we are likely to end up mapping a landscape peopled only by men, mostly elite men' (Enloe 1989: 1).

In drawing women into IR, some critics have concentrated upon the prevalence of a logic of *militarism*, expressing a peculiarly male approach to the management of international conflict and disagreement. They have emphasized the possibilities for greater cooperation that would flow from a fuller involvement by women in international decision-making (Ruddick 1990). More generally, there has been an aspiration to bring into view those women and their interests 'hidden' by the conventions of traditional IR and its 'high politics' agenda. In *Bananas, Beaches and Bases* (1989), Enloe pursues this insight in discussing the role of some of those unseen women – ambassadors' wives, prostitutes servicing military bases, low-paid domestic servants, female workers in tourism – who make the international world go round. She shows how high and low politics (and economics) are intimately related and how the conventional remit of IR largely ignores what women do and their systematically disadvantaged position. Increasingly complex international economic relationships – from the international fruit trade to the global sex industry – often rely, at their base, upon the poorly paid or unpaid work of women. The business of international diplomacy would be impossible without an unseen army of female workers. Without these women in subordinate positions, the 'high politics' and the 'big players' could not go on. It is only a prejudice about what 'counts' as IR that allows these women (and their interests) to be discounted.

Finally, feminist writers draw attention to the distinctive position of women within a (restructured) global political economy. In part theirs is a critique of the ways in which what counts as 'economic activity' and 'rational behaviour' within neo-realist discussion is presented as gender-neutral when in fact it inscribes assumptions which marginalize the participation and contribution of women (by disregarding production within the household, for example). But this literature also points to the ways in which the costs of restructuring the international economy under globalizing imperatives have fallen disproportionately upon women. Women were already over-represented among the world's poorest people. As unskilled work has migrated to less developed regions of the world, so women have found themselves making up an increasing proportion of the world's worst paid wage labourers (in Asia's highly deregulated Export Production Zones, as much as 85 per cent of the workforce: Steans 1998: 136). At the same time, feminists have evolved a critical view of the logic (and rhetorics) of 'international development'. While development was for long seen as a 'good thing' for less developed countries (more or less uniformly advocated by the Western institutions that had control of such things), a more critical attitude has emerged among those who are sceptical about how much real welfare is delivered to those who are supposedly the beneficiaries of these processes. This has contributed to a more nuanced view, in which the claims of the developers are regarded much more sceptically and where space is demanded for the poorest to articulate their own sense of what development requires. As we shall see in Chapter 7, the interplay of 'top-down' and bottom-up' in the international developmental arena is now quite complex. (See, for example, the heated debate over the World Bank's *Voices of the Poor*; World Bank 2001.)

### *'Realism' does not reflect 'reality' but one world-view (among many) in the service of particular interests*

The problem that feminists identify here is not just about a 'reality' of deep-seated and gendered patterns of inequality. It is quite as much about the ways in which the language of traditional IR, above all in its realist forms, has failed to acknowledge these relationships. In large part, so its feminist critics argue, this is because realism, despite the claims of its advocates, is not a description of social reality but one highly partisan and selective reading of it (a view which draws its inspiration, at least in part, from the work of Foucault; see above, pp. 75–6). It is this same claim – that realism is not a synopsis of the real world but a highly selective interpretation of it – that underpins the criticism of many social constructivists. At the more radical pole of this social constructivist critique there lies a growing body of 'postmodernist' writing on international politics. The more general postmodernist sensibility stresses diversity, uncertainty, the impossibility of fully grounded truth-claims, the ungraspability of the 'essence of things'. It reserves its fiercest criticism for those who defy this sensibility and insist upon the possibility of seizing upon the one objective truth and using this knowledge to direct political action. Classical realism (along with many of its critics) falls more or less unreservedly into this latter camp and, as such, it is the object of the postmodernists' withering scepticism. More specifically, postmodernist critics have challenged the realists' understanding of the 'Great Texts' (of Thucydides, Machiavelli, Hobbes and so on), insisting that the 'timeless' endorsement of the realist approach which they find there is just one way of reading these sources. Postmodernists challenge many of the core conceptions with which realists operate: the unitary state, sovereignty, the one-dimensional conception of political power. All of these are theoretical constructs or conventions rather than descriptions of an external reality. Realist accounts of the world derive much of their authority from being 'objective', 'scientific' and 'rational'. But postmodernists reject the claimed epistemological priority of these categories and move to replace the realists' preferred language of logic and objectivity with anecdote, irony and happenstance.

For many postmodernist critics, realism is not a quest to describe things 'as they really are', but rather an attempt to invoke and legitimate a distinctive view of the world order in the service of particular powerful interests. It is simply the story that one especially powerful group tells to itself about the way in which the world works (not coincidentally, to its advantage).

Among the IR postmodernists (or those who were once postmodernists or those who once allowed themselves to be described as postmodernists), there is also a sense that realists and others fail to grasp the *real* nature of contemporary (perhaps postmodern) warfare. The newness of this experience was crystallized in the First Gulf War. Writers such as Jean Baudrillard (author of the 'notorious' *Did the Gulf War Happen?*) and James Der Derian stressed that war in the era of virtual reality is different. In the face of the conventional assumption that there was a war in the Gulf which was then reported to a world audience, postmodernists such as Der Derian argue that, in effect, the televisual representation of the conflict (with its arcade-game graphics and persistent games analogy) *was* the 'reality' of the Gulf War. So, too, with the Second Gulf War. Today's 'wars are fought in the same manner as they are represented, by military simulations and public dissimulations, by real-time surveillance and TV "live-feeds"', and 'as war goes virtual, through infowar, netwar, cyberwar, through a convergence of the PC and the TV, its foundations as the ultimate reality-check of international politics begins to erode' (Der Derian 2000: 772). The intention is absolutely not to suggest that in modern wars no one *really* dies. Rather the purpose is to disclose that wars are still bloody and destructive and cruel and messy but that there is an attempt to *conceal* this through the ways in which the experience of conflict is represented/created. The intention is that we should be 'virtually distanced' from violent death, so that the virtuousness of modern warfare (always said to be defending the cause of democracy or the human rights of an oppressed minority) should itself not be questioned.

The postmodernists' approach is primarily de(con)structive. In George's evaluation, 'what postmodernism has exposed . . . is international relations . . . as a discursive process, a process in which identities are formed, meaning is given, and status and privilege are accorded – a process of knowledge as power' (George 1994).

In the hands of Der Derian, it brings a critical scrutiny to bear upon the 'official' version of 24/7, live-feed war. Whether postmodernist IR might also have a more constructive aspect – beyond a rather limp appeal for diversity and tolerance – is something about which postmodernists themselves are appropriately sceptical (Der Derian 1992, 1995, 2000).

## Conclusion

It is an extremely unfortunate division of intellectual labour which has typically seen the study of IR *between* states and social, economic and political relationships *within* states pursued as if these defined two quite distinct spheres. On the one hand, it has allowed internationalists to focus too exclusively upon questions of national security. At the same time, it has permitted too many sociologists, economists and political scientists to underplay the role of force and violence in the domestic life of nation-states. In the face of a reality which corresponds ever less convincingly with this division, the barriers between the study of domestic and foreign affairs are breaking down. What is revealed is an extraordinarily complex interplay of local, regional, national, transnational and global forces with nation-states as strategic, but not always as privileged actors. The jury may still be out on whether these changes are best described as an intensification of internationalization or as defining a 'new' stage of globalization. But there can be little doubt that transnational forces, above all in the economy but also in such troubled areas as the global environment, have come to exercise an increasing influence and that states' control over their own territorial domain has weakened. Held (1995) points out there is an important sense in which, because of both internal and external changes, nation-states no longer represent 'a community of fate' in the sense in which it was once supposed that they did. And this represents a huge challenge to our traditional understanding of what a sovereign political association should look like.

## Further reading

Der Derian, J. (2000) 'Virtuous war/virtual theory', *International Affairs* 76, 4, 771–88.
Keohane, R. O. (1989) *International Institutions and State Power*. London: Westview Press.
Morgenthau, H. (1978) *Politics Among Nations*. New York: Knopf.
Steans, J. (1998) *Gender and International Relations*. Cambridge: Polity.
Waltz, K. (1979) *Theory of International Politics*. Reading, MA: Addison-Wesley.
Wendt, A. (1999) *Social Theory of International Politics*. Cambridge: Cambridge University Press.

# 7 States of the twenty-first century

It is clear enough at the start of the twenty-first century that modern states are very far from 'withering away'. The earliest years of the new century give us plenty of evidence of the enduring importance of the state in its traditional form, quintessentially in the shape of the USA. Yet the environment of states' action is clearly changing, radically and, in some instances, swiftly. In this chapter, we explore this changing environment and establish that political circumstances are subject to change both 'domestically' and 'globally' (in as much as these two can still be usefully distinguished). In what follows, we proceed from changes in the 'internal' environment of states through the regional/intergovernmental level towards an assessment of the new global framework. We shall finish by considering one of the first really radical and truly global analyses of states' governance in the new century – Michael Hardt and Antonio Negri's epic *Empire* (2000).

## Governance: governing without government

In Chapter 4, we considered the emergence of the 'new public management' and new forms of government-mandated regulation. We can consider these as special cases of a more general phenomenon of the late twentieth-/early twenty-first-century political order – that is, the development of new modes of governance or what is sometimes called 'governing without government' (see Rhodes 1997; Pierre and Peters 2000; Pierre 2000). As we shall see, governance is an aspect of governing at both state and supra-state level.

Even in the hands of its most articulate sponsors, 'the concept of governance is notoriously slippery' (Pierre and Peters 2000: 7). Its essence lies in the idea that governing – that is, the business of making binding and effective collective decisions for a given political community – is less and less the exclusive business of the state and its agencies (including law enforcement) and more and more a matter of the negotiation of decision-making (and implementation) between state actors (at various levels) and societal interests, a process mediated through both formal and informal channels. There is some disagreement about the extent to which governance represents a wholesale disempowering of the state or simply a reorganization of its governing capacity. According to Pierre and Peters (2000: 68), 'the new governance . . . does not mean the end or decline of the state but the transformation and adaptation of the state to the society it is currently embedded in.' In Rhodes's less state-centric view, governance 'refers to self-organizing, interorganizational networks characterised by interdependence, resource exchange, rules of the game and significant autonomy from the state' (Rhodes 1997: 15). What is quite clear, however, is that governance in whichever of these forms represents a very clear challenge to the 'traditional' view of states' rule (built around the ideas of sovereignty, authority, constitutionality and impersonal power exercised through a public bureaucracy) outlined in Chapter 1. In so far as it is states that still rule (if anyone does), the literature of governance suggest that they rule in quite different (and, in general, much more mediated) ways. At the very least, if states are to get their way, they will have to coax, cajole, persuade and bribe their societal 'partners', both domestic and international, to make things happen. (Of course, this was always to a significant extent the way in which states got their business done.)

Why does the state find itself driven towards the new adventure of governing through governance? Pierre and Peters (2000: 52–67) identify a number of causes. First, there is the idea (retraceable in its current form to the 1970s) that states have become 'overloaded', required to deliver levels of services (especially welfare services) which democratic publics are increasingly reluctant to fund (at least knowingly). Second, there is the idea that 'managing' increasingly complex societies outruns the 'command and control' capacities of existing states (a key idea in Giddens's call for a 'Third Way'; see Giddens 1998). Societies are just too complex to be effectively managed by a single central authority. Third, there is the impact – nebulous but probably real – of a shift in faith from states to markets. This new faith is provisional, ideological and often misplaced. But it has certainly had an impact upon the ways in which both state and societal actors see the 'problems' and 'solutions' of effective government. Fourth, all states have felt the impact of economic globalization, even if they have also had a hand in creating it (both of which we discussed in Chapters 4 and 6). Cumulatively, globalization has weakened the immediate domestic authority of the nation-state (though it may have given states new forms of *collective* agency at the international level). Fifth, governance has emerged as a seemingly attractive alternative where states are seen to have 'failed' in a string of policy areas, ranging from transport infrastructure to drug addiction. (Although, as Moran (2001) rightly points out, governance already has its own considerable repertoire of policy catastrophes ranging, in the UK, from BSE to the Millennium Dome.) Finally, we might add that, for governments themselves, governance solutions may have the attractive quality of distancing politicians from the opprobrium that goes with unpopular decisions/outcomes. Interest in governance has grown because 'the state no longer has a monopoly over the expertise nor over the economic or institutional resources necessary to govern' (Pierre 2000).

Governance is not entirely new. National corporatist regimes have long shared certain governing capacities with key societal actors in exchange for their members' compliance. 'Pre-governance' states often allowed *greater* autonomy to key social interests (for example, in the long-standing self-regulation of professions such as medicine and law). Despite this, we can find something 'new' in the 'new' forms of governance. First, governance is widely seen as a 'multi-level' process or set of processes. It reaches down to the sub-national level and outwards and upwards towards transnational actors. Labour governments in Britain, following their electoral success in 1997, restored the parliament in Scotland (after a 300-year gap), created an assembly for Wales and (re-)created a governing authority and executive mayor for the capital city. In the USA under Clinton, much of the responsibility for the management of welfare policy was handed back to the states (a classic example of blame/responsibility avoidance). At the same time, a number of governing functions have been transferred from national governments to international organizations – most clearly, though still far from unambiguously, in the case of the EU. Some competencies have simply been transferred to non-government agencies – as with Labour's decision in 1997 to transfer the responsibility for setting interest rates to a committee of the Bank of England. In other cases, a government function has been reallocated to an agency at arm's length from government itself – as with the transfer of the system of state schools' inspection in the UK from HMI (Her Majesty's Inspectors of Schools) to OFSTED (the Office for Standards in Education). In a somewhat Foucauldian twist, governments have sought to introduce a 'self-auditing' culture in which institutions are rewarded for generating their own internal systems of surveillance and review. Cumulatively, these moves, alongside the widespread privatization of public utilities, are sometimes said to add up to a 'hollowing out of the state' (Rhodes 1997: 33).

Governance also dictates a change in the mechanisms through which governments seek to enforce their will. Of course, a 'command and control' model of states' action was always, to a significant degree, a convenient constitutional fiction. The long history of policy failure is very often a story of the substantial distance that lies between ambitious policy and disastrous implementation. Indeed, this experience of policy failure is itself a source of impetus to new forms of governance. It is of the essence of the newer forms of governance that, even where state actors still seek to lead, they are obliged to negotiate with societal partners, rather than simply to command. The ambition of state actors under the imperatives of governance is not to rule but to 'steer' the policy process (even if this brings in its wake an orgy of auditing, as governments seek to exercise 'indirect' control of policy through a plethora of targets and 'standards').

Once again, the newness of this relationship can be overstated. States have always negotiated with really powerful interests (and not always from a position of strength). In the case of subaltern states, they have often been on the receiving end of the chain of authority, frequently from more powerful states and their agencies or armies. There is still plenty of command in contemporary states' action – for example, in the new and more personalized relationship of the state with individual 'jobseekers'. But, as Foucault pointed out, even the 'powerless' have some resources on their side (even if it is little more than stubborn foot-dragging). The mechanisms of governance are seen to require states to engage in qualitatively new levels of negotiation with key societal actors. In complex societies, states are chronically reliant upon the active compliance of a range of non-state actors if they are to realize their policy ambitions. This means also that the 'classic' device associated with securing the will of the modern state in its 'traditional' form – that is, the law – is an increasingly ineffective tool. Characteristically, success derives not from formal legal authority but from 'entrepreneurialism and political skill' (Pierre and Peters 2000: 24). This does not necessarily mean that states are becoming weaker. The real issue is the extent to which states can realize their policy ambitions. It may just be that leading a coalition of social forces (domestic and international) is more *effective* than commanding that one's will be obeyed. (After all, it never did King Canute any good.)

## Policy networks

Crucial to this understanding of the shift from government to governance has been a renewed emphasis upon the idea of *policy networks* as the medium through which policy is made and implemented. In older models of government, it was assumed that governing was the product of a hierarchy in which authoritative decisions taken at the peak of government cascaded downwards to the various levels at which they were to be implemented. A number of critics insist that this is quite inadequate as a way of (even quite approximately) modelling how government works now. Central to contemporary forms of government (and thus of governance) is the idea of networks – that is, the idea that policy is made and implemented not by a governing authority *independent* of social actors but in the context of on-going exchange of information, resources and opportunities between elements in the governing apparatus and more-or-less organized interests in society. Relationships within the networks thus created are not uni-directional and hierarchic but based on negotiation and exchange, in a web of relationships which is consciously maintained across time.

The origins of the idea of policy networks lie in an earlier literature on the inter-action between governments and organized social interests (whether in pluralist or corporatist form; see above, pp. 56–8, 69). But the idea of governance through networks is now seen to go far beyond the traditional domain of interest group politics. Indeed, it penetrates to the very heart of government itself. Thus (in Rhodes's treatment), the top-down hierarchical model of government increasingly gives way to a 'differentiated polity' in which the 'core executive' at the heart of national government can be redescribed as 'the set of networks which police the functional policy networks' (Rhodes 1997: 14). Beneath the 'meta-network' of the 'core executive' lie a whole series of other policy networks through which government is made to happen in an unending and open-ended process of negotiation and exchange. Of course, this is not at all the same as saying that we now live in an age of 'open government' in which the government is open to the negotiation of its agenda with each and every societal interest. Government is interested in those network actors who have resources to offer, and these are, as we know, very unevenly distributed. Moreover, the informal process of endless negotiation may make for *less* open government, as privileged interests 'carve up' decisions with key government actors. The crucial issue here, however, is the way in which governing has changed under a policy network regime. Although states are still crucial (after all, they have many of the most important resources, including the power to tax and a monopoly of legitimate force), they are no longer privileged in the way that traditional theories of state sovereignty suppose. In Rhodes's account (1997: 33), governance refers to 'self-organizing, interorganizational networks' which enjoy 'a significant degree of autonomy from the state. Networks are not accountable to the state.' Upon this account, 'the state becomes a collection of interorganizational networks made up of governmental and societal actors able to steer or regulate' (Rhodes 1997: 57).

## Transnational policy networks and policy transfer

Policy networks are not just domestic. Writing of the emergence of a new pattern of *global* governance, Held and McGrew (2002) identify three key developments: 1) the end of the Cold War and the 'frozen' international regime it helped to entrench, 2) the process of globalization itself, and 3) the emergence of new forms of governance *within* states. As in its domestic variant, global governance is marked by multiple layers, multilateralism, pluralism and structural complexity. And increasingly it gives rise to a matrix of policy networks informing public policy at the international or global level. Typically, these networks are '*transgovernmental* (such as the Basel Committee on Banking Supervision and the Financial Action Task Force), *trisectoral* (public, corporate, and NGOs), and *transnational* (such as Medecins sans Frontières)' (Held and McGrew 2002: 11). At the same time, the level of intergovernmental activity has intensified, and this is perhaps most clearly seen in a significant growth in *policy transfer*, the process through which governments (or their policy networks) are increasingly influenced by policies undertaken elsewhere, elements of which can be transferred from one state to another (see Dolowitz and Marsh 1996).

Policy transfer is not new. The ancient Greeks had many imitators as well as admirers, and the impact of Roman imperial outreach (and its legal code) can still be seen across Europe and beyond. But if it is not entirely new, there is still reason to think that policy transfer has become more important in recent years. In significant part, this is because globalization and, in differing ways, greater regionalization have intensified both the possibilities and the incentives for policy transfer. First, there is just so much more information around and it is so much more readily transmissible. Policy-makers (and their clients) know more about what is happening elsewhere. Information technology makes it much easier and quicker and cheaper to study the policy experience and initiatives of others, both for governments and for other policy stakeholders. It is also widely supposed that globalization has led to a greater convergence of national experiences (and policy challenges). The demise of the Soviet Empire is supposed to have left us with one model of a successful economic order – a more or less lightly regulated private market economy (even if continuing diversity in the 'varieties of capitalism' argues against this: see Kitschelt *et al.* 1999; Coates 2000). Economic problems (and solutions) are now widely understood to be of the same kind for differing national economies. Furthermore, the spread of internationalization or globalization means that national economic circumstances are increasingly tied in to a world economic order. Nations who want to be on board have increasingly to learn the rules and mimic the successful institutional arrangements of the big players. The emergence of regional authorities – the Association of South-East Asian Nations (ASEAN), the Common Market of the South

(MERCOSUR) and, above all, the European Union (EU) – with community-wide standards and practices has provided a further incentive for states to converge on standardized practices and procedures.

Globalization has also clearly had an impact upon the wider policy-making community. In many policy areas (in social policy, for example) there now exists an extensive international policy community of key players. The senior public servants and policy advisers in this virtual community share a common vocabulary. They move through the same international agencies, conferences and airport lounges. New forms of instantaneous global communication make the sharing of information easier and quicker. The reform of labour market and welfare policies in a number of developed states over the past twenty years provides an excellent example of the policy transfer process in action. Not just policy ideas, but detailed policy mechanisms, even the wording of legislation have been transferred between jurisdictions. (On the example of social policy transfer between the USA, Australia, New Zealand and the UK, see Dolowitz 1998; Pierson 2003).

Of course, policy transfer has never been an entirely voluntary process. The Romans and later the British *imposed* their legal and administrative orders on their respective empires by force of arms. Policy transfer by imposition remains crucial. To take a contemporary example, many of the world's poorest countries find themselves on the receiving end of economic policies manufactured in Washington by the IMF and the World Bank. Similarly, post-conflict states may find their political and legal systems being dictated by the Pentagon, as the world's one remaining superpower imposes what it understands to be governing 'best practice' upon a howsoever reluctant client.

Finally, and as we might expect, policy transfer is not just an intergovernmental practice. Other actors in a global civil society are able to learn and adapt international lessons. It is as likely to be reformers *outside* government as those within who seek to draw on experience elsewhere, as the networking of the anti-globalization lobby suggests (see Keane 2003).

## Multi-level governance

The growing transmissibility of ideas and policies between polities, the 'hollowing out of states' and the increase in 'governing by network' bring us to a consideration of what has come to be called *multi-level governance*. At its simplest, this describes 'the dispersion of authoritative decision making across multiple territorial levels' (Hooghe and Marks 2001). In this sense, multi-level governance is a familiar enough feature of states with long-standing federal political arrangements, states such as Australia, Germany and the USA. What is new in the current situation is the suggestion that multi-level governance is emerging as a form that routinely goes *beyond* the nation-state (and is something much more than military alliance or *ad hoc* cooperation of states on particular policy issues). For Europeans at least, the most important site of this emergent transnational multi-level governance has come in the protean form of the European Union. Of course, the nature of the Union and the issue of whether or not it is destined to end up as a United States of Europe have been fiercely contested. Its expansion eastwards has simply served to make these discussions more confusing. Nonetheless we can find very widespread agreement that the growth of the EU has brought about real political changes, among which the development of forms of multi-level governance is central.

In Hooghe and Marks's (2001) account, for example, European integration is a polity-creating process in which authority and policy-making influence are shared across multiple levels of government – sub-national, national, and supra-national. This multi-level governance involves at least four key changes:

1. *Decision-making competencies are shared by actors at different levels rather than monopolized by national governments.* Supranational institutions – the European Parliament, the European Commission and the European Court – have an independent influence upon decision making within the EU.

2. *Collective decision making among states involves a significant loss of control for individual national governments.* Growing numbers of EU decisions require less than unanimity amongst state members (through various forms of qualified majority voting). In this sense, decisions have moved outside the competence of individual member states.

3. *Political arenas are interconnected rather than nested.* Subnational political (and economic) actors do not interact with European level institutions exclusively through the medium of (and under the watchful eye of) national governments. Subnational, national and supranational political agencies are interconnected in a variety of ways. National governments are not now able to maintain an effective monopoly/veto upon decision-making authority.

4. *An emergent individual rights' framework for citizens at the EU level places significant constraints upon what individual nation states may do to their citizens.* This is an important constraint upon what has often been seen as a *sine qua non* of statehood, that is the capacity to act as the final arbiter in the treatment of citizens within its borders.

(Hooghe and Marks 2001: 3–4; emphasis added)

There is some measure of disagreement about just how important these changes are (see, for example, Hix 1998; Hix and Goetz 2001; Hooghe and Marks 2001). Some persist in seeing the EU as essentially intergovernmental, with individual nation-states cooperating in order to strengthen their domestic positions and to cope effectively with supra-national challenges (whether economic or social). Nonetheless, it is hard to believe that multi-level governance has no purchase in the real world when a majority of EU member states have decided to opt for economic and monetary union.

The European Union offers particularly compelling evidence of multi-level governance, but it is a process with a much wider relevance. In this more general context, Keane (2003: 98–104), for example, writes of the dispersion of decision-making power into three levels: *micro-government*, *meso-government* and *macro-government*. At the micro-level, we find 'sub-territorial state institutions' and local and regional governments. The meso-level is occupied by traditional nation-states and supra-state institutions, such as the EU, ASEAN and CARICOM (the Caribbean Community). At the macro-level, we find globe-spanning political arrangements, arising from institutions such as the OECD or the emergent International Criminal Court. Together the interaction of these institutions helps to create what Keane calls a *cosmocracy* – 'the first-ever world polity' – 'a conglomeration of interlocking and over-lapping sub-state, state and supra-state institutions and multidimensional processes that interact, and have political and social effects, on a global scale' (see also Held 1995, on the idea of a multi-levelled cosmopolitan democracy).

We may well feel uncertain that we are standing at the threshold of a European super-state or that the interconnectedness of transnational governing processes is such that we have now entered into the world of cosmocracy. We can, however, be reasonably sure that multi-level governance has reached a point at which it begins meaningfully to impinge upon the powers and discretion of traditional nation-states (with the possible exception of the one extant super-state, the USA). As ever, we need to bear in mind that such a change is not 'pure loss' for nation-states. In ceding some *formal* authority to others, the state may in practice increase the actual *capacity* to realize its policy ambitions (whatever these may be).

Whether the process is driven by an increase in multi-level governance or by the rather broader progress of a multifaceted globalization, it is clear that these changes have also helped to invoke new forms of oppositional politics at the transnational level. This kaleidoscope of differing interests, methods and peoples is most often referred to as the 'anti-globalization movement'. At one level this makes sense. Many of those who mobilize through the loose association of groups that make up 'the movement' are indeed concerned about the consequences (economic, environmental, cultural and even spiritual) of the global outreach of 'turbocapitalism' and especially the impact of its flagship transnational corporations (most famously criticized under the 'No Logo' rubric of Klein 2000). A global economy that has escaped the countervailing powers of political authority (especially that of the nation-state) is a key concern. But these critics are rarely advocates of a return to greater national autonomy. Generally they want to alter the direction of globalization, not simply abandon it. Indeed, one of the (few) things that unites the anti-globalization movement is its committed internationalism, and its practitioners are for the most part adept in the innovative use of globalization's newest technologies (from the Internet and mobile phone to the stage-managed world media event).

In fact, the 'anti' label has stuck so effectively to 'the movement' precisely because it is so diverse and amorphous (or, in Green and Griffith's borrowed usage, because it is a 'movement of movements'; Green and Griffith 2002: 49). It has no fixed organizational structure. Its membership ranges from mildly reformist business leaders through 'concerned' mainstream politicians to the outer limits of anti-capitalist direct action. Among its characteristic concerns are globalization and economic inequality (including issues of fair trade and indebtedness), the environment, political rights, issues of race and gender, and cultural and religious diversity. Anti-capitalism and anti-Americanism are important but far from universal themes. One source of the movement is scepticism/disillusionment with the efficacy of 'mainstream' political activity, and correspondingly the movement's supporters are much more likely to be found within and/or acting through (internationalist) NGOs than traditional political parties (or in new partnerships of government and INGOs). This 'anti-political politics' is important for us – in terms of its organization, agenda and methods – because it tells us something about the way in which politics and the international order (and nation-states) have changed in the early years of the new century. States have certainly not disappeared, but they do operate within a significantly reconfigured landscape.

## States and migration

One key development driving the process of transnational multi-level governance is the emergence of a range of problems which cannot be effectively addressed at the level of the nation-state. In part these are issues relating to the management of the global economy (or rather the lack of such management), concerns which are heightened by a growing sense of the complex interconnectedness of the world's economic forces (an issue discussed in Chapter 4 and to which we return in the closing pages of this chapter). But the drive to multi-level governance also arises from a series of issues which are not so immediately 'economic' (though each of them has a crucial economic component). These include the challenge of a degrading natural environment, the control of global pandemics (such as AIDS and SARS) and the enforcement of international controls on the illegal trafficking of drugs (and its laundered proceeds). By way of example, we explore here another of these key issues: the transnational management of migration.

The politics of migration has had a much heightened profile (especially within the more developed states) in recent years. The displacement of peoples following what Keane (2003: 149) has called 'uncivil wars', the rise of populist parties of the right (and the attempt to outmanoeuvre them) and, most recently, the fear of the globally itinerant terrorist have all increased the levels of political attention (and capital) devoted to the international movements of people. Of course, migration is almost by definition an international issue (though in recent years increasing attention and concern has been focused upon the status and welfare of 'internally displaced' persons, that is, those who are made refugees *within* their own borders). It is also of long standing. Human populations have been on the move ever since Adam and Eve left the Garden of Eden, and mass migration has been commonplace in modern times, with some modern states – such as Australia and the USA – clearly the creation of migrant populations (generally with scant regard for indigenous peoples or their forms of governance). But recent years have seen migration achieve a new salience as an issue for the states of modernity. The politics of migration are crucial because defining who counts as a citizen and determining who may and who may not enter and remain within a given territory are core elements of what it has meant to be a state in modernity (as we saw in Chapter 5).

As we might anticipate, globalization and the challenge this poses to the integrity of the nation-state are high on the agenda of the recent politics of migration. The greater movement of persons around the globe (whether for business or pleasure) has been one of the key indicators of accelerated globalization. Air passenger and air freight miles have grown rapidly over the last forty years (at close to 10 per cent per annum; International Civil Aviation Organization 2003) and the International Organization for Migration estimates that, at the start of the twenty-first century, almost 3 per cent of the world's population (175 million) is made up of international migrants, a number that has doubled since 1965 (International Organization for Migration 2003). But the freedom to move (at least, to do so legally) is very unevenly distributed. While tourists from the affluent West, alongside those who have money to invest, are welcomed almost everywhere, the world's very poorest people find it increasingly difficult lawfully to access the world's richer countries. The latter is reflected in the growing scale of 'irregular migration', which has grown into a lucrative international criminal business which the IOM estimates to involve between one and two and a half million people annually (International Organization for Migration 2003). Increasing economic inequality on a global scale is a major 'push' factor in the growth of both legal and illegal migration (Dollar and Collier 2001: 43–6). Remittances of migrant workers, for example, are a key source of economic survival for many less developed countries, with workers' remittances exceeding the sum of foreign aid plus foreign direct investment in a number of African countries.

This challenge was intensified in the 1990s – particularly for potential 'recipient' states in Western Europe – by a huge growth in the number of persons applying for political asylum. This was a consequence both of the break-up of the Soviet Union, releasing an aspiration for westward movement, especially into the more affluent western half of Germany, and, a little later, of the succession of internal struggles within the former Yugoslavia, which again created hundreds of thousands of refugees *inside* Europe's south-easternmost corner. Largely as a result of these changes (loosely if not directly associated with globalization), applications for asylum in Europe rose from fewer than 200,000 in 1987 to a peak of 830,000 in 1992 (Levy 1999). In Britain, asylum applications reached a peak (of just over 80,000) in 2000, though by this time the applicants were principally escaping civil disorder in Afghanistan, Iraq, Somalia and Sri Lanka (Home Office 2003).

If globalization helped to create new pressures to migrate it also, upon some accounts, changed the ways in which states and other actors responded. Saskia Sassen (1998) is among those who have argued that a new global order has, in fact if not in law, changed the circumstances under which states make immigration policy. In part, she argues that a global economic regime which frees up the movement of capital while further restricting the mobility of labour is likely to prove to be unsustainable. (Something like the same argument appears in a much radicalized form in Hardt and Negri's *Empire*.) At the same time, she also insists that immigration policy-making is shifting into supra-national institutions (especially though not exclusively within the EU) and that domestic governments are more and more constrained in their choice of domestic policy instruments by an emergent (and global) human rights regime which is itself increasingly a point of reference for domestic judiciaries. Thus, 'under human rights regimes states must increasingly take account of persons *qua* persons, rather than *qua* citizens':

When it comes to immigration policy, states under the rule of law increasingly confront a range of rights and obligations, pressures from both inside and outside, from universal rights to not-so-universal ethnic lobbies. The overall effect is to constrain the sovereignty of the state and to undermine old notions about immigration control.

(Sassen 1998: 71, 57)

The idea that in this most quintessential area of states' rights – the right to determine who shall live within one's borders and upon what terms – power is being transferred to transnational actors has not gone unchallenged. Both Joppke (1998, 2001) and Freeman (1995, 1998) insist that nation-states remain fiercely and determinedly in control of their own immigration policy. Indeed, in the face of growing pressure on their borders, Joppke (1998: 109) identifies 'an increasing willingness and insistence of states to maintain their sovereignty over the determination of entry and expulsion'. This does not necessarily mean, as is sometimes popularly supposed, that the stance of all states is becoming increasingly 'restrictionist'. In fact, states are caught between the opposing imperatives of popular opinion (which, it is suggested, is broadly hostile to rising immigration) and a human rights regime, both domestically and internationally, which is inclined to recognize the entitlements of oppressed persons to political refuge. This dilemma is further complicated by the fact that dwindling population replacement rates in Europe alongside escalating pension commitments make further immigration quite compelling on economic grounds. It is these countervailing pressures (alongside the sheer persistence and guile of desperate displaced persons) that may help to explain why immigration regimes turn out never to be quite so 'draconian' as succeeding generations of politicians promising to be 'firm but fair' insist that they will be. Indeed, Freeman (1998), while seeing the drivers of immigration policy as essentially domestic, insists that domestic opinion is complex and far from uniformly 'restrictionist' (although this is probably more true of the USA than of Europe; on which, see Guiraudon and Lahav 2000). As ever, politicians and those who put pressure upon them are keen to distinguish between 'good' and 'bad' incomers and to put in place regimes that discriminate accordingly.

At the same time, migration policy gives us an interesting insight into multi-level governance in action. According to Guiraudon and Lahav (2000), migration policy within Europe in the 1990s saw a threefold shift: *upwards* towards intergovernmental fora, *downwards* towards local authorities and *outwards* towards non-state actors such as airline carriers, private employers and refugee agencies. (Guiraudon (2000) refers to states seeking out the most effective level and site for governance as 'venue shopping'.) Interestingly, this is seen to reflect not so much a *weakening* of the nation-state as a strategic relocation of its efforts. By devolving activities outwards, downwards and upwards, nation-states are able to protect certain activities from the scrutiny of domestic agencies (especially the courts), to pre-empt political resistance (for example, by preventing asylum-seekers ever leaving their home country) and to deflect criticism for unpopular decisions upon other social and political actors (airlines and haulage companies).

The consideration of migration policy reveals some by now familiar themes in the dynamics of the twenty-first-century state. Clearly, we are on the terrain of governance – where state actors interact with other interested parties both domestically and internationally not in law-like relationships but in varying forms of partnership and policy regime. But this takes place within a context in which states still control many of the most important resources (including the formal authority to permit and prohibit movement across international borders). Migration policy is multi-tiered. But once again this cannot be read as a simple abdication of nation-state power or, indeed, as a zero-sum game of any kind. As the idea of 'venue shopping' suggests, the state may well find advantages in passing responsibility (and blame) on to someone else. Finally, we can see that globalization really does make a difference. But this is not most effectively caught by the idea of a simple decline in state power. Globalization affords modern states quite as many opportunities as pitfalls.

## The 'outward face' of the twenty-first-century state

Throughout this book we have stressed that the attempt to draw a watertight division between the 'inward' and 'outward' faces of the modern state, while always misconceived, has become ever more difficult to maintain (as our discussions of the rise of governance, policy networks, policy transfer and the multifaceted impact of globalization have clearly demonstrated). In the early years of the new century, such a recognition has come to have an increasing impact upon those who have seen themselves as specialists in the workings of the international political order. If the international is always present in the domestic, so, we must suppose, is the domestic always present in the international.

### *New world order?*

In these debates, the key point of reference is (still) the end of the Cold War. As a sub-discipline that grew up in the post-war world and largely under the tutelage of North Americans, it is perhaps understandable that IR was strongly shaped by the world historical stand-off that characterized relations between the USA and the Soviet Union in the second half of the twentieth century. Michael McGwire (2001 and 2002) has characterized the dominant IR approach still more narrowly as embodying a 'national security' paradigm, arising from the particular and peculiar conditions that American foreign policy faced in the formative post-war period between 1945 and 1953. Such a view, he suggests, helps to explain why 'realism' was so dominant as the orthodoxy of both policy-makers and academics over the past half-century. A world without the Soviet Union has begun to breed a newer, though as yet unconsolidated paradigm. This still proceeds as did its Cold War predecessor more or less directly from a view of the importance (and desirability) of securing the dominance of American interests, but it places an increasing emphasis upon 'homeland security' (rather than securing America's interests, as in the past, by always fighting its wars on someone else's soil). The events of 11 September 2001 certainly gave a powerful impetus to this new perspective, but they did not create it.

Crucial to this newer view is the idea that a post-Soviet world is in many ways more dangerous and certainly much more messy and unpredictable than its Cold War predecessor. There is now no state that can hope credibly to challenge the war-fighting machinery of the USA. But states, often the least powerful and effective in conventional terms, are still critically important to the new security situation, though they now belong within a much more complex security landscape that is not exclusively occupied by state actors. To some extent, we can still see international political business between states as usual, with the deployment of the usual repertoire of diplomacy, alliances, trade and aid. But in the North American view, the international situation in the early years of the new century is complicated – and made much more dangerous – by the emergence of two 'new' types of state. These are *'rogue states'* (or, as they have now been euphemistically recast, 'states of concern') and *'failed states'*.

Now that no state can hope to defeat the USA in a conventional war – a truth given rather banal authority by the complete mismatch of the Second Gulf War (of 2003) – the USA is seen to be increasingly likely to face opponents engaged in 'asymmetric warfare'. Asymmetric warfare describes those forms of conflict which avoid set-piece trials of strength and direct engagement with military personnel (which invite certain defeat). It operates through informal structures and the targeting of cultural, political and/or civilian targets, often with no immediate military purpose. Increasingly, such asymmetric warfare is prosecuted not by states or quasi-states but by loose associations of decentralized, non-state actors, 'non-national and transnational groups based on ideology, religion, tribe, culture, zealotry, and illegal economic activities' (Grange 2000). In the parlance of military commentators, this is 'fourth-generation warfare', or '4GW' (for example, Vest 2001). Outside the metropolitan world, this is likely to emerge in violent, episodic, low-intensity conflict of the kind Keane describes as 'uncivil war'. When it is directed at the West and, more especially at the USA, it is likely to take the form of 'terrorist' attacks directed at symbolic targets (usually, though not universally, of no military significance). A characteristic fear of commentators is that fourth-generation warriors will exploit the technical sophistication (and vulnerability) of the most developed states to wreak havoc (cheaply and anonymously) upon or through its information technology infrastructure. Following the story line of a dozen Hollywood movies, 4GW hackers will turn the hi-tech capacity (and enormous destructive capability) of the USA in upon itself.

Although these fourth-generation warriors are characteristically viewed as non-state actors, they are seen to operate (and indeed only to be able to operate) in a supportive context provided by the presence of varying dysfunctional states ('state sponsors of terrorism') – either rogue states or failed states. Although both have historical precursors – Henriksen's (2001) historical survey has the Gauls as the first rogue warriors! – the concern with these dysfunctional states is much more manifest since 1989. Before this time, 'pariah' states were generally those which were excluded from the family of international states either because of the appalling ways in which they treated their own populations or because they sought to equip themselves with nuclear arms in the face of the disapproval of key Western powers

(Litwak 2000). Although today's rogue states still mistreat their populations, it is their *outward* face that gives rise to the greatest concern. Attention was directed towards 'problem' states and 'state-sponsored terrorism' throughout the 1980s, but current usage dates from the first Clinton administration and the perceived necessity of 'confronting backlash states' (Lake 1994). Backlash states are said to have certain common characteristics:

> Ruled by cliques that control power through coercion, they suppress basic human rights and promote radical ideologies . . . their leaders share a common antipathy toward popular participation that might undermine the existing regimes. These nations exhibit a chronic inability to engage constructively with the outside world, and they do not function effectively in alliances – even with those like-minded . . . they share a siege mentality. Accordingly, they are embarked on ambitious and costly military programs – especially in weapons of mass destruction (WMD) and missile delivery systems.
>
> (Lake 1994: 46)

Identified as backlash states at this time by the US administration were Cuba, North Korea, Iran, Iraq and Libya. Rogue states are those which 'have large conventional military forces and that condone international terrorism and/or seek weapons of mass destruction, including nuclear, biological, and chemical armaments' (Tanter 1999). The failure to comply with a United Nations mandate to eliminate such weapons of mass destruction was, of course, the much-disputed justification for the USA and its allies to invade Iraq in March 2003. A second rationale was provided by the largely unproven connection between Saddam Hussein's Iraqi regime and the al-Qaeda terrorist network.

A second source of concern (to the USA at least) has been the (growing) number of so-called *failed states*. Although use of the term is rather imprecise and selective, in essence a failed state describes a political entity which is no longer able to maintain authority or political order, a society in which the basics of public order and the maintenance of law and order have collapsed (see Jackson 1998; Brinkerhoff and Brinkerhoff 2002). According to Susan Rice (2002), failed or failing states at the time of writing included Afghanistan, Somalia, the Democratic Republic of Congo, Sudan, Angola, Bosnia, Sierra Leone, Zimbabwe, Liberia, Burundi, Côte d'Ivoire and Colombia. Others – among them Pakistan, Georgia, Albania, Yemen and Nigeria – were 'weak, if not yet clearly "failing" states'. In part, the anxiety over failed states concerns the appallingly dangerous, insanitary and impoverished circumstances in which the luckless citizens of such states are forced to live. But at least as important for the architects of national security policy in the West is the security challenge that failed states present to Western interests. As Bush's National Security Strategy so succinctly puts it: 'America is now threatened less by conquering states than we are by failing ones.' It continues:

> The events of September 11, 2001, taught us that weak states, like Afghanistan, can pose as great a danger to our national interests as strong states. Poverty

does not make poor people into terrorists and murderers. Yet poverty, weak institutions, and corruption can make weak states vulnerable to terrorist networks and drug cartels within their borders.

(cited in Rice 2002)

The challenge is not so much from the failed states themselves as from their failure to control their own territory or to prevent its being used as a safe base for terrorist groups. Even states which are not the sponsors or tolerators of terrorist activity within their borders may contribute to a general lack of order and thus pose a threat to the integrity of the global political system (and lay themselves open to 'therapeutic' intervention by the USA and its allies).

The identification of both of these types of 'deviant' state is more or less uniquely of American provenance. Critics (such as Noam Chomsky 2000) insist that the labelling of states as 'rogues' or 'failed' is almost entirely a product of US geopolitical interests – providing a justification for US intervention in places where it considers its vital interests are at stake. Chomsky insists that the biggest rogue among the world's sovereign states is the USA itself – willing to act unilaterally in the face of international law and the express wishes of the United Nations. Others see the 'failed state' as itself a failed concept – one which does not capture the real nature of political authority (and its breakdown), particularly in African states (Spanger 2000). The function of the idea of the 'failed state' is seen to be to provide a justification for unilateral US intervention (or multilateral intervention in those circumstances in which others can be persuaded to back US interests). The critics certainly have a point. The USA is highly selective in those states it identifies as rogues (and, of course, those individuals it identifies as 'rogues' *within* these states also vary very considerably through time, as the USA's changing relationship to Saddam Hussein and Osama Bin Laden demonstrates). Arab opinion is consistently outraged by the failure of the USA to identify Israel as one of the Middle East's leading rogues. The terminology of 'rogue states' and 'failing states' certainly serves to legitimate intervention by the USA, while allowing her to maintain the moral high ground as the world's number one police authority. At the same time, we should recognize that state failure is a *real* problem. Life in a society with no 'common power' is likely to prove, as Hobbes (1968: 186) famously feared, 'solitary, poore, nasty, brutish and short'. And critics have frequently complained of the *failure* of the USA (or the UN) to intervene adequately, or in time, where state authority has clearly broken down (as experience at different times in Rwanda, Somalia, Bosnia and the Congo attests).

## The twenty-first-century state as *Empire*?

Our survey of the state at the start of the twenty-first century identifies a number of key trends – an increasingly complex governing order made up of multiple layers, overlapping jurisdictions and interlocking networks; the seemingly relentless progress of globalization and the movements of money, ideas and people that this brings in its wake; and an international order in which the terrifying stalemate of bipolar nuclear confrontation has given way to the little less frightening prospect of a single superpower trying to keep its collective eye on a bewildering kaleidoscope of diverse and sometimes ill-defined causes and actors, many of whom turn out to be armed and extremely dangerous. All of these elements (and others) are brought together and given a very radical and somewhat counter-intuitive twist in Michael Hardt and Antonio Negri's survey entitled *Empire*.

First published in 2000, *Empire* is an attempt to grasp in all its puzzling complexity the new international governing order that prevails at the start of the twenty-first century – and to anticipate and advocate its overthrow. The central claim of the book is that we are living in a new age of empire. But this new world of empire owes very little to extant traditions of imperialism – and more to ancient Rome than to modern Britain or France. Indeed, according to Hardt and Negri, the nation-states that made the empires of modernity are largely in retreat. The new order owes much to globalization but, while globalization does much to undermine the political authority of nation-states (including even the USA), it does not undermine political power itself. The new form taken by political power in the twenty-first century is empire.

> Over the past several decades, as colonial regimes were overthrown and then precipitously after the Soviet barriers to the capitalist world market finally collapsed, we have witnessed an irresistible and irreversible globalization of economic and cultural exchanges. Along with the global market and global circuits of production has emerged *a global order, a new logic and structure of rule – in short a new form of sovereignty*. Empire is the political subject that effectively regulates these global exchanges, the sovereign power that governs the world.
>
> (Hardt and Negri 2000: xi; emphasis added)

Thus the declining political effectiveness of nation-states does not mean that politics – or sovereignty – has been eclipsed by economics. ('Politics does not disappear', Hardt and Negri insist; 'what disappears is any notion of the autonomy of the political'.) Instead, 'sovereignty has taken a new form, composed of a series of national and supranational organisms united under a single logic of rule. This new global form of sovereignty is . . . Empire.' While truly global in its scope and impact, this empire owes nothing to traditional imaginings of 'world government'. It is a radically 'decentred and deterritorializing apparatus of rule'. It knows no territorial borders or boundaries. It 'manages hybrid identities, flexible hierarchies, and plural exchanges through modulating networks of command' (xii–xiii). It 'operates on all registers of the social order extending down to the depths of the social world' (xv).

Empire is ubiquitous and amorphous. It is present at the global level but also in the interstices of everyday life. It is the governing principle of an economic order that is increasingly about what Hardt and Negri (here following Foucault) call 'biopolitical production' – 'a new economic-industrial-communicative machine' – yielding an economy which is about the production and reproduction of life itself (40). It aims to rule over 'social life in its entirety', and 'thus Empire presents the paradigmatic form of biopower' (307). Empire is 'continually bathed in blood', but its aim is always to maintain (or impose) peace – 'a perpetual and universal peace outside history' (xv). Here Hardt and Negri point towards the (new) mechanisms and justifications of 'humanitarian intervention'. Empire replaces the idea of international law with a permanent policing role – an 'international community' permanently watchful and ready to intervene. It revives the idea of 'just war' to warrant its repeated intervention in the 'internal' affairs of those states which 'threaten' the peaceful world order (in which the interests of empire are entrenched). Humanitarian NGOs (such as Amnesty International and Oxfam) are recast as 'the most powerful pacific weapons of the new world order', preparing public opinion for the 'just' interventions of the 'secular wing' of empire (36). Thus, 'intervention is an effective mechanism that through police deployments contributes directly to the construction of the moral, normative, and institutional order of Empire' (38).

Although empire is a network not a hierarchy and appears in varying shapes and forms, Hardt and Negri see it as having a clear constitutional structure. In their reading, the idea of empire is (in general form, rather than specific content) the project of the US constitutional order writ large (where the US constitution refers to a set of governing practices and ambitions rather than simply to a historic document). Above all, 'the fundamental characteristic of imperial sovereignty is that *its space is always open.*' In embodying this principle historically, US constitutional government is seen as 'a moment of great innovation and rupture in the genealogy of modern sovereignty' (161). The US constitution envisages political authority as 'constituted by a whole series of powers that regulate themselves and arrange themselves in networks' (162) Unlike the imperialisms of old Europe, empire grows not by the formal conquest of foreign dominions (and peoples) but by extending its coverage and maximizing the number of people who come under its influence. Thus, empire can be redescribed as 'the global expansion of the internal US constitutional project' (182). In this way (but only in this way) can the USA be said to have a privileged place in the process of begetting empire.

The institutional structure of empire is complex and protean. In part it is pyramidical, with the USA, the G7 (or G8) nations and their (economic, military and cultural) organizations at its comparatively narrow peak. Below this come the networks of transnational corporate capitalism and 'second-tier' nation-states. Below this again lies a third level inhabited by 'groups that represent popular interests in the global power arrangement' (311), such as the United Nations General Assembly and various international NGOs. In this new order, political command 'is exercised no longer through the disciplinary modalities of the modern state but rather through the modalities of biopolitical control: . . . the bomb, money and ether' ( 344, 347).

Hardt and Negri work with what are by now familiar ideas (the decline of nation-state authority, the ubiquity of global capitalism, the importance of networks, new information technologies and the extension of new forms of governance). But they use these to build a quite distinctive account of global governance under the biopolitics of empire. Their account of how we may expect (and hope) to get beyond empire is still more imaginative. In the face of thirty years' orthodoxy (on both right and left), they see the coming of the new global order as an expression of the *strength* of popular forces in the preceding period both in terms of anti-colonial struggles and of workers' and students' movements.

> The construction of Empire and its global networks is a *response* to the various struggles against the modern machines of power, and specifically to class struggle driven by the multitude's desire for liberation. The multitude called Empire into being.
>
> (Hardt and Negri 2000: 43; emphasis added)

They welcome the coming of empire much as Marx welcomed the transition from feudalism to capitalism – as the inauguration of a new order which 'increases the potential for liberation' (44). Globalization should be welcomed (rather than resisted) by those seeking radical change because it constitutes the new terrain on which the struggle for liberation can be prosecuted anew. The conflicts that characterize empire are not so clearly defined and delineated as they were for the workers' movement in the classical age of industrial capitalism. But it is the very distinctiveness and diversity of these forms and sites of resistance – riots in Los Angeles, student protest in Tiananmen Square, strikes in France and South Korea, the Palestinian Intifada – that make such struggles 'leap vertically and touch immediately on the global level' (55). Furthermore, these struggles are by their very nature anti-systemic. They are 'at once economic, political, and cultural – and hence they are biopolitical struggles, struggles over the form of life' (56).

The agent of change under empire is 'the multitude'. If implicitly for the most part, 'the multitude' takes the place in the biopolitical economy of empire that the proletariat occupied in Marx's account of the revolutionary overthrow of capitalism. Thus, 'the creative forces of the multitude that sustain Empire are also capable of autonomously creating a counter-Empire, an alternative political organization of global flows and exchanges' (xv). The multitude is altogether more amorphous and diverse than the classical industrial proletariat. A key source of its strength lies in the distinctive character of labour under empire – increasingly engaged in mental labour and the production of virtual goods and services. The multitude is more truly universal (*and* diverse) than the industrial proletariat could ever hope to be. And it expresses itself (and its discontents) through its movement around what is now an unambiguously global economy – through the disruptive mechanisms of 'nomadism', 'desertion' and 'exodus'. Giving a radical twist to the dynamics of large-scale migration, Hardt and Negri place especial stress upon the transformative impact of globally mobile labour in the struggle to establish counter-empire. The global economy of empire requires labour to be a highly mobile 'factor of production', but it cannot live with the disruptive consequences that the heightened mobility of real workers brings. Again echoing Marx in the *Communist Manifesto*, they insist that 'a specter haunts the world and it is the specter of migration' (213). 'Through circulation the multitude reappropriates space and constitutes itself as an active subject' (397). Eventually these struggles of the multitude will carry us forward from the 'modern republic' of empire to the '*postmodern posse*', Hardt and Negri's characteristically original shorthand for the future form of governance – 'the power of the multitude and its telos, an embodied power of knowledge and being, always open to the possible'. As with Marx's anticipation of a transition to communism, there are no models of this future: 'Only the multitude through its practical experimentation will offer the models and determine when and how the possible becomes real' (411).

*Empire* is an extraordinary *tour de force*. It embraces many of the changes we have delineated earlier in this chapter: the displacement of government by governance and of hierarchy by network; the emergence of complex patterns of multi-layered governance; rapid changes in the nature and distribution of labour; the centrality of the politics of migration; the diversity of contemporary oppositional movements and counter-cultures. Above all, it recognizes the permanence and impermanence of change (the sense that 'all which is solid melts into air' which Marx originally identified as the hallmark of capitalist modernity). It is a suitably provocative end-point for our survey of the emergent twenty-first-century political order. But it leaves many questions unanswered, while on other issues we may suspect that its answers, though bold and challenging, are probably wrong. Above all, we are still left wondering just how different states will look in the twenty-first century. This is the question which we shall attempt to answer in Chapter 8.

## Further reading

Hardt, M. and Negri, A. (2000) *Empire*. London: Harvard University Press.

Hooghe, L. and Marks, G. (2001) *Multi-level Governance*. Lanham, MD: Rowan & Littlefield.

Joppke, C. (ed.) (1998) *Challenge to the Nation State*. Oxford: Oxford University Press.

Litwak, R. S. (2000) *Rogue States and U.S. Foreign Policy: Containment after the Cold War*. Baltimore: Woodrow Wilson Center Press.

Marsh, D. and Rhodes, R. (1992) *Policy Networks in British Government*. Oxford: Clarendon Press.

Pierre, J. and Peters, B. G. (2000) *Governance, Politics and the State*. London: Macmillan.

# 8 Conclusion

## States of the future and the future of the state

At a number of points in this book, and more especially in the preceding chapter, our attention has been drawn towards the changing character of the modern state. In Chapter 2, I described the emergence of the modern state as a historical and in some sense contingent development. We saw both that there were states before modernity and that even these more primitive forms of the state were of comparatively recent origin. There was no reason in principle to believe that humankind, having once managed its collective affairs without the necessity of a state apparatus, might not in the future find ways of living that were 'beyond the modern state'. Such an expectation is not entirely new. Marx and some of the more pacific-minded schools of nineteenth-century liberalism shared, albeit in their rather differing ways, a belief in the eventual 'withering away of the state'. Assorted anarchists and utopians have always longed for just such an outcome, and, from time to time, voices in the political mainstream (Ernest Renan in the 1880s, John Herz in the 1950s) have supposed that changing international circumstances might be moving us towards the redundancy of the nation-state. In some recent accounts, as we have seen, globalization is said already to have carried us to the very threshold of such an epochal change. Thus, Tony McGrew (1992a: 87), for all his cautious qualifications, accepts that 'there is a powerful argument which indicates that globalization is dissolving the essential structures of modern statehood.'

Throughout the later chapters of this book, and more especially in discussion of the international order and the changing state–economy relationship, we have found plenty of evidence of a profound attenuation of the powers of the traditional state form of modernity – the nation-state. Held (1995) has written of

> a set of forces which combine to restrict the freedom of action of governments and states by blurring the boundaries of domestic politics, transforming the conditions of political decision-making, changing the institutional and organizational context of national polities, altering the legal framework and administrative practices of governments and obscuring the lines of responsibility and accountability of national states themselves.

Yet, for a number of reasons, it is clear that we cannot equate these profound changes with a tendency for the state to 'wither away', and there are at least three qualifications to be entered against the logic of 'state decline'. First, there is clearly a temptation to (over-)generalize from particular areas of the state's activity in which change has been most striking. Thus, for example, some commentators have identified the decline in the state's ownership of industry or in traditional forms of the public administration of welfare with a general withdrawal of the state. But such a conclusion is not warranted. These sorts of changes have not only been concentrated upon particular sectors of the state's activity but have often also been complemented by *new* functions for the state (e.g. in the *regulation* of privatized industries or the *juridification* of industrial relations). Second, there are strategic areas of state activity in which the 'withdrawal' of the state is much less marked. This is true, above all, of the state's military and national security functions. There have admittedly been some limited moves towards 'privatization' of the management of courts and the prison service, but in the conduct of military and national security policy the state remains fiercely jealous of its sovereign powers. Of course, states enter into alliances and pacts which commit them to joint action with other sovereign states, and their effective autonomy (the power to decide for themselves what they will do) is sharply qualified by the actual disposition of military strength. But this has been true throughout the era of modern states. While states may agree to act multilaterally, they are extremely reluctant to pool *effective control* over their military forces, as even the briefest consideration of the experience of the United Nations as an armed force should demonstrate. Discussion of a European Security Force may hold out the prospect of a supra-state alternative but, on the other hand, the military conduct of the USA in the opening years of the new century serves to reinforce older assumptions. The bottom line is that 'the modern state is still able in principle to determine the most fundamental aspects of people's life-chances – the question of life and death' (Held 1991: 212).

Finally, we should not suppose that a decline in the *nation-state* form is the same as a decline in the modern state *per se*. Although the nation-state has been the fairly ubiquitous form that the modern state has come to take, and although we tend to identify the classical nation-state with the model of centralized polities such as France and the UK, neither of these associations is a necessary one. In practice, states have always been multi-levelled. In federal states (such as Germany and the USA), this is explicitly and constitutionally recognized. A sociologically informed view of the state (similar to that developed in Chapters 3 and 4) makes it clear that the state is not a single unified actor, but rather an ensemble of forces intermingled with its social and economic context. State effects (to borrow Jessop's usage) are generated at multiple levels, on many sites and by a multitude of social actors. State activity may be relocated away from the level of the nation-state without our assuming that 'state-effectivity' has been correspondingly weakened. Certainly, the *idea* of a unitary state sovereignty has been extremely important, effectual and (some would suppose) harmful in the modern period. But, here following Foucault, we should not allow this significance to persuade us that it has ever been a very useful empirical generalization about what actually happens.

# Changing states

On balance, it seems appropriate to suggest that over the past thirty years there has been an accelerating change in the circumstances in which states have to act. Transnational forces in general and a globalized market economy in particular have decisively limited the free hand of states in both domestic and foreign policy. At the most general level, we can speak of a decisive weakening of certain strategic competencies of the state, and at times this seems to add up not just to a quantitative, but also to a qualitative change in the nature of states' activity. Nonetheless, if their powers have been reduced, states are still decisive players in both the domestic and international arena and it remains the case that there are enormous differences *between* states in terms of their capacity to act autonomously on the world stage. In several areas (such as welfare, labour markets and industrial policy) we have seen that states have often abandoned some traditional functions only to take on new ones. In Michael Mann's judgement, nation-states are 'diversifying, developing, not dying', and the weakening of the state in Western Europe is 'slight, *ad hoc*, uneven, and unique' (Mann 1993b: 115–16). In the closing pages, I want to consider three ways in which contemporary states are likely to be subject to a process of continuing change. These are:

1   the resiting of state activity;
2   changes in the functioning of the state; and
3   the replacement of states by other social forces.

## *Resiting of state activity*

We have become so used to the nation-state form that we are inclined to see any diminution of its powers as a weakening of the state *per se*. But such an assumption is misplaced, for at least some of the powers of the nation-state are being reallocated to state institutions at either a sub-national or a supra-national level. The first of these changes (decentralizing state activities) can be seen quite clearly in the reform agenda of Labour governments in Britain since 1997. One of the new government's earliest measures was to legislate devolved government for Scotland and Wales. Rather more faltering (though still on the agenda) were moves to set up assemblies within the English regions. Labour also provided for the election of mayors with executive powers in major cities and the (re)institution of an assembly for London. At the same time, leaders of local government in the regions have continued to establish new forms of public–private sector partnership within their regional economies. They have sought to bypass central government and establish direct links with EU institutions in Brussels and with other regional governments, a process which is seen much more clearly in the continental experience of Germany's *Länder* or Spain's *autonomias*. Meanwhile, national government has continued its efforts, especially within the field of social welfare, to devolve authority (and responsibility) for the management of resources down to the most local level (though this is done in the context of new and highly intrusive mechanisms of 'accountability', generally to central government rather than to end-users). In all these areas it is important to see that power is not just 'given away'. In general, the devolution of authority from central government is matched by a wholesale transformation of the apparatuses of surveillance through which government centrally seeks to hold these new 'power-holders' to account.

A still more important change in the most recent period is the transfer of state functions to a supra-national level. We saw in Chapters 6 and 7 how the accelerating transnationalism of the past fifty years has brought into being (or at least enhanced the activity of) a number of international political authorities. Among the best known of these have been the UN and its off-shoots: the International Monetary Fund (IMF), the World Bank, the General Agreement on Tariffs and Trade (GATT) and latterly the World Trade Organization (WTO). Less prominent (though increasingly important) are a myriad of smaller or more specialized international authorities concerned with the technical or political coordination of cross-border relations. There has even been, as we have seen, some internationalization of political lobbying (as evidenced by the activities of groups such as Greenpeace and Amnesty International). And we can see examples emerging of new forms of political interaction about new sorts of political issues – as evidenced in the negotiations between Toronto's civic authorities and the World Health Organization (WHO) over the city's health status following an acute outbreak of SARS.

Many of these organizational developments are a response to the need to manage more extensive transnational processes – above all, those relating to the world economy and the global environment. As we have already seen, very few commentators have supposed that they are part of an (evolutionary) logic that is carrying us towards 'world government'. Indeed, the prospect of a global authority claiming the sorts of sovereign powers which have been commonplace in nation-states is unimaginably far away. In this context, the international relations 'realists' are right to see these new fora as settings within which, for much of the time and *in so far as they are able*, nation-states will continue to pursue their own distinctive agendas. On the other hand, we have already seen that nation-states are *not* unitary-rational agents, nor are they the *only* effective actors on the global stage. Furthermore, the new international order is one in which nation-states are increasingly, and for a whole variety of reasons, *not* able to pursue their own agendas. This does not betoken a simple transfer of powers from the nation-state to international political authorities. At least one account of globalization suggests that national governments are losing their power but that *no one* is inheriting them (leaving the world, its economy and its environment increasingly 'ungoverned and ungovernable'). An alternative view suggests that nation-states can actually *enhance* their individual powers (in the face of the globalizing challenge) by pooling their sovereignty in international institutions. Upon this account, the *de facto* powers of the nation-state are protected by surrendering a part of their *de jure* claim to sovereignty. But there is also a third possibility: that we are moving towards a world order in which at least some forms of authoritative decision-making take place beyond the framework of inter-state relations, with national governments as one among several stakeholders. (Examples given by Held and McGrew include the Global Water Partnership, the World Commission on Dams and the Global Alliance for Vaccines and Immunization; Held and McGrew 2002: 11.) In a world in which governing is increasingly about governance, the exercise of political authority is likely to appear (and indeed to become) more complex, more elusive and multi-sited. The old IR metaphor of the world order as a series of billiard balls crashing into each other will no longer do. The current world game looks much more like a high-tech pinball machine without a player.

### Changes in the functioning of the state

One of the most important developments of the past decade, and one which is continuing apace, is a change in the characteristic *mode of delivery* of state services. In Chapter 1 we saw how, under the authoritative influence of Weber, the bureaucratic form of organization became almost a defining element of the modern state. Indeed, state and public bureaucracy became terms which were often used interchangeably. With a measure of regret, Weber saw the bureaucracy as the indispensable means of public administration in large-scale societies because of its machine-like efficiency. In more positive accounts, the civil service was seen to be impregnated with a powerful sense of public duty, staffed by public servants with a self-effacing interest in promoting the greatest common good. We saw in Chapter 3 how this model of bureaucratic public service came under withering attack from the neo-liberals. Public officials were no different (and no better) than the rest of the population. They were utility-maximizers who simply used their monopolistic control over the apparatus of compulsory state provision to extract a rent from a disempowered citizenry who had nowhere else to go. It hardly needs repeating that for neo-liberals the 'solution' to this problem lay in a greater reliance upon markets. Neo-liberals believe that, in almost every conceivable situation where goods and services are to be supplied, markets allowing for the freest possible exchange of economic factors will normally guarantee the most efficient and effective use of resources. Under a system of private ownership and with financial rewards tied to market performance, markets will generate the greatest available output from any given input. Their solution to a perceived lack of productivity in the public domain is therefore 'markets' wherever possible and, where not, a solution that approximates the workings and logic of a market.

Throughout the 1980s and much of the 1990s, this sentiment had a profound impact upon the reform of public administration in a range of quite differing political regimes. In circumstances where governments found themselves under increasing pressure to deliver services to their electorates (often in the face of 'unfavourable' demographic changes) but with a limited resource base (squeezed by sluggish economic growth and/or the international mobility of capital), they looked for every possible way of extracting a greater *output* of goods and services from a fairly static *input*. Privatization was the very clearest way of making this move from states to markets (often with the additional incentive of an immediate cash injection for governments from the cut-price sale of assets), and privatization was a global phenomenon of the 1990s (but one that may now have passed its peak, as we saw in Chapter 4). In other areas, where for economic or political reasons such a transfer has not seemed possible, governments have tried *to bring the market into the state*. At various points in this study, we have seen evidence of these sorts of initiatives. They have included partial transfer of activity into the private sector or the creation of public authorities insulated from electoral pressure (both of which have been seen in UK housing policy), the 'contracting out' of non-core activities to outside suppliers and the creation of an 'internal market' for public services (e.g. in health and education). In the UK (and more modestly elsewhere), the size of the civil service has been reduced and there have been fewer 'jobs for life', more short-term contracts and the introduction of performance-related pay. As we saw in Chapter 4, the UK civil service has been substantially remade since the late 1980s, with the implementation of policy transferred into a series of partially autonomous executive agencies, run along quasi-commercial lines. Much the same aspiration captured the heart and soul of the US political class, with Clinton's vice-president, Al Gore, being charged in the early 1990s with the responsibility for *reinventing government* (the title of Osborne and Gaebler's best-selling reformer's handbook, published in 1992).

At the start of the new century, it is clear that the high tide of 'classic' neo-liberalism has passed – even though it continues to have a profound impact upon the newer governing institutions and practices. At one time, it appeared that Britain's dominant party (or at least influential sections of it) was committed to the wholesale replacement of the welfare state with private market alternatives. In New Zealand, in the 1980s and 1990s, this experiment was carried further than anywhere else, making it the number one destination for would-be reformers across the Western world (see Kelsey 1995). This moment has passed. In part, this is because the tide has turned in favour of (nominally) social-democratic parties. In part, it is a response to some spectacular failures – such as the meltdown of the national rail system in the UK following privatization or the faltering pace of New Zealand's economic growth. Perhaps more than anything else, though, it is a recognition that, in democracies, public services (though not their funding) are popular. Now increasingly parties find themselves fighting over the 'old' terrain of who can provide the best (and most cost-effective) public services. But the *methods* through which they claim to be able to deliver these *desiderata* have changed. In the area of labour markets, for example, the somewhat discredited idea of 'market failures' has been revived. But the failures are now seen to lie not so much with an absence of demand but rather with the inadequacy of factors of supply, above all, labour. Aptly named 'active labour market programmes' concentrate upon making the unemployed 'job ready', and this is seen increasingly as the responsibility of the unemployed (or 'not job-ready') themselves. Thus Labour's New Deal (unlike its famous US forerunner) is not about funding public works but about allowing as many people as possible (including many of those who were previously 'excluded' by their health status or family responsibilities) to participate in the 'new economy'. Increasingly, the agencies that are to deliver the government's agenda belong not to the state but to 'social partners', to whom the state's 'social' work is now sub-contracted. In all these ways, states are becoming more 'regulating' than 'producing'. They are increasingly inclined to use market-like mechanisms and contracts to realize their policy objectives. But we are still an enormous distance from the neo-liberals' dream of government meeting once a year to hand out the annual contracts! As we saw in Chapter 4, and for better or worse, we still live in an era of big government.

### *Replacing the state?*

A third and perhaps the most radical agenda for change rests upon the aspiration to replace the modern state with other institutional forms. Sometimes this is presented as a purely normative argument (describing the institutions by which the state *should* be replaced) and sometimes as an empirical argument (these are the forms which are *actually* replacing the state). Often, it is a mixture of the two (these are the changes that are taking place and this is why we should encourage them). At the risk of very considerable oversimplification, we can think in this context of two main alternatives to the state: markets and 'the community' (Miller 1989). We have seen the case for markets replacing states at various points in this book. There is a normative argument (markets maximize freedom and choice), an argument from utility (markets maximize overall welfare) and an empirical argument (in the 'new' global economy, international markets are increasingly independent of the jurisdiction of nation-states). The case for replacing the state with 'communal' action is rather more diffuse. At least some of the advocates of an empowered civil society see this as the site of communal forms of activity replacing the state. Socialists hostile to the logic of 'the capitalist state' have wished to see power transferred to communities of workers (variously defined). In its more conservative forms, the argument from community has been one for the restoration of traditional forms of the family (and traditional forms of authority *within* the family) to countermand the 'dissolution' of kinship responsibilities which it is supposed the interventionist state has precipitated. These widely differing advocates of community all tend to argue that there is no combination of state and market which exhaustively defines a satisfactory basis for the allocative and authoritative ordering of our collective life.

I do not want, at this late stage in the book, to open up a discussion of the myriad claims surrounding market, state and community. (I have discussed these issues extensively elsewhere: Pierson 1993, 1995, 1998.) Rather, I confine myself here to a brief consideration of whether market, community, family or indeed anything else is likely in the foreseeable future to replace the state. I focus upon the area in which these disputes have been most vigorously engaged – i.e. over the future of the welfare state.

In earlier chapters, we have seen that welfare was the single most important sector of growth in both state budgets and state employment throughout the twentieth century and, more especially, after 1945. We have also seen how it is upon the administration of welfare and the taxation regime required to fund it, that much of the fiercest criticism of the modern state has been focused. Furthermore, it is in respect of welfare activities (in health, education and pensions) that we have seen the most active attempts to reallocate responsibilities from the state to markets and/or families and communities. It is here then that we might most naturally look for signs of a coming replacement of the state. Yet, in fact, the evidence is rather mixed, or, more properly, the outcomes are complex. Governments have certainly encouraged their citizens to make greater provision for their own present and future welfare (though this has often required the state to subsidize preferred forms of 'private' activity). They have introduced market-mimicking devices in the allocation of health and educational provision (though at considerable cost, with widely contested gains in efficiency and without persuading ever larger numbers of citizens to choose an alternative private option). They have, perhaps, succeeded in lowering expectations of future pension provision, but without as yet solving the problem of how the larger retired population of the future is to have an adequate income (or enjoy adequate standards of housing and health care). An entire generation of secretaries of state for social security committed to reducing the 'burden' of welfare expenditure has found it impossible to do anything more than stem the pace of growth in the welfare budget.

This does not mean that 'nothing much has changed'. As we have seen, the social security regime has been subject to almost continuous reform to bring it into line with a labour market profoundly changed by (among other things) the new international political economy. Policies for 'care in the community' have had profound effects upon the circumstances and expectations of millions of older people. But there is no straightforward 'replacement' of the state. State, market, community and family have always been entwined in the provision of social welfare. The present reordering of that relationship does not add up to a simple movement away from the state. For example, at the same time as the state places an increasing responsibility upon the family to support its members (e.g. in retirement or full-time education), there are a growing number of lone individuals, one-parent families and single-person households who fall outside this network of support. The reduction of state support may be real enough, but it has to be understood in terms of reconstructing a complex mixed economy of welfare, rather than in terms of a straightforward shift from state to market or community.

## End states?

A similar story might be told about other major areas of the state's activity. Circumstances have changed, state competencies have changed, perhaps even the character of the state itself is being altered. The sorts of economic policies which were routinely followed by advanced capitalist nation-states in the post-war period are now regarded as 'undo-able'. States now exercise much less control over their external economic environment (with the considerable qualification that all but the most powerful of states have *always* been policy-takers rather than policy-makers). But this is not the same as saying that states have become less active or that states are simply making way for markets. The state that tries to make itself more attractive to inward investors is often intensely active in shaping its working population, its labour markets, its industrial relations, its transport infrastructure, its educational curricula, and its tax structure to suit these new objectives. States still redistribute income and opportunities on a massive scale. It is the (less progressive) character of this redistribution as much as its size that has changed. We have also seen how the processes of globalization, while weakening individual nation-states, create new problems of political coordination which have had increasingly to be addressed at the transnational level. Indeed, our growing awareness of the global limits to economic growth generates a new and powerful imperative for collective decision-making (and self-control) at the global level.

At the same time, modifications of states' capacities do not all run one way. The same technology that allows capital to be instantly mobile around the global economy allows the state instantly to access the most intimate details about its individual citizens. Technological change has also had a profound effect upon the ways in which we perceive states and the ways in which they speak to us. An issue at the founding of the USA was how representatives in Washington could hope to keep in touch with their remote electors in far away New Hampshire. Now virtually everything is instantly transmissible everywhere – and news is available twenty-four hours a day, every day. While both the utopias and dystopias of the virtual world are over-written, this undoubtedly changes what it is to govern and be governed. Now, more than ever, the business of government is a banal spectacle. At the start of the century – and more especially after 11 September 2001 – there is a temptation to look away from states towards other types of political actors, not least as a threat to citizens' lives and well-being. But the nature of the 'security threat' is differentiated. Around the world, many populations still have more to fear from state actors – either their own or those that have been the victims of non-state assaults. And alongside the dreadful loss of life perpetrated by non-state actors we should remember the much more systematic and mundane toll exacted by states themselves. In the 1990s, states around the world executed on average 2,400 of their own citizens every year (Amnesty International 2003).

One last lesson of the present period is that we need to abandon our almost exclusive concern with the state as nation-state. Undoubtedly, 'the death of the nation-state' is an immeasurably long way off, but, at the same time, we need to be aware of the other contexts (above and below the nation-state level) in which state effects are generated and the ways in which these might be made accountable to *their* potential citizens. Here, the traditional apparatus of modern political theory is rather unhelpful. From the early modern period, problems of political obligation, obedience, representation, consent and so on have tended to be set in the context of a unitary, sovereign nation-state authority. Correspondingly, citizenship has been represented as a singular quality (with 'dual citizenship' as a peculiar exception). As Held (1995) points out, globalization means that our citizenship can no longer be exhaustively defined by membership of the nation-state, nor democracy by participation in purely national political processes. And in an era in which 'abnormal' political action (direct action, boycotts, even suicide bombings) is increasingly 'normal', it makes less and less sense to think of our political activity exclusively in terms of the 'transmission belt' logic of traditional forms of representation.

If the state, in both its older and newer forms, is not going away, we need to think much harder about how it might be more effectively directed and controlled by its citizens. We need to do this in the context of multiple political orders and multiple forms of citizenship. One of the most remarkable complacencies of contemporary political thought is the supposition that the extension of the suffrage around the turn of the twentieth century 'completed' the transition to the fullest practicable democracy. In fact, this was a vital, indispensable, but essentially incremental step in the right direction. Above all else, the changing form of the modern state is a challenge to our democratic imagination.

# Bibliography

Abrams, P. (1988) 'Notes on the difficulty of studying the *state*', *Journal of Historical Sociology* 1, 1, 58–89.

Adam Smith Institute (2003) *Tax Freedom Day*. http://www.adamsmith.org/cissues/tax-and-economy/tax-freedom-day-2003.htm (accessed 4 Sept 2003).

Albertsen, N. (1988) 'Postmodernism, post-Fordism and critical social theory', *Environment and Planning D: Society and Space* 6, 339–65.

Allen, J. (1990) 'Does feminism need a theory of "the state?"', in S. Watson (ed.) *Playing the State*. London: Verso, 21–37.

Allison, G. (1971) *The Essence of Decision*. Boston: Little, Brown.

Almond, G. A. and Verba, S. (1965) *The Civic Culture*. Boston: Little, Brown.

Almond, G. A., Nordlinger, E. A., Lowi, T. J. and Fabbrini, S. (1988) 'The return to the state', *American Political Science Review* 82, 3, 853–901.

Alt, J. E. and Chrystal, K. A. (1983) 'Political business cycles', in J. E. Alt and K. A. Chrystal, *Political Economics*. Brighton: Wheatsheaf.

Amnesty International (2003) http://web.amnesty.org/pages/deathpenalty-facts-eng (accessed 10 Sept 2003).

Anderson, B. (1991) *Imagined Communities*. London: Verso.

Anderson, J. (ed.) (1986) *The Rise of the Modern State*. Brighton: Wheatsheaf.

Anderson, P. (1974) *Lineages of the Absolutist State*. London: New Left Books.

Andrews, G. (ed.) (1991) *Citizenship*. London: Lawrence & Wishart.

Ardant, G. (1975) 'Financial policy and economic infrastructure of modern states and nations', in C. Tilly (ed.) *The Formation of National States in Western Europe*. Princeton, NJ: Princeton University Press.

Aristotle (1946) *The Politics*. Oxford: Clarendon Press.

Ashford, D. E. (1986) *The Emergence of the Welfare States*. Oxford: Blackwell.

Axelrod, R. M. (1984) *The Evolution of Co-operation*. New York: Basic Books.

Bacon, R. and Eltis, W. (1978) *Britain's Economic Problem: Too Few Producers*. London: Macmillan.

Barber, B. (1984) *Strong Democracy*. Berkeley: University of California Press.

Bardach, E. (1984) 'Implementing industrial policy', in J. Chalmers (ed.) *The Industrial Policy Debate*. San Francisco: Institute for Contemporary Studies.

Beetham, D. (1985) *Max Weber and the Theory of Modern Politics*. Cambridge: Polity.

Berger, P. L. (1987) *The Capitalist Revolution*. Aldershot: Wildwood House.

Berki, R. N. (1989) 'Vocabularies of the state', in P. Lassman (ed.) *Politics and Social Theory*. London: Routledge.

Beveridge, W. H. (1942) *Social Insurance and Allied Services*. London: HMSO.

Bishop, M., Kay, J. and Mayer, C. (eds) (1994) *Privatization and Economic Performance*. Oxford: Oxford University Press.

Bobbio, N. (1986) *Which Socialism?* Cambridge: Polity.

Bodin, J. (1967) *Six Books of a Commonwealth*. Oxford: Blackwell.

Braun, R. (1975) 'Taxation, sociopolitical structure, and state-building: Great Britain and Brandenburg–Prussia', in C. Tilly (ed.) *The Formation of National States in Western Europe*. Princeton, NJ: Princeton University Press.

Brinkerhoff, D. W. and Brinkerhoff, J. M. (2002) 'Governance reforms and failed states: challenges and implications', *International Review of Administrative Sciences* 68, 4, 511–31.

Brownlie, I. (1971) *Basic Documents on Human Rights*. 1st edn, Oxford: Clarendon Press.

—— (1992) *Basic Documents on Human Rights*. 3rd edn, Oxford: Clarendon Press.

Brubaker, R. (1992) *Citizenship and Nationhood in France and Germany*. Cambridge, MA: Harvard University Press.

Bull, H. (1972) 'The theory of international relations: 1919–1969', in B. Porter (ed.) *The Aberystwyth Papers: International Politics 1919–1969*. Oxford: Oxford University Press.

—— (1977) *The Anarchical Society*. London: Macmillan.

Burke, E. (1909) 'On American taxation', in *Speeches*. London: Macmillan.

Burton, J. (1972) *World Society*. Cambridge: Cambridge University Press.

Butler, D., Adonis, A. and Travis, T. (1994) *Failure in British Government: The Politics of the Poll Tax*. Oxford: Oxford University Press.

Butler, J. and Scott, J. W. (eds) (1992) *Feminists Theorize the Political*. London: Routledge.

Cable, V. (1995) 'The diminished nation state', *Daedalus* 124, 2, 23–53.

Cahill, K. (2001) *Who Owns Britain*. London: Canongate.

Carr, E. H. (1939) *The Twenty Years Crisis, 1919–1939*. London: Macmillan.

Cerny, P. (1990) *The Changing Architecture of Politics*. London: Sage.

—— (1991) 'The limits of deregulation: transnational interpenetration and policy change', *European Journal of Political Research* 19, 173–96.

Chomsky, N. (2000) *Rogue States: The Rule of Force in World Affairs*. London: Pluto Press.

Coates, D. (2000) *Models of Capitalism: Growth and Stagnation in the Modern Era*. Cambridge: Polity.

Cohen, J. L. and Arato, A. (1992) *Civil Society and Political Theory*. London: MIT Press.

Collins, P. H. (2000) *Black Feminist Thought: Knowledge, Consciousness and the Politics of Empowerment*. London: Routledge.

Connell, R. W. (1990) 'The state, gender, and sexual politics', *Theory and Society* 19, 507–44.

Cox, R. (1993) 'Gramsci, hegemony and international relations: an essay in method', in S. Gill (ed.) *Gramsci, Historical Materialism and International Relations*. Cambridge: Cambridge University Press.

—— (1994) 'Global restructuring', in R. Stubbs and G. Underhill (eds) *Political Economy and the Changing Global Order*. London: Macmillan.

CSO (Central Statistical Office) (1993, 1994, 1995) *Economic Trends*. London: HMSO.

—— (1995) *Social Trends* 25, London: HMSO.

Dearlove, J. and Saunders, P. (1991) *An Introduction to British Politics*. Cambridge: Polity.

Denham, A. and Garnett, M. (1998) *British Think Tanks and the Climate of Opinion*. London: UCL Press.

Der Derian, J. (1992) *Antidiplomacy*. Oxford: Blackwell.

—— (ed.) (1995) *International Theory*. New York: New York University Press.

—— (ed.) (1998) *The Virilio Reader*. Oxford: Blackwell.

—— (2000) 'Virtuous war/virtual theory', *International Affairs* 76, 4, 771–88.

Dobash, R. E. and Dobash, R. P. (1992) *Women, Violence and Social Change*. London: Routledge.

Dollar, D. and Collier, P. (2001) *Globalization, Poverty and Growth*. Washington, DC: World Bank.

Dolowitz, D. P. (1998) *Learning from America: Policy Transfer and the Development of the British Workfare State*. Sussex: Sussex Academic Press.

Dolowitz, D. P. and Marsh, M. (1996) 'Who learns what from whom: a review of the policy transfer literature', *Political Studies* 44, 343–57.

Downs, A. (1957) *An Economic Theory of Democracy*. New York: Harper & Row.

Dunleavy, P. and O'Leary, B. (1987) *Theories of the State*. London: Macmillan.

Dyson, K. (1980) *The State Tradition in Western Europe*. Oxford: Martin Robertson.

Earle, J. S., Frydman, R. and Rapaczynski, A. (1993) *Privatization in the Transition to a Market Economy*. New York: St Martin's Press.

Easton, D. (1981) 'The political system besieged by the state', *Political Theory* 9, 3, 303–25.

Eisenstadt, S. N. (1963) *The Political Systems of Empires*. Glencoe, IL: Free Press.

Ellison, N. and Pierson, C. (eds) (2003) *Developments in British Social Policy 2*. London: Palgrave.

Engels, P. (1978) 'The origin of the family, private property, and the state', in R. C. Tucker (ed.) *The Marx–Engels Reader*. 2nd edn, London: Norton.

Enloe, C. (1989) *Bananas, Beaches and Bases*. Berkeley: University of California Press.

Esping-Andersen, G. (1985) *Politics Against Markets*. Cambridge: Polity.

European Commission (1994) *European Economy, 3: Towards Greater Fiscal Discipline*. Brussels: EC Directorate-General for Economic and Financial Affairs.

Evans, M. (1995) 'Elitism', in D. Marsh and G. Stoker (eds) *Theory and Methods in Political Science*. London: Macmillan.

Evans, P. B., Rueschemeyer, D. and Skocpol, T. (eds) (1985) *Bringing the State Back In*. Cambridge: Cambridge University Press.

Foucault, M. (1994) *Power*. New York: New Press.

Freeman, G (1995) 'Modes of immigration politics in liberal democratic states', *International Migration Review* 29, 4, 881–902.

—— (1998) 'The decline of sovereignty? Politics and immigration restriction in liberal states', in C. Joppke (ed.) *Challenge to the Nation State*. Oxford: Oxford University Press, 86–108.

Gamble, A. (1985) *Britain in Decline*. 2nd edn, London: Macmillan.

Gardiner, K. (1993) *A Survey of Income Inequality over the Last Twenty Years – How Does the UK Compare?* London: LSE Welfare State Programme.

Garrett, G. (1998) *Partisan Politics in the Global Economy*. Cambridge: Cambridge University Press.

George, J. (1994) *Discourses of Global Politics*. Boulder, CO: Lynne Rienner.

Giddens, A. (1981) *A Contemporary Critique of Historical Materialism*, Volume 1. London: Macmillan.

—— (1982) 'Class division, class conflict and citizenship rights', in A. Giddens, *Profiles and Critiques in Social Theory*. London: Macmillan.

—— (1984) *The Constitution of Society*. Cambridge: Polity.

—— (1985) *The Nation-State and Violence*. Cambridge: Polity.

—— (1998) *The Third Way*. Cambridge: Polity.

Gilpin, R. (1981) *War and Change in World Politics*. Cambridge: Cambridge University Press.

Gordon, D. (1988) 'The global economy: new edifice or crumbling foundations?', *New Left Review* 168, 24–65.

Gramsci, A. (1971) *The Prison Notebooks*. London: Lawrence & Wishart.

Grange, D. L. (2000) 'Asymmetric warfare: old method, new concern', *National Strategy Forum Review*, winter; http://www.nationalstrategy.com/nsr (accessed 10 Sept 2003).

Green, D. and Griffith, M. (2002) 'Globalization and its discontents', *International Affairs* 78, 1, 49–68.

Greenfeld, L. (1992) *Nationalism: Five Roads to Modernity*. London: Harvard University Press.

Grieco, J. (1988) 'Anarchy and the limits of cooperation', *International Organization* 42, summer, 485–507.

Guiraudon, V. (2000) 'European integration and migration policy: vertical policy-making as venue shopping', *Journal of Common Market Studies* 38, 2, 251–71.

Guiraudon, V. and Lahav, G. (2000) 'A reappraisal of the state sovereignty debate', *Comparative Political Studies* 33, 2, 163–95.

Hailsham, Lord (1976) *Elective Dictatorship*. London: BBC.

Hall, S. and Held, D. (1989) 'Citizens and citizenship', in S. Hall and M. Jacques (eds) *New Times*. London: Lawrence & Wishart.

Halliday, F. (1987) 'State and society in international relations: a second agenda', *Millennium* 16, 2, 215–29.

Hammouya, M. (1999) *Statistics on Public Sector Employment*. Geneva: ILO.

Hardt, M. and Negri, A. (2000) *Empire*. London: Harvard University Press.

Harrington, M. (1987) *The Next Left: The History of the Future*. London: Tauris.

Hawkins, G. and Zimring, F. F. (1988) *Pornography in a Free Society*. Cambridge: Cambridge University Press.

Hayek, F. (1976) *The Road to Serfdom*. London: Routledge & Kegan Paul.

—— (1982) *Law, Legislation, and Liberty*, 3 vols. London: Routledge & Kegan Paul.

Heady, C., Mitrakos, T. and Tsakloglou, P. (1999) *The Distributional Impact of Social Transfers in the European Union: Evidence from the ECHP*. Florence: European Research Institute.

Heater, D. (1990) *Citizenship: The Civic Ideal in World History, Politics and Education*. London: Longman.

Held, D. (1987) *Models of Democracy*. Cambridge: Polity.

—— (1989a) 'Power and legitimacy', in D. Held, *Political Theory and the Modern State*. Cambridge: Polity.

—— (1989b) 'Citizenship and autonomy', in D. Held, *Political Theory and the Modern State*. Cambridge: Polity.

—— (1991) 'Democracy, the nation-state and the global system', in D. Held, *Political Theory Today*. Cambridge: Polity.

—— (1992) 'The development of the modern state', in S. Hall and B. Gieben (eds) *Formations of Modernity*. Cambridge: Polity.

—— (1993) 'Democracy: from city-states to a cosmopolitan order?', in D. Held, *Prospects for Democracy*. Cambridge: Polity.

—— (1994) 'Inequalities of power, problems of democracy', in D. Miliband (ed.) *Reinventing the Left*. Cambridge: Polity.

—— (1995) *Democracy and the Global Order*. Cambridge: Polity.

Held, D. and McGrew, A. (1993) 'Globalization and the liberal democratic state', *Government and Opposition* 28, 2, 261–85.

—— (2002) 'Introduction', in D. Held and A. McGrew (eds) *Governing Globalization*. Cambridge: Polity, 1–21.

Henriksen, T. H. (2001) 'The rise and decline of rogue states', *Journal of International Affairs* 54, 2, 349–73.

Henshall, D. (1992) *The Myth of Absolutism*. London: Longman.

Hinsley, F. H. (1986) *Sovereignty*. 2nd edn, Cambridge: Cambridge University Press.

Hintze, O. (1973) 'The state in historical perspective', in R. Bendix (ed.) *State and Society: A Reader in Comparative Political Sociology*. Berkeley: University of California Press.

Hirst, P. and Thompson, G. (1995) 'Globalization and the future of the nation state', *Economy and Society* 24, 3, 408–42.

Hix, S. (1998) 'The study of the European Union II: the "new governance" agenda and its rival', *Journal of European Public Policy* 5, 1, 38–65.

Hix, S. and Goetz, K. H. (2001) 'Introduction: European integration and national political systems', *West European Politics* 23, 4, 1–26.

HM Treasury (2003) *Public Expenditure.* www.hm-treasury.gov.uk.economic_data_and_tools (accessed 4 Sept 2003).

Hobbes, T. (1968) *Leviathan.* Harmondsworth: Penguin.

Hobsbawm, F. (1990) *Nations and Nationalism since 1780.* Cambridge: Cambridge University Press.

Hogwood, B. W. (1992) *Trends in British Public Policy.* Buckingham: Open University Press.

Hollis, M. and Smith, S. (1991) *Explaining and Understanding International Relations.* Oxford: Clarendon Press.

Home Office UK (2003) *Immigration and Asylum.* http://www.homeoffice.gov.uk/rds/immigration1.html (accessed 10 Sept 2003).

Honoré, A. M. (1961) 'Ownership', in A. C. Guest (ed.) *Oxford Essays in Jurisprudence.* Oxford: Oxford University Press.

Hooghe, L. and Marks, G. (2001) *Multi-Level Governance.* Lanham, MD: Rowan & Littlefield.

Human Rights Watch (2003) http://www.hrw.org/campaigns/race/nationality.htm (accessed 10 Sept 2003).

Hutton, W. (1995) *The State We're In.* London: Cape.

International Civil Aviation Organization (2003) *Statistical Yearbook.* www.icao.int/icao/en/atb/sea/yearbk.htm (accessed 11 Sept 2003).

International Organization for Migration (2003) *Managing Migration for the Benefit of All.* http://www.iom.int (accessed 10 Sept 2003).

Jackson, R. H. (1998) 'Surrogate sovereignty? Great power responsibility and "failed states"'. Working Paper no. 25: Institute of International Relations, University of British Columbia.

Jessop, B. (1988) *Conservative Regimes and the Transition to Post-Fordism: The Cases of Britain and West Germany.* Colchester: Essex Working Papers in Politics and Government.

—— (1989) *Thatcherism: The British Road to Post-Fordism.* Colchester: Essex Working Papers in Politics and Government.

—— (1990) *State Theory: Putting Capitalist States in their Place.* Cambridge: Polity.

—— (1994) 'The Schumpeterian workfare state', in R. Burrows and B. Loader (eds) *Towards a Post-Fordist Welfare State.* London: Routledge.

Johnson, C. (1982) *MITI and the Japanese Miracle: The Growth of Industrial Policy, 1925–1975.* Stanford, CA: Stanford University Press.

Joppke, C. (1998) 'Asylum and state sovereignty', in C. Joppke (ed.) *Challenge to the Nation State.* Oxford: Oxford University Press, 109–52.

—— (2001) 'The legal-domestic sources of immigrant rights', *Comparative Political Studies* 34, 4, 339–66.

Keane, J. (1988) *Democracy and Civil Society.* London: Verso.

—— (2003) *Global Civil Society?* Cambridge: Cambridge University Press.

Kelsen, H. (1961) *General Theory of Law and State.* New York: Russell & Russell.

Kelsey, J. (1995) *The New Zealand Experiment.* Wellington: Bridget William Books.

Keohane, R. O. (1984) 'The world political economy and the crisis of embedded liberalism', in J. Goldthorpe (ed.) *Order and Conflict in Contemporary Capitalism.* Oxford: Oxford University Press, 15–38.

—— (1989) *International Institutions and State Power*. London: Westview Press.

Keohane, R. O. and Nye, J. S. (1977) *Power and Interdependence*. Boston: Little, Brown.

King, D. (1987) *The New Right: Politics, Markets and Citizenship*. London: Macmillan.

Kitschelt, H., Lange, P., Marks, G. and Stephens, J. D. (eds) (1999) *Continuity and Change in Contemporary Capitalism*. Cambridge: Cambridge University Press.

Klein, N. (2000) *No Logo*. London: Flamingo.

Knutilla, M. and Kubik, W. (2000) *State Theories: Classical, Global, and Feminist Perspectives*. 3rd edn, London: Zed Books.

Korpi, W. (1983) *The Democratic Class Struggle*. London: Routledge & Kegan Paul.

Krasner, S. (1999) *Sovereignty: Organized Hypocrisy*. Princeton, NJ: Princeton University Press.

—— (2001) 'Rethinking the sovereign state model', *Review of International Studies* 27, 17–42.

Kymlicka, W. and Norman, W. (1994) 'Return of the citizen: a survey of recent work on citizenship theory', *Ethics* 104, 3, 52–81.

Lake, A. (1994) 'Confronting backlash states', *Foreign Affairs* 73, 2, 45–55.

Lenin, V. I. (1960) 'The state and revolution', in *Collected Works*, Volume 25. London: Lawrence & Wishart.

Levy, C. (1999) *Asylum Seekers and the European Union in the 1990s*. http://www.zmk.uni-freiburg.de/EuropeanSocialStructure/SeminarvorlessungSS99/ (accessed 10 Sept 2003).

Lindblom, C. (1977) *Politics and Markets*. New York: Basic Books.

Lister, R. (1993) 'Tracing the contours of women's citizenship', *Policy and Politics* 21, 1, 3–16.

Litwak, R. S. (2000) *Rogue States and U.S. Foreign Policy: Containment after the Cold War*. Baltimore: Woodrow Wilson Center Press.

McGrew, A. (1992a) 'Conceptualizing global politics', in A. McGrew and P. G. Lewis (eds) *Global Politics*. Cambridge: Polity.

—— (1992b) 'Globalization', in S. Hall, D. Held and A. McGrew (eds) *Modernity and its Futures*. Cambridge: Polity.

McGwire, M. (2001) 'The paradigm that lost its way', *International Affairs* 77, 4, 777–803.

—— (2002) 'Shifting the paradigm', *International Affairs* 78, 1, 1–28.

Machiavelli, N. (1961) *The Prince*. Harmondsworth: Penguin.

McIntosh, M. (1978) 'The state and the oppression of women', in A. Kuhn and A. Wolpe (eds) *Feminism and Materialism*. London: Routledge & Kegan Paul.

McKay, D. (1993) *American Politics and Society*. 4th edn, London: Blackwell.

Mackinnon, C. A. (1989) *Toward a Feminist Theory of the State*. Cambridge, MA: Harvard University Press.

Maclean, F. (1978) *Holy Russia*. London: Weidenfeld & Nicolson.

Maine, H. (1890) *Ancient Law*. London: John Murray.

Majone, C. (ed.) (1990) *Deregulation or Re-regulation?* London: Pinter.

Mann, F. K. (1943) 'The sociology of taxation', *Review of Politics* 5, 225–35.

Mann, M. (1970) 'The social cohesion of liberal democracy', *American Sociological Review* 35, 3, 423–39.

—— (1986) *The Sources of Social Power*, Volume I: *A History of Power from the Beginning to AD 1760*. Cambridge: Cambridge University Press.

—— (1993a) *The Sources of Social Power*, Volume II: *The Rise of Classes and Nation-States, 1760–1914*. Cambridge: Cambridge University Press.

—— (1993b) 'Nation-states in Europe and other continents: diversifying, developing, not dying', *Daedalus* 122, 3, 115–40.

Marquand, D. (1988) *The Unprincipled Society*. London: Fontana.

Marsh, D. (1992) *The New Politics of British Trade Unionism*. London: Macmillan.

Marsh, D. and Rhodes, R. (1992) *Policy Networks in British Government.* Oxford: Clarendon Press.

Marsh, D. and Stoker, C. (eds) (1995) *Theory and Methods in Political Science.* London: Macmillan.

Marshall, T. H. (1964) *Class, Citizenship and Social Development.* London: University of Chicago Press.

Martin, A. (1997) *What Does Globalization Have to Do with the Erosion of Welfare States: Sorting Out the Issues.* Bremen: Zentrum für Sozialpolitik.

Marx, K. (1965) *Capital,* Volume 1. London: Lawrence & Wishart.

—— (1973a) 'The Communist Manifesto', in K. Marx, *The Revolutions of 1848.* Harmondsworth: Penguin.

—— (1973b) 'The Eighteenth Brumaire of Louis Bonaparte', in K. Marx, *Surveys from Exile.* Harmondsworth: Penguin.

—— (1975) 'Critique of Hegel's doctrine of the state', in K. Marx, *Early Writings.* Harmondsworth: Penguin.

Meehan, F. (1993) *Citizenship and the European Community.* London: Sage.

Michels, R. (1962) *Political Parties.* New York: Free Press.

Miller, D. (1989) *Market, State and Community.* Oxford: Oxford University Press.

Mills, C. W. (1956) *The Power Elite.* New York: Oxford University Press.

Milner, H. (1992) 'International theories of cooperation among nations', *World Politics* 44, 466–96.

Milward, A. S. (1992) *The European Rescue of the Nation State.* London: Routledge.

Mitchell, T. (1991) 'The limits of the state: beyond statist approaches and their critics', *American Political Science Review* 85, 1, 77–96.

Moran, M. (2001) 'Not steering but drowning: policy catastrophes and the regulatory state', *Political Quarterly* 72, 4, 414–27.

Morgenthau, H. (1978) *Politics Among Nations.* New York: Knopf.

Mosca, C. (1939) *The Ruling Class.* New York: McGraw Hill.

Mulgan, G. (1993) 'Reticulated organization: the birth and death of the mixed economy', in C. Crouch and D. Marquand (eds) *Ethics and Markets.* Oxford: Blackwell.

Nielsen, K. (1991) 'Towards a flexible future – theories and politics', in B. Jessop, H. Kastendiek, K. Nielsen and O. Pedersen (eds) *The Politics of Flexibility.* London: Edward Elgar.

Niskanen, W. A. (1971) *Bureaucracy and Representative Government.* New York: Aldine-Atherton.

—— (1973) *Bureaucracy: Servant or Master?* London: Institute of Economic Affairs.

Nordlinger, F. A. (1981) *On the Autonomy of the Democratic State.* Cambridge, MA: Harvard University Press.

Nugent, N. (1993) 'The European dimension', in P. Dunleavy, A. Gamble, I. Holliday and C. Peele (eds) *Developments in British Politics 4.* London: Macmillan.

O'Connor, J. (1973) *The Fiscal Crisis of the State.* New York: St Martin's Press.

OECD (Organization for Economic Cooperation and Development) (1989) *Economies in Transition.* Paris: OECD.

—— (1995) *The OECD Jobs Study.* Paris: OECD.

—— (2001) 'Recent privatisation trends', *Financial Market Trends* 79.

Ogus, A. I. (1994) *Regulation: Legal Form and Economic Theory.* Oxford: Oxford University Press.

Ohmae, K. (1990) *The Borderless World.* London: Collins.

Oldfield, A. (1990) 'Citizenship: an unnatural practice?', *Political Quarterly* 61, 177–87.

Olson, M. (1965) *The Logic of Collective Action.* Oxford: Oxford University Press.

—— (1982) *The Rise and Decline of Nations.* New Haven, CT: Yale University Press.

Osborne, D. and Gaebler, T. (1992) *Reinventing Government.* Reading, MA: Addison-Wesley.

Panitch, L. (1994) 'Globalisation and the state', in R. Miliband and L. Panitch (eds) *Socialist Register* 30.

Parris, H., Pestieau, P. and Saynor, P. (1987) *Public Enterprise in Western Europe.* London: Croom Helm.

Pateman, C. (1988a) *The Sexual Contract.* Cambridge: Polity.

—— (1988b) 'The patriarchal welfare state', in A. Gutmann (ed.) *Democracy and the Welfare State.* Princeton, NJ: Princeton University Press.

Peacock, A. and Wiseman, J. (1961) *The Growth of Public Expenditure in the UK.* Oxford: Oxford University Press.

Perraton, J., Goldblatt, D., Held, D. and McGrew, A. (1997) 'The globalisation of economic activity', *New Political Economy* 2, 2,

Peters, G. (1999) *Institutional Theory in Political Science: The 'New Institutionalism'.* London: Pinter.

Phillips, A. (1991) *Engendering Democracy.* Cambridge: Polity.

—— (1993) 'Citizenship and feminist theory', in A. Phillips, *Democracy and Difference.* Cambridge: Polity.

—— (ed.) (1998) *Feminism and Politics.* Oxford: Oxford University Press.

Pierre, J. (ed.) (2000) *Debating Governance.* Oxford: Oxford University Press.

Pierre, J. and Peters, B. G. (2000) *Governance, Politics and the State.* London: Macmillan.

Pierson, C. (1986) *Marxist Theory and Democratic Politics.* Cambridge: Polity.

—— (1993) 'Social policy', in P. Dunleavy, A. Gamble, I. Holliday and C. Peele (eds) *Developments in British Politics 4.* London: Macmillan.

—— (1994) 'Continuity and discontinuity in the emergence of the "postFordist" welfare state', in R. Burrows and B. Loader (eds) *Towards a PostFordist Welfare State.* London: Routledge.

—— (1995) *Socialism After Communism.* Cambridge: Polity.

—— (1998) *Beyond the Welfare State? The New Political Economy of Welfare.* Cambridge: Polity.

—— (2001a) *Hard Choices: Social Democracy in the Twenty-First Century.* Cambridge: Polity.

—— (2001b) 'Globalisation and the End of Social Democracy', *Australian Journal of Politics and History* 47, 4, 459–74.

—— (2002) '"Social Democracy on the back foot": the ALP and the new Australian model', *New Political Economy* 7, 2, 179–97.

—— (2003) 'Learning from Labor? Welfare policy transfer between Australia and Britain', *Journal of Comparative and Commonwealth Politics* 41, 1, 77–100.

Pierson, C. and Castles, F. G. (2001) 'Australian antecedents of the Third Way', *Political Studies* 51, 4, 683–702.

Pirie, M. (1985) *Privatization.* Sydney: Centre 2000.

Poggi, G. (1978) *The Development of the Modern State.* London: Hutchinson.

—— (1990) *The State: Its Nature, Development and Prospects.* Cambridge: Polity.

Polanyi, K. (1944) *The Great Transformation.* New York: Rinehart.

Poulantzas, N. (1978) *State, Power, Socialism.* London: Verso.

Radosh, R. and Rothbard, M. N. (1972) *A New History of Leviathan.* New York: Dutton.

Randall, V. (1987) *Women and Politics.* London: Macmillan.

Regan, S. (2003) 'Paying for welfare', in N. Ellison and C. Pierson (eds) *Developments in British Social Policy 2.* London: Palgrave.

Rein, M. (1985) 'Women, employment and social welfare', in R. Klein and M. O'Higgins (eds) *The Future of Welfare.* Oxford: Blackwell.

Rhodes, R. (1997) *Understanding Governance: Policy Networks, Governance, Reflexivity and Accountability.* Buckingham: Open University Press.

Rice, S. E. (2002) *U.S. Foreign Assistance and Failed States*, Washington, DC: Brookings Institution; http://www.brook.edu/views/papers/rice (accessed 10 Sept 2003).

Rose, R. and Peters, C. (1978) *Can Governments Go Bankrupt?* New York: Basic Books.

Rosenau, J. N. (2000) 'Change, complexity, and governance in globalizing space', in J. Pierre (ed.) *Debating Governance*. Oxford: Oxford University Press, 167–200.

—— (2003) 'Governance in a new global order', in D. Held and A. McGrew (eds) *Global Transformations Reader*. Cambridge: Polity, 223–33.

Rousseau, J. J. (1968) *The Social Contract*. Harmondsworth: Penguin.

Ruddick, S. (1990) *Maternal Thinking: Towards a Politics of Peace*. London: Women's Press.

Salvadori, M. (1979) *Karl Kautsky and the Socialist Revolution: 1880–1938*. London: New Left Books.

Sanders, D. (1990) 'Government popularity and the next election', *Political Quarterly* 62, 235–61.

Sargisson, L. (1996) *Contemporary Feminist Utopianism*. London: Routledge.

Sassen, S. (1998) 'The *de facto* transnationalizing of immigration policy', in C. Joppke (ed.) *Challenge to the Nation State*. Oxford: Oxford University Press, 49–85.

Scharpf, F. W. (1991) *Crisis and Choice in European Social Democracy*. New York: Cornell University Press.

Schmitter, P. (1974) 'Still the century of corporatism?', *Review of Politics* 36, 85–131.

Schumpeter, J. (1954) 'The crisis of the tax state', *International Economic Papers* 4, 5–38.

—— (1976) *Capitalism, Socialism and Democracy*. London: Allen & Unwin.

Scott, J. (1991) *Who Rules Britain?* Cambridge: Polity.

—— (2001) *Power*. Cambridge: Polity.

SIPRI (Stockholm Peace Research Institute) (2002) *Worldwide Military Expenditure*. http://first.sipri.org (accessed 10 Sept 2003).

Skinner, Q. (1989) 'The state', in T. Ball, J. Farr and R. L. Hanson (eds) *Political Innovation and Conceptual Change*. Cambridge: Cambridge University Press.

Skocpol, T. (1992) *Protecting Soldiers and Mothers*. Cambridge, MA: Harvard University Press.

Smith, A. D. (1986) 'State-making and nation-building', in J. A. Hall (ed.) *States in History*. Oxford: Blackwell.

Smith, M. (1995) 'Pluralism', in D. Marsh and C. Stoker (eds) *Theory and Methods in Political Science*. London: Macmillan.

Spanger, H.-J. (2000) *Failed State or Failed Concept? Objections and Suggestions*. http://www.ippu.purdue.edu/failed_states/2000/papers/spanger.html (accessed 10 Sept 2003).

Spruyt, H. (1994) *The Sovereign State and its Competitors*. Princeton, NJ: Princeton University Press.

Steans, J. (1998) *Gender and International Relations*. Cambridge: Polity.

Stewart, A. (1995) 'Two conceptions of citizenship', *British Journal of Sociology* 46, 1, 63–78.

Strange, S. (1995) 'The defective state', *Daedalus* 124, 2, 55–74.

Stubbs, R. and Underhill, G. (1994) *Political Economy and the Changing Global Order*. London: Macmillan.

Sylvester, C. (1994) *Feminist Theory and International Relations in a Postmodern Era*. Cambridge: Cambridge University Press.

Tanter, R. (1999) *Rogue Regimes: Terrorism and Proliferation*. London: Macmillan.

Therborn, C. (1977) 'The rule of capital and the rise of democracy', *New Left Review* 103.

Thucydides (1982) *The Peloponnesian War*. Harmondsworth: Penguin.

Tilly, C. (1975) 'Reflections on the history of European state-making', in C. Tilly (ed.) *The Formation of National States in Western Europe*. Princeton, NJ: Princeton University Press.

—— (1990) *Coercion, Capital, and European States, AD 990–1990*. Oxford: Blackwell.

——(1994) 'The time of states', *Social Research* 61, 2, 269–95.

Tullock, C. (1976) *The Vote Motive*. Princeton, NJ: Princeton University Press.

Turner, B. S. (1990) 'Outline of a theory of citizenship', *Sociology* 24, 2, 189–217.

Underhill, G. (2000) 'State, market and global political economy: genealogy of an (inter-?) discipline', *International Affairs* 76, 4, 805–24.

United Nations (2002) *World Economic and Social Survey 2002*. New York: United Nations.

Vartiainen, J. (1995) 'The state and structural change: what can be learnt from the successful late industrializers?', in H.-J. Chang and R. Rowthorn (eds) *The Role of the State in Economic Change*. Oxford: Oxford University Press, 137–69.

Vest, J. (2001) 'Fourth-generation warfare', *Atlantic Monthly*, December 2001. http://www.theatlantic.com/ (accessed 10 Sept 2003).

Viotti, P. R. and Kauppi, M. V. (eds) (1993) *International Relations Theory*. New York: Macmillan.

Vogel, D. (1987) 'Political science and the study of corporate power', *British Journal of Political Science* 17, 385–408.

Vogel, U. (1991) 'Is citizenship gender-specific?', in U. Vogel and M. Mann (eds) *The Frontiers of Citizenship*. London: Macmillan.

Wade, R. (1995) 'Resolving the state–market dilemma in East Asia', in H.-J. Chang and R. Rowthorn (eds) *The Role of the State in Economic Change*. Oxford: Oxford University Press, 114–36.

Wallerstein, I. (1993) 'Patterns and prospectives of the capitalist world-economy', in P. R. Viotti and M. V. Kauppi (eds) *International Relations Theory*. New York: Macmillan.

Waltz, K. (1959) *Man, the State and War*. New York: Columbia University Press.

——(1979) *Theory of International Politics*. Reading, MA: Addison-Wesley.

Weber, M. (1970a) 'Politics as vocation', in H. H. Gerth and C. W. Mills (eds) *From Max Weber*. London: Routledge & Kegan Paul.

——(1970b) 'Bureaucracy' in H. H. Gerth and C. W. Mills (eds) *From Max Weber*. London: Routledge & Kegan Paul.

——(1978a) *Economy and Society*, Volume I. New York: Bedminster.

——(1978b) *Economy and Society*, Volume III. New York: Bedminster.

Weir, M. and Skocpol, T. (1985) 'State structures and the possibilities for "Keynesian" responses to the depression in Sweden, Britain and the United States', in P. B. Evans, D. Rueschemeyer and T. Skocpol (eds) *Bringing the State Back In*. Cambridge: Cambridge University Press.

Wendt, A. (1999) *Social Theory of International Politics*. Cambridge: Cambridge University Press.

Wilson, C. (1977) *Special Interests and Policy Making*. London: John Wiley.

World Bank (2001) *World Development Indicators*. New York: World Bank.

Wright, V. (1994) 'Reshaping the state: the implications for public administration', *West European Politics* 17, 3, 102–37.

# Index

Learning Resources
Centre